Peter Norton's DOS Guide

Revised & Expanded

To Walter
Peter Norton

Other Brady Books by Peter Norton

Inside the IBM PC, Revised and Enlarged
PC-DOS: The Guide to High Performance Computing
Peter Norton's Assembly Language Book for the IBM PC

Peter Norton's DOS Guide

Revised & Expanded

Peter Norton

A Brady Book
New York, New York 10023

The first edition of this book was published under the title:
MS-DOS and PC-DOS: User's Guide

 BRADY

Simon & Schuster, Inc.
Gulf+Western Building
One Gulf+Western Plaza
New York, NY 10023

DISTRIBUTED BY PRENTICE HALL TRADE

Manufactured in the United States of America

3   4   5   6   7   8   9   10

Library of Congress Cataloging-in-Publication Data

Norton, Peter, 1943–
    Peter Norton's DOS Guide, Revised & Expanded

    "A Brady Book."
    Rev. ed. of: MS-DOS and PC-DOS. 1st ed. ©1984.
    Includes index.
    1. MS-DOS (Computer operating system)   2. PC DOS
(Computer operating system)   I. Norton, Peter, 1943–
MS-DOS and PC-DOS.   II. Title.   III. Title: DOS guide.
QA76.76.063N68   1987   005.4   87-1222

ISBN 0-13-662073-6

Contents

Part III   Deeper into Disks   107

Chapter 9   Understanding Disks   109

Chapter 10   Hard Disk Set Up   129

Chapter 11   Working with Subdirectories   141

Chapter 12   Advanced Disk Commands   157

Limits of Liability and
Disclaimer of Warranty

The author and publisher of this book have used their best efforts in preparing this book and the programs contained in it. These efforts include the development, research, and testing of the theories and programs to determine their effectiveness. The author and publisher make no warranty of any kind, expressed or implied, with regard to these programs or the documentation contained in this book. The author and publisher shall not be liable in any event for incidental or consequential damages in connection with, or arising out of, the furnishing, performance, or use of these programs.

Trademarks

Introduction

This book is about getting started with PC-DOS, the disk operating system for the family of IBM Personal Computers, but it doesn't stop with DOS. It is about much more beside, because there are two halves to this book, even though you won't find them broken out in separate sections. One half of the book—the part you would expect to find—teaches the things you need to know about getting started with DOS and getting the most out of it. The other part, equally valuable, teaches what you need to know in order to be a wily, smart, and effective user of a small personal computer.

On the one hand, this book tells you about DOS and how to make good use of the commands that are built into it. On the other, it also gives you information on such topics as how to choose intelligently among the hundreds of programs offered for sale.

Both halves of this book are based on something that sets it apart from many others: practical advice. In these pages, you'll find out how to make your personal computer work for you. You'll learn what works and what doesn't, what to buy, what to use, and none of this advice is theoretical. It's based on my experience. Specifically, on:

- More than a decade of experience with all sorts of computers.
- Fairly recent conversion to working with a small computer. That means my experiences as a beginner haven't yet been lost in the swamps of time.
- Heavy, full-time use of a personal computer for the last few years. (Actually, more like ten hours a day, six or seven days a week, so lots of personal-computer experience has been compressed into a short span.)
- A healthy dose of common sense—something we all rely on, and something this book will help you develop in terms of DOS and your personal computer.

Help When You Need It

Perhaps you are the enthusiastic first-time owner of a personal computer. Perhaps your work is forcing you to use a computer you aren't really sure you want to deal with. Perhaps you are considering getting a small computer, and you want to learn a little of what computers are all about (and how to spend your money wisely). If you fit into any of these three descriptions, then this book is for you.

This is a help book for beginning computer users—people who will be working the IBM PC family of computers. How can you get the most help from it?

- If you are completely new to computers and don't understand them at all, read Chapter 1; it explains the fundamental ideas about how a computer and its operating system (DOS) work. Also, make use of the narrative glossary in Chapter 25; it defines some of the most commonly used technical terms related to computers, but it ties the definitions together in a narrative, rather than dictionary-like, form, so it's easier to read and understand.
- Check the chapter headings. They will guide you into the material you need.

Most of all, this book is here to help you through the small traumas of beginning to use your computer. Every new experience brings its pleasures and pains, but the pains tend to come first. And the problems of "computer phobia" are now legendary. Whether you are a reluctant beginner or a starting enthusiast, this book will help make your use of DOS easier. Computers are now for everyone.

This book won't, by the way, go into all the technical details of using DOS. Your computer's manuals do that nicely. What it will do is help you understand what those manuals are about and, more importantly, it will help you get started. And it will do something more that your computer's manuals cannot, or dare not, do: It will give you advice about what's good and bad in software that you may be thinking about buying.

Variations in DOS

Like everything else mankind has created, DOS has a history, and that history is reflected in the version numbers, such as 2.11 and 3.20, which indicate what edition of DOS you have. You need to know at least a little about these version numbers, to know where you stand with DOS.

The major changes to DOS are reflected in the whole numbers, like the three in Version 3.20. The lesser numbers indicate minor, less important changes in the progress of DOS. Of course there are improvements and additions made in each version of DOS; the only really important thing is that you have a version no earlier than 2.00. The one-series was really the infancy of DOS and if by any chance you have one of those, you should trade it in for a newer version, but it's unlikely that you do. Whatever version of DOS came with your computer, it's almost certainly the right one for you to use.

The most popular versions seem to be 2.11, which is widely used with non-IBM brand "clones," and any of the three's, particularly 3.10 and 3.20. Quite likely you have one of those. This book describes the features of the latest version of DOS, and if you have an earlier version, such as 2.10 or 2.11, just a few of the things mentioned here may not apply to your computer and your DOS. Not to worry, as long as you have a version later than the one-series, you should be just fine.

There are several ways you can find out which version of DOS your computer is using. One way is to look at your DOS manual. It will have the version number on the cover or title page. There are also two ways your computer can tell you which version of DOS it has. When you start up your computer with DOS, you ordinarily see the version number at the beginning of your session. There is also a DOS command called VER that tells DOS itself to report its version number to you. I'll be discussing how to start your computer with DOS and how to use the VER command early in the book.

DOS and Your PC

Just before I end this introduction and plunge into DOS, let's pause to define two terms: DOS and the IBM Personal Computer family.

DOS is the name used by IBM for the main operating system that runs on the IBM PC family. DOS was created for IBM by Microsoft, a leading company in software for personal computers. Microsoft also provides versions of DOS for many other computers; these other versions are usually called MS-DOS (short for Microsoft DOS).

To distinguish the IBM version, many people call it PC-DOS. In fact, this version has been called PC-DOS so much that many people believe PC-DOS is IBM's official name for the product; not true. Whether we call it DOS, PC-DOS, or MS-DOS, we're essentially talking about the same thing. The differences between DOS for one computer and DOS for another are quite minor. However, since this book is for use with the IBM Personal Computer family and the IBM version of DOS, we'll follow the IBM standard when there are differences between one version of DOS and another.

Now, what about the computers that use DOS? There are several models of IBM Personal Computer, so we refer to them collectively as the IBM PC family. The foundation of this family was the original model of PC introduced in 1981. Later additions included the PC-XT (which introduced large-capacity hard disks to the family), the discontinued PCjr and the Portable PC, the Convertible PC, and the high-performance PC-AT. IBM also makes other models, some of them quite specialized.

Actually, the PC family has grown beyond what IBM itself offers. Other companies have broadened our choices by producing models that are highly compatible with the IBM products and offer combinations of features that aren't exactly matched by any IBM model. Notable among these extended members of the family are many models by Compaq, Tandy, and Toshiba. In truth, there are more good variations on the basic PC than we could wiggle a floppy disk at. All of these machines can be considered legitimate members of the full PC family; and they all use the same DOS operating system that you'll learn about in this book.

PART I

Setting the Stage

1

BASIC COMPUTER CONCEPTS

Introduction

To use your computer successfully you need to have an idea of what it is and how it functions. By this I don't mean the computer technician's understanding of what's going on under the cover of your machine. I mean just a simple, practical, working idea of what's what: the sort of working knowledge that you need of a car in order to be a safe driver—not what a mechanic needs to know, but what a driver needs to know. As the "driver" of a small computer, you need a basic understanding of what's going on in your machine.

This chapter will lay out some basic computer concepts for you. I'll cover these concepts in four parts: First, we'll look at the computer metaphorically, as if it were a human office worker. Then, we'll consider what this "office worker" can do and what it can't. Next, I'll look at the importance of an operating system like our DOS. Finally, we'll wrap up this chapter with a practical matter—the two quite different ways you can use your computer.

The Computer as Worker

The best way I know to explain how a computer works, to help make sense of its parts, and to show how they work together, is to pretend the computer is an office worker. Let's suppose you are at work. Your boss tells you that you will have a new personal assistant with only one task to perform: to help you with your work. But, the boss tells you privately, this assistant isn't very bright. Conscientious, yes; hard-working, yes; but bright, intelligent, imaginative? Absolutely not. A helper to assist with whatever you ask to be done, but has to be given instructions in laborious detail. A worker with lots of energy but absolutely no initiative, no common sense, no independence.

You don't need me to tell you the identity of your new assistant; obviously, it's your computer. Let's see, then, what your computer assistant has to offer, what it needs to get any work done, and what you'll have to do to get any useful work out of it.

Parts of the Computer

Your computer has, as they say, an electronic brain. This brain (and as you'll see, it's a "pea brain," for sure) goes by various names in computer terminology. Basically, it is the **central processing unit**, or just the **processor**, for short. This "brain" is the central, fundamental part of a computer, and sometimes people refer to just this one part as being the computer itself. That description is pretty accurate, but naturally it can be confusing to refer to one of many parts as *the* computer, so I'll mostly call it the **processor**.

If we choose to ignore intelligence and creativity, which humans have and computers don't, we can say that your computer's processor is analogous to a brain. It is a fair analogy, because the computer's processor, like a person's brain, is what has the ability to comprehend and carry out instructions.

So far, then, we have your computer assistant's brain: the processor. What comes next? If your assistant is going to get any work done, it needs a place to work. For an office worker that place would be a desk. What part of your computer is its work space, its desk? You might be surprised to find it is the part we call the computer's **memory**.

Memory

Now we all know that a person has a memory, and most people have heard a computer also has something known as its memory, so it is natural to think that the computer's memory is analogous to our own. Wrong. Our memory is where we remember things; it is our brain's more or less permanent record of information, but the memory of a computer is not a permanent record of anything. Instead, the computer's memory is the part it uses as a work space. The memory is where the computer places the information it is working on at the time. This is just like the desk of an office worker. When people perform work, information is spread out on as much of the desk as is needed. When the work is finished, the desk is cleared and made ready for another task. So it is with the computer's memory, the computer uses its memory on a temporary basis. When the current job is done, the memory can be cleared for another task.

This analogy between the computer's memory and an office worker's desk goes even further. In principle, all of your desk is work space, but part of it is probably taken up by a telephone or a pencil cup. It is the same way with a computer's memory. On the whole, most of the memory is available as working space for the computer, but certain parts of the memory are dedicated to one specialized use or another.

Some things that you do at a desk require very little space. You don't need much space to scribble a letter. But if you are writing a report, you need more space—space for your writing pad, for your notes, for a dictionary. Nearly any desk has room for that sort of work. But if you are doing a very complicated task, let's say some complex accounting job that requires looking up information in all sorts of account books and journals—then you need much more space. Maybe more space than there is on an ordinary desk.

Things are the same way with a computer's memory. First, the more complicated the task, the more memory the computer needs as a working space. Second, like desks, computer memory usually comes in standard sizes. For a computer, the size of its memory is usually measured in "K," or thousands of characters of memory capacity. One K is exactly 1,024 characters (**bytes**, in computer terminology). For convenience, we can think of each K as simply a thousand characters—the amount of space taken up by 150 words of English, that's about the size of this paragraph.

A typical amount of memory for home hobby computers is around 48K. In the past, professional-class PCs commonly had 64K of memory. Nowadays, personal computers for professional use usually start at 128K and often have 256K or even more. These are the most common work space sizes for personal computers—64K, 128K, and 256K. Larger sizes are available, and it is not unusual for a personal computer to have 512K. The standard models of the PC family can accommodate up to 640K of memory, and the advanced AT model can handle 3,072K bytes (which is called, when the numbers get that big, three megabytes).

But back to our analogy. There is another way that a computer's memory is like a worker's desk. For common, simple tasks, not much of the memory/desk is used. For more complex jobs, more and more memory is used until, finally, we encounter some job that is too large to fit into the available space. This is why it is good to have plenty of memory in your computer; since memory is relatively cheap, having plenty is inexpensive insurance against bumping up against a problem that is too large to fit. And again, as with an office worker, having more work space generally doesn't affect how fast the work gets done—speed relates to the worker's brainpower. The size of the work space mostly affects how large and complicated a job can be done.

So far in understanding the parts of our computer, we've covered the **processor** (brain) and the **memory** (desk/work space). What about the rest of the computer parts? Let's consider what **disk storage** represents to your computer.

Disk Storage

Disk storage is the computer's equivalent of the office worker's filing cabinet. Disk storage comes in several forms: flexible **floppy diskettes**, rigid disk cartridges, or permanently mounted, nonremovable fixed **hard disk systems**. Depending on which one you're talking about, these may be called disks, diskettes, fixed disks, hard disks, Winchester disks, cartridges, or mini-disks. Functionally, they all do the same job for our computers. They act as a place to store information when the computer is not actually working on it. The information can be either data or programs. When the computer is working on the information, it is in memory (on the desktop); when the computer is not using the information, it is in disk storage.

Disk storage not only acts like a filing cabinet for the computer, it even borrows some of the terminology of filing cabinets. Within disk storage, our information is organized into **files**. Each file contains whatever kind of data is appropriate to its purpose: written text, accounting numbers, sets of instructions (**programs**) for the computer, and so on. When the computer needs information from a file, it "opens" the file, reads it or writes to it, and then "closes" the file.

Here, the computer terminology closely matches what human workers do with files. There is only one major difference in the way a computer uses a file and the way a person does. If you or I work with a file from a filing cabinet, we generally place the whole file folder on our desk. The computer's way of using a file is different. The computer works with small parts of a file—similar to our taking only a page at a time from a file folder. Part of the reason a computer works this way is to reduce the amount of memory needed to get the work done.

Peripherals

I've already mentioned that computers "read" and "write" when they're working with files. They can read and write in another sense, too, and even talk on the telephone. They do this through what are called **input/output (I/O)devices**, or **peripheral devices**.

A personal computer usually has a display screen to write information onto, and it often has a printer as well. A printer is the computer's equivalent of having a typewriter at hand. Both the display screen and the printer are I/O devices . The computer does most of its reading (other than from its disk filing cabinet) from its keyboard. It reads what we type on the keyboard. The disk storage on a computer is another I/O device.

The computer also can use the telephone to talk to other computers or write to distant peripheral devices (for example, writing through a telephone line to a printer that is located somewhere else). To use a telephone, a computer needs special parts to connect it to the phone lines. These special parts are called a **communications adapter** and a **modem**; they perform the translation necessary to change computer talk into telephone talk and back again. These parts, the adapter and the modem, may be built into your computer, or they may be attached separately.

In addition to those I've mentioned, there are many other possible types of I/O or peripheral, devices that can be connected to your computer. Many of them are designed for very special purposes. There are special printers, called **graphics printers** or **plotters**, which are designed to draw pictures. There are special input devices that the computer can read, such as a **light pen** (which can read a position on the display screen), a **joystick** (mostly used for games), or a **mouse** (which is a joystick for people who are too serious to play games); and, naturally, there is much, much more.

That is basically the full set of a computer's parts: the processor (brain), the memory (desk), the disk storage (filing cabinet), telephone (adapter and modem), typewriter (printer), and so on. That is the **hardware**—the physical computer as worker. What about the computer software we hear so much about?

Software

The analogy of our computer as a faithful, but not very bright, assistant helps to explain **software**—computer programs—as well. Normally, people have a general education, general mental skills, and knowledge that we call job skills. A computer has few job skills of its own, but this loyal, if dim-witted assistant can do anything that we can explain in meticulous detail.

The computer doesn't know how to do anything by itself. It needs programs to tell it what to do—this is one assistant that literally "goes by the book." To accomplish any work, the computer must first turn to its disk file for the program instructions that will tell it exactly what to do.

When we use the computer, our first step in getting it to work is to tell it which program—which book of instructions—to follow. The program can be anything that people have taught computers to do, from accounting calculations to game playing. (Some of the programs we run on our computers are aids to make it easier for us to write more programs.)

Introducing DOS

One of the programs a computer can run is a master program, a program that makes it easier to run other programs. This master program is called an **operating system**, and it is the computer's equivalent of a human worker's general education or an office worker's general office skills. If you or I were working as clerks in an office, we would be expected to have training in specific jobs, such as bookkeeping. For jobs like these, a computer has programs that tell it how to do specific work.

But as clerks we would also be expected to know how to do common, ordinary things: sharpen a pencil, close an envelope, or even how to find things in a filing cabinet. These types of very basic skills are given to a computer by its operating system. The operating system takes care of the ordinary tasks that all programs need to carry out. Notice that I used the word "basic," not "unimportant." It is the operating system that handles the very important task of taking care of the filing cabinet, the computer's disk storage.

And so we come to the main subject of this book: an operating system, the Disk Operating System, called DOS from Microsoft.

The Computer at Work

Now we are ready to see how a personal computer works as a whole. To make things easier, we'll keep to our analogy of the dumb-but-faithful computer assistant.

When we arrive at the office and first need our computer, we turn it on. Our assistant reports to work. The first task we give it is to start up its operating system. Our assistant has forgotten everything overnight, so its first task in the morning is to take its general instruction manual (operating system) out of the filing cabinet (disk storage), and place it on its desk (memory).

Once the computer is running, our assistant is ready for work and we can tell it what to do next. We give it the name of a program. This might be a word-processing program, such as Microsoft Word, or it might be a spreadsheet program, such as Lotus 1-2-3. Given the name of the job to be done, our worker can take the specific instructions (program) out of the filing cabinet (disk) and get everything ready on its desk (memory). For a while, we have our computer help with that kind of work. When we're done, we tell it to put the program away. When we want to do something else, we give our computer the name of another program—and so it goes.

As the computer works for us, it uses its disk storage to fetch and save our information. It uses the display screen to speak to us; it uses the printer to give us a written record; it uses the keyboard to take our commands. It may use the telephone to pass information to and from another computer. But whatever it does, it is still just a simple helper.

What a Computer Can and Can't Do

There are times when a computer can be very helpful and times when it is more of a nuisance than an aid. We have to teach it how to do things (which is laborious), and we have to learn the limitations of its ways (which can be equally time consuming). For some jobs, it helps; for others, it doesn't.

On the whole, a computer can be very useful, but it pays to remember that there are some things it can do and many, many things it can't. Even more important, there are many things you might try to do with a computer that are better done by hand.

First, let's consider what the computer can do, and very well. It's a real whiz at arithmetic—fast and unfailingly accurate. Arithmetic is what computers do best. In fact, when you are using a computer for something else, such as writing a letter with a word-processing program, most of what the computer is doing behind the scenes is arithmetic. So when we need arithmetic done, the computer is just dandy at it. The computer's most famous and best success with arithmetic has been with **electronic spreadsheets**, such as Lotus 1-2-3.

1-2-3 is a fine example of computing at its best: It is quick and handy, and it makes it possible for many people to do all sorts of financial planning and numeric calculations, which they wouldn't have even tried before there were programs like this. Doing the kind of work that 1-2-3 does, only doing it by hand, was so difficult that we might as well say it was impossible. In short, computers can make impossibly lengthy calculations as easy to do as scratching your nose.

Another thing computers are very good at is record keeping, but only certain kinds of record keeping. With their large disk storage, computers can save large amounts of data. And under the right circumstances, computers can be efficient about searching out just the information that we need. But it is also true that many kinds of simple record keeping are more work to keep on a computer than they are to keep by hand.

This is something worth knowing. Once you fall even a little in love with what a computer can do, it is easy to become infatuated and try to get it to do everything for you. Beware. You don't turn to your computer to add 2 + 3, but you do use it to add the square roots of a hundred numbers—that's more in its line of work. It's the same with keeping records. If you have any information that is reasonably easy to keep organized by hand, then it would probably be more work to use your computer to keep track of it. On the other hand, when your manual records get out of hand, it's time to call in the computer.

People are still learning how to master the talents of computers, and so we are expanding the range of things it is practical to have computers do for us. Some things that don't even fit into a computer's natural skills of arithmetic and record keeping have turned out to be very good things to have a computer do, anyway. The best example of this is word processing, which means computer work related to the written word: accepting written text, changing (editing) it, keeping track of it, checking its spelling and grammar, and formatting it so the printed pages are nice and tidy. This is one type of work that the computer learned (through programming) how to do fairly recently, and yet it has become one of the computer's greatest successes. So there are now, and will be in the future, many jobs a computer can do well, even though they don't involve much computation.

There are some jobs, though, that computers can't and may never be able to do, and these include anything that involves intelligence and judgment. Computers do very well by rote. But when a task calls for imagination, intuition, or creativity, it is, at least for now, a job for people—perhaps a job with which a computer can assist, but still a job for humans.

What it all boils down to is this: You can expect your computer to be able to handle any task that is mechanically straightforward, but you can't expect it to perform any job that involves judgment. Likewise, you can expect success with your computer in any work that falls in the right scale—neither too big for your computer to handle, nor too small for it to be worth putting on your computer. Don't blame the machine if you ask it to do something it was not meant to do.

The Importance of an Operating System

So far you've seen what a computer is and the sorts of things that it can do, and you've had a little bit of explanation of the role of the computer's operating system, DOS. But that is all; at this point, it might seem that the operating system is no big deal. Actually, the operating system is a very big deal, and for several reasons.

First, an operating system is very important because it sets *both* the environment in which you interact with the computer and the environment in which your programs work. That means the operating system establishes the working character of your computer, as much or more than does the particular kind of computer you have. Likewise, the operating system sets many of the practical limits of your computer's usefulness, just as the specific hardware does.

The operating system completes your computer. Without it, your computer is a useless hunk, like a car with no fuel. With it, your computer takes on both life and a particular character. Your friends who grew up in big cities have different characters and styles, on the whole, than your friends who grew up in the country. It's the same with operating systems. With one, your computer will have one style; with another, it will have another style. And because this style permeates much of your interaction with your computer, the character of your operating system affects the way you use the computer.

Here's another reason why your operating system is important. Computer programs will not work with just any operating system. They generally have to be matched to the operating system used by the computer on which they run, and this means the number of programs available for your computer is heavily influenced by the popularity of the operating system that it uses. Thanks partly to the enormous success of the IBM Personal Computer, which pioneered the DOS operating system, and partly to the strong reputation of Microsoft, DOS has become the dominant operating system for the current 16-bit generation of computers.

In many ways, it does not matter to us if our operating system is better or worse than some other system. What does matter is how popular our operating system is—that is, how many programs are available for it, and how many different computers use it. The popularity of the operating system is mostly what determines how good a choice of tools (programs) we have available. In DOS we have a runaway winner.

Yet another reason why our operating system is important has to do with the future. An operating system can either be open to expected developments in computing, or it can cut itself off from the future. Again, fortunately for us, DOS has a well-planned and orchestrated future ahead of it, based upon a compatible family of operating systems.

There's a related advantage, too. When you change from one personal computer to a newer one, you do not want to have to discard all of the computer skills and experience you have acquired. Here again, DOS is a plus. Because it is the dominant operating system in its part of the computer world, the chances are great that your next computer will use either DOS or a big brother to DOS. This "upward compatibility" salvages not only the usefulness of your skills, but probably the usefulness of your programs as well.

Two Ways of Using a Computer—Interactive and Batch

Before we finish this chapter on computer fundamentals, you should learn about one subject that will become increasingly important as your use of a personal computer widens: the two basic ways you can use a computer.

When you first start using your computer, you will probably give it your full attention. You will work with the computer *interactively*, which means that you do something (such as type at the keyboard), and then the computer does something (such as show a result on the screen). You type something else, the computer does something else, and so on, and so on. This is **interactive computing**, one of the two fundamental modes in which computers can operate. The interactive mode is, and feels, so natural that you may wonder why you would ever want the computer to work in any other way.

But the simple fact is when you are working with the computer interactively, the computer is keeping you busy just as much as you are keeping it busy. This isn't always ideal.

When you need some computer help with your work, it is natural to work interactively with your computer. But there are some things that the computer can do—print a string of files, for example—that need not require your constant attention. This is when the computer can do its work more or less on its own, unattended and, thankfully, not needing attention. This style of computer operation is called, for no particularly important reason, **batch mode.**

Thus, your computer can work either in interactive mode or batch mode. There isn't a strict division between the two, it's just a matter of degree: how much attention your computer requires when it is doing some work.

There is a very good reason why I am pointing out that computers can, under the right circumstances, work on their own, unattended. You may begin by using your computer only occasionally, but inevitably, as time goes by, you will want your computer to do more and more work for you. Does this extra work have to take up more and more of your own time? Not if you are aware of the possibilities of the computer's unattended batch-processing capability.

The secret to successful batch operation lies in two things: programs that don't require unnecessary interaction, and good use of DOS's batch-processing capability, which you will begin to learn about in Chapter 7.

As a real-life example, consider an accounting program that I use. One of its operations is quite lengthy. Unfortunately for me, when the program is doing this lengthy operation it repeatedly asks me if I want it to continue. I always do, but the darned thing won't carry on without my say-so. This wastes my time, just sitting around telling the program to get on with its business. If this program had been written with a batch mode in mind, it would be enormously more useful and convenient for me.

The moral of this story is twofold. First, it points out the possibilities of unattended batch operation (wouldn't it be nice if I could just have my computer tell my accounting program, "yes, continue," "yes, continue," till the job was done). Second, the story shows that you should be careful when buying or writing programs; make sure that they do not require unnecessary attention from people. People have better things to do than pay attention to fussy programs.

This, then, has been a quick look at the fundamentals of computers, with emphasis on the parts that are most likely to end up being useful to you. Let's move on to getting started with DOS.

2

GETTING STARTED WITH DOS

Introduction

Life often seems topsy-turvy when you are getting started at some new endeavor, usually it seems as though you need to know everything at once. What do you learn first? What do you do first? We'll grapple with this problem, as you learn how to get started with DOS.

The very best way to start using DOS and your computer is not to do it alone. If you can find a patient someone who knows the ropes, ask this person to lead you by the hand through the basic steps. With the help of someone experienced, you can skim the rest of this chapter. The second best way to start is to continue reading.

Setting Up DOS

There are some fairly important things you need to do before you get started with DOS. Well, not really before you get started, but still quite early in the game. But you can't, or shouldn't try to, do these early steps, which have to do with safeguarding your DOS system, until you are at least slightly comfortable with your computer.

If this is beginning to sound like the "chicken or the egg" riddle, it's not. So that you don't feel lost right at the start, this is what you are working toward: First, you're going to get a little working knowledge of what DOS does when you work with it. Second, you're going to learn the fundamental steps you need to get going—getting diskettes ready for use (called formatting), and making copies of your data, so you don't have to worry about damaging your only copy of DOS (or anything else, for that matter).

Once you have an idea of what you should do, you are going to do it. You'll step through the basic diskette operations: formatting, copying, testing, and, of course, using the diskettes. Let's get to work.

What You Need to Know First

The very first things you need to know are these:

- How DOS settles in at its desk when it begins its working day.
- How you tell DOS to do some work.
- What special problems you face when starting out.
- How the safeguards against these problems work.
- What setting up diskettes is all about.

Let's begin with what DOS does when it starts its working day. When your computer "wakes up," it doesn't know very much, because it doesn't have an ordinary program loaded into it. Your computer does, however, have two special built-in programs it can rely on, and it does know how to do two things: how to do a little self-testing to see that things are in working order, and how to start up DOS. This start-up program is usually called a **bootstrap loader**, since it "pulls DOS up by the bootstraps."

This bootstrap operation works in two stages. First the tiny program built into your computer goes to work. This simple start-up program reads the very first part of a diskette which, if it has been prepared for start up, is where DOS has left a program of its own—a program that knows how to get DOS itself all set up. The program in your computer doesn't actually know anything about DOS. It just knows how to read the beginning of a diskette and run whatever it finds there as a program. The program doesn't know, or care, if it is starting DOS or some other operating system. It just reads the beginning of a diskette, where DOS's own starting routine is.

The second part of this start-up routine, which is part of DOS, is just smart enough to get the rest of DOS going; it reads the rest of DOS from the disk and voilà—DOS is running. All this goes on behind the scenes, however, you don't see the details. You just watch the computer working away until DOS is started up.

When DOS is ready to start, it first asks for the current date and time, so it can keep track of both. It's a good idea to put in the right date and time faithfully, because that lets DOS keep track of when your data is created, and such information can become very important later on.

The exact form DOS asks for the date and time may vary slightly from version to version, but here is a typical opener. DOS displays this on your screen and waits for you to key in the date:

```
Current date is Tue 1-01-1980
Enter new date:
```

You key in the date, using the hyphen (-) or the slash (/) to separate the month, day, and year. (You can, by the way, type a date such as July 4, 1987 as 7/4/87—you needn't type it as 7/04/1987 unless you want to.)

After you type the date and press Enter, DOS displays the same type of request for the time:

```
Current time is 0:00:12.34
Enter new time:
```

Again, you key in the time, using a colon (:) to separate hours, minutes, and seconds. DOS uses a twenty-four-hour clock, which means that if the time is past noon, you enter a number of 12 or more. For example, 2 PM is 14, and so forth.

At this point, I ought to mention that your computer can be equipped with hardware that will automatically set the date and time. The AT and most later models of IBM PC come with this feature, and such a clock/calendar can also be installed in most PCs. Therefore, you may find that the time and date are set automatically for you.

There is a way to bypass these starting operations, but I'll cover that later. Right now, I don't want to get lost in details. It's enough for you to know that if your computer is set up with certain hardware or software, the starting-up messages you see could be quite different from what I've illustrated.

After the preliminaries are taken care of, DOS announces it is ready for work with a short message that usually gives the brand of your computer and the version of DOS you have. This is a typical example:

```
The IBM Personal Computer DOS
Version 3.20 (C) Copyright International Business Machines Corp 1981, 1986
              (C) Copyright Microsoft Corp 1981, 1986
```

This example shows version 3.20 of DOS; yours might be 2.00, 2.10, or something else. As I mentioned in the Introduction, you can also find your version number on the cover or title page of your DOS manual.

(By the way, this display is called DOS's **starting message**. You can change it if you want, as you'll see in Chapter 24.)

Date, time, and starting message. This, in simple terms, is how DOS begins its working day. Next, let's see how to tell DOS to do some work. The process is a simple, if very terse, dialogue between DOS and you. DOS tells you it is ready to accept a command, and then you tell DOS what to do.

Getting DOS to Work

DOS tells you it is ready for a command by displaying what is called the DOS **prompt**, which, literally, prompts you to type in a command.

The typical prompt looks like this: A>, a capital letter A followed by a greater-than symbol. The A part of the prompt indicates which disk drive DOS is using to get and save information. You might see another letter of the alphabet, but the effect is the same. (We'll dig further into what this letter means in Chapter 3.)

When you see the DOS prompt, probably A> or C>, then you know you are talking to DOS and it wants you to tell it what to do; it wants an instruction. On the other hand, if you see something else on the display screen, you know it isn't DOS that's waiting for a command, it's some *other* program asking for instructions.

The prompt is DOS's part of the dialogue. To actually get DOS to do some work, you must give it a **command**. What are commands and what can they do? In the simplest terms, a command is the name of a program that you want the computer to carry out. That program/command might be the name of a program you've written, or it might be the name of a program you've bought, such as Lotus 1-2-3 or WordPerfect. It might be the name of a program that is a part of DOS itself, such as TIME, which lets you change the current time. Finally, it might be the name of a special type of DOS program called a **batch-execution** file, which you'll begin learning about in Chapter 7 and causes work to be done in batch mode, as discussed in Chapter 1.

Essentially then, you might say there are four types of commands: your own programs, store-bought programs, DOS's own programs, and DOS batch programs. If you're a little bit fuzzy on the distinctions at this point, don't worry about it. Dividing commands into four categories just gives us a way to think about them logically. There is very little difference among these four. They are all just programs that we can tell DOS to carry out for us.

Now, how do you get commands to work? It's simple: You key in the name of the command and press your computer's Enter key. DOS takes it from there, figuring out what type of command it is, finding the program, and making the program work. DOS does it all. All you have to do is type in the command name.

Giving Yourself a Sense of Security

So far you've seen how DOS gets started, and how it takes commands from you. Now, what are the special problems I mentioned at the beginning of this chapter? How serious are they, and how do you protect yourself?

The problems actually are few, and are mostly concerned with the possibility of losing data. It's pretty hard to break the computer itself, short of dropping it out the window, or pouring coffee inside it. If you were driving a car, rolling along at a good speed, and then suddenly shifted into reverse, you'd break your car pretty quickly. Driving into a tree would do a lot of damage, too. But you can't break a computer by "bad driving." You can damage it by physical abuse, but not by typing the wrong thing at the keyboard.

The major problem you face as a computer user is losing your only copy of some information. You can lose data in two ways. One is by physically damaging a diskette on which the data is stored, the equivalent of taking a phonograph record and breaking it. The other is by mistakenly telling the computer to throw data away, the equivalent of taking a cassette recording of some music and erasing it. There are ways you can reduce the chance that you'll do the computer equivalent of breaking a record or erasing a tape, but the most important safeguard against losing data is simply to keep extra copies around. That is the reason why the first thing to do is make copies of your DOS diskette: so you can start working with the copy, knowing that if you do anything wrong, the original is safe.

There is one more thing to learn before you can begin—you need to know the basics of setting up diskettes. You copy diskette data, including the data on the DOS diskette, onto blank diskettes. But a blank diskette can't be used just as it comes out of the box. It has to be **formatted** first.

Formatting

What is formatting? It is something like taking a blank piece of paper and ruling lines on it, to give you guidelines to make your handwriting even. A brand-new diskette is just like a blank piece of paper, but your computer needs the equivalent of guidelines written onto the diskette, to create a framework for your data. Formatting creates this framework—the guidelines for DOS to use in writing on your diskettes. You can copy your data onto a formatted blank diskette; you cannot copy data onto an unformatted blank diskette.

When you format a diskette, you have a choice of including or not including a copy of DOS on it. Here's the reason for the choice: If you format your diskettes with DOS, you can use these diskettes to start your computer system. That can be very handy, because it means you don't have to look for or keep track of a special start-up diskette. The only tradeoff is that having a copy of DOS on a diskette takes up some space, so there is less room for your data.

When we get deeper into the subject, you'll learn how to decide when it's a good idea to put DOS onto a diskette and when it's better not to. You'll see more about that in Chapter 6, Basic Disk Commands, and in Chapter 9, Understanding Disks. You'll also find out the advantages and disadvantages of a shortcut called DISKCOPY. For now, though, follow the simplest and safest rule: Put DOS on all of your diskettes.

This ends the background part of this chapter. Now let's proceed to safeguard and play with DOS.

The First Things to Do with DOS

You're ready to start DOS for the first time. To begin, you'll need four things. The first, naturally, is your computer. The second is the computer's introductory instruction manual, so you can see how each operation is done on your particular computer. The third is the DOS diskette that came with your computer's DOS manual, and the fourth is four or five blank diskettes.

With these parts ready, place the DOS diskette in the opening of your computer's first disk drive, close the latch, and turn your computer on. Most computers take a short while to warm up and then perform a little self-testing. When that is done, the computer will begin reading the DOS diskette. Finally, DOS will start as described earlier, by asking you for the date and the time like this:

```
Current date is Tue 1-01-1980
Enter new date: XX/XX/XXXX     (Type the date where the X's are.)
Current time is 0:00:12.34
Enter new time: XX:XX          (Here, too, type where the X's are.)
```

Then, DOS will show you its beginning message like this:

```
The IBM Personal Computer DOS
Version 3.20 (C) Copyright International Business Machines Corp 1981, 1986
             (C) Copyright Microsoft Corp 1981, 1986
```

When this start-up message appears, DOS is ready for you to begin work, and tells you so by giving the command prompt, A>.

Using Disk Drives

If you have read your computer's beginner's manual, you've probably seen a discussion of what to do if you have one or two diskette drives. DOS and your computer need two diskette drives, so you can do things like copy data from the diskette in one drive to another diskette in the other drive.

Your computer probably has two diskette drives. But does that mean you're stuck if it has only one? No, DOS's solution is to pretend that the computer has two drives, anyway. It does so by first treating your single disk drive as drive number 1 (known as the "A" drive), and then treating the same drive as if it were drive number 2 (known as the "B" drive). If you actually have two disk drives, the two just merrily work away. If not, every time DOS switches back and forth, treating the one real drive as A or B, it stops and tells you to change the diskette from the one that is supposed to be in the A drive to the diskette that is supposed to be in the B drive (or vice versa). So, with only one disk drive, DOS switches the use of it between the two drives that it needs, A and B.

From now on, I'll always just refer to your computer's A drive (the first one) and B drive (the second one). If you have only one real drive, DOS will maintain the pretense that there are two drives, as long as you cooperate by switching the diskettes in and out of the single drive. (When this happens, by the way, you'll quickly discover the advantages of having two drives.)

Now that you have DOS ready to work, you can format some diskettes to get them ready for use. Formatting diskettes is a basic everyday operation, you might as well get some practice right now.

First, give DOS the command to format a diskette. The command, as you type it, looks like this:

```
FORMAT B: /S
```

There are three parts to this command. First, there is the command itself, FORMAT. Then there are two parameters, **specifications**, that tell FORMAT just how to operate. The first parameter, B: , tells the FORMAT command to format the diskette in the B drive. The second parameter, /S, tells the FORMAT command to place a copy of DOS onto the formatted diskette.

After you type the command, press the Enter key and FORMAT itself comes into play. When FORMAT is ready to start formatting our diskette, it will stop and ask you to put your diskette into the B drive, and then press a key:

```
Insert new diskette for drive B:
and strike ENTER when ready
```

(It may tell you to press any key, or as here, it may tell you to press the Enter key in particular. Don't be concerned: That's one of the minor variations among different versions of DOS.)

After you insert the diskette and press Enter or another key, the FORMAT command program will work away, formatting the diskette. When it is finished, it will give a little report on its work. The exact nature of the report will depend upon your computer and the kind of diskettes that it uses, but this is typical:

```
Format complete
System transferred
   362496 bytes total disk space
    40960 bytes used by system
   321536 bytes available on disk
Format another (Y/N)?
```

You should take this opportunity to format several diskettes, so answer Y to the question about formatting another. FORMAT will again remind you to put a new diskette into the B drive and tell you to press Enter or to press any key.

Keep repeating this formatting procedure until you have a small supply, four or five, of working diskettes. They will soon come in handy. When you have enough, answer N to the "Format another" question, so that the FORMAT command will come to an end.

You should now have several diskettes, each formatted and each with a copy of DOS on it. Copying DOS onto a diskette with the /S parameter, however, does not mean that all the parts and tools of

DOS are copied onto the diskette. It means that the most fundamental parts of DOS are copied.

Even though you have created a number of diskettes you can use to start DOS, you do not yet have a duplicate copy of the DOS that's on your original diskette. Your next step, then, is to copy everything from your original DOS diskette onto one of these newly formatted diskettes. This copy will become your main working copy of DOS, then you can put the original away for safekeeping.

Duplicating Your DOS Diskette

To duplicate your DOS diskette, you'll get a chance to try another DOS command, COPY. As you'll see in Chapter 5, the COPY command, like many others in DOS, has more than one use. But for now the feature of the COPY command you will use is the most simple and straightforward one there is: copying data from one diskette to another.

If you have two disk drives, place one of your formatted diskettes in drive B. If you have one disk drive, leave your DOS diskette in your disk drive.

The COPY command, as you'll use it to copy everything from the diskette in drive A to the diskette in drive B, is typed like this:

```
COPY   A:*.*   B:
```

We'll put off the full details until the next chapter, but you can easily see the main parts of what is going on here. It's not much different from what you saw with the FORMAT command. Again, there are three parts: the command name (COPY), and two parameters.

In this case, the first parameter indicates what to copy from, and how much to copy. In effect, the A: part of this parameter says, "copy from drive A." The *.* part is a shorthand way of saying "copy everything that's on the diskette in drive A." The second parameter, B: , simply says, "copy to drive B."

Notice that the first parameter has a *.* part to indicate that everything should be copied, but the second parameter doesn't have any such specification. Why? Because you've implied that whatever is found on A should be copied as it is to drive B.

Type this command, then, and press the Enter key. The DOS COPY command will dutifully copy everything it finds on the diskette in drive A to the diskette in drive B (requesting you at appropriate points to switch diskettes if you have only one disk drive).

When the COPY procedure is complete, you will have in drive B a diskette that contains everything on the diskette in drive A. Use this new diskette as your working copy of DOS, and put the original copy of DOS away. From now on, you won't have to worry about doing it any harm.

This finishes your short lesson on how to get started in DOS. It has done several things. For one, it "got your feet wet." Without having to understand too much about DOS, you've been able to put it to work and get something useful out of it—some formatted diskettes to work with and a copy of the DOS diskette to use without worry. Now you're ready to understand the principles behind what you've done, and you're ready to learn more about the commands of DOS, both ordinary and advanced. All this will occupy us for the next few chapters.

3

FUNDAMENTALS OF DOS COMMANDS

Introduction

Before you can move on to really start looking at the DOS commands, you have to learn the fundamentals of how they are laid out and used. In this chapter, we'll pause to master the basics of DOS commands. My real goal in this book is to help you become familiar with DOS: to speed you as quickly as possible toward thinking of DOS as an old friend, a needed tool that you use easily and with hardly a second thought. One thing that will help you most in getting comfortable with DOS is an understanding of how important disk drives are to DOS.

DOS is, after all, a disk operating system, and disks are at the core of the way DOS operates and organizes itself. If you want to understand DOS, you need to understand the way DOS thinks about disks.

Keeping Track of Drives

One of the first things you need to realize about how it works is that DOS focuses more on the disk drive than it does on the diskette in the drive. Whether your computer has one or two diskette drives, or even a high-capacity hard-disk system, DOS needs a consistent and uniform way of keeping track of this disk gear. It does this, as you saw in Chapter 2, by giving a letter "name" to each of the drives.

The first drive is referred to as A, the second as B, and so forth. As I mentioned in the last chapter, DOS will turn a single drive into a "let's-pretend" pair of drives, A and B. Many DOS command operations need two disk drives and when there is only one drive, it is easier and more consistent for DOS to fake a second drive, B drive, than to try to do everything with only the A drive.

By the way, if your computer has a high-capacity hard-disk system, the hard disk is probably identified as drive letter C, while the letters A and B stand for two floppy diskette drives (or one floppy drive masquerading as two). The XT model of the IBM Personal Computer and most AT models have these high-capacity, non-removable hard disks. (IBM calls them **fixed disks**, because unlike floppy diskettes, you can't move them in and out of the drive.)

If you have a hard disk, most of the work you do with the computer will be centered around drive C. When you do operations that involve floppy diskettes, you'll use drives A and B.

Such background aside, let's assume you have a diskette you want to work with. If you put that diskette in your A diskette drive, then you tell DOS to look to the A drive to find what is on that diskette. You'd get the same result if you put the same diskette in the B drive and told DOS to look there. The point is simple: DOS doesn't know what you're doing with diskettes, which you might even be switching around behind its back. DOS *does* know what's what with the disk drives, so that is where its focus is.

This means that whenever you do anything with data or programs on a disk, you have to let DOS know which drive you want it to look to. You do this by typing the drive letter, followed by a colon, like this — A:. That tells DOS to work with drive A. You'd do the same for drive B by typing B: , or drive C by typing C: . (By the way, DOS will happily take either upper- or lowercase letters and treat them the same. In my examples, I'll always show what you type in uppercase, but you can type it either way.)

When any of your computer manuals refer to the **drive specification**, they are referring to the drive letter, followed by a colon. So remember, A: , B: , and so on are also known as drive specifications.

The Default Drive

Much of what you do with the computer involves disk data, so it could be a real nuisance to have to keep typing in the drive specification all the time. DOS simplifies the process by having what's called a **default drive**—a drive that DOS looks to, unless you say otherwise. DOS keeps track of the current default drive, and any time you or a program refer to a disk without giving a drive specification, DOS assumes you intend to use the default drive.

I've already mentioned that DOS prompts for commands with something like this:

```
A>
```

So you're probably able to guess that the A in this prompt refers to the current default drive. If the default drive were changed to B, then DOS's prompt would be:

```
B >
```

This prompt is really quite clever, when you think about it. Since the default drive can be changed, it's very helpful to have DOS remind us of where the default is. But it would be a nuisance to have DOS repeatedly display a message such as:

```
The default drive is now X.
```

Instead, the DOS command prompt is a compact, handy, and unobtrusive way for DOS to remind you of the current default drive.

What if you want to change the default drive? It's simple: Just type in a drive specification all by itself. DOS interprets the drive specification as a command to change the default drive and away you go. Here is a dummy example:

```
A >     (the DOS prompt, saying the default drive is A)
  B :   (you enter a B drive spec, with no other command, and press Enter)
B >     (DOS changes the default drive)
```

Whenever you are working with disks, you have free choice: Use the default drive or specify a different one. In fact, you can specify the drive even if it is already the default—there is no harm in that. The upshot is, if you want to be very specific about a drive, for whatever reason, you can type the letter of the drive you want to use, and it will work just fine, default or not.

Interval versus External Commands

The next thing to cover about commands in general is where they come from. As I've mentioned, commands that we ask DOS to carry out are, in one way or another, programs. The question is: What kind of programs are they and where are they located? This brings us to the topic of internal versus external commands.

DOS faces a quandary you might never think of. In itself, DOS has a large number of services, or commands, available for us to use. Given a choice, we would like to have these command services on tap, instantly, at all times. But for us to have this, the programs that provide these services would have to be resident in memory. That means they would be taking up some of our computer's working memory space all of the time—when we were using them and when we were not. On the other hand, we want to have as little as possible of our computer's memory (its working desktop) taken up by these command programs that we might or might not need to call upon, because we have plenty of other uses for the memory.

The conflict is obvious, and to resolve it DOS provides us with a compromise. A handful of the smallest and most useful command programs are a resident part of DOS. These are called the **internal commands**. They are in memory all the time, once DOS has been read off the disk and started up. And because they are in memory, they are always available—DOS "knows" these commands and can call upon them as easily as you can muster up your name or telephone number. When you used the FORMAT and COPY commands, you used internal commands.

All of the other command programs in DOS are called **external**, and they are kept on the disk until they are needed. When you call for one of these commands, DOS must refer to the disk to "refresh" its memory, much as you might look up the recipe for your grandmother's Christmas cookies.

In terms of computers, the internal commands are built right into DOS, and there is no question that they are a part of DOS. The external commands are also provided with DOS, and they are rightly considered to be part of it as well. But aside from the fact that they come on your DOS disk, they are actually little different from any program that can be used from disk. In reality, there is only a fuzzy distinction between the external commands that are part of DOS and all other external programs, which are also types of commands you call up from disk. Shortly you'll see a list of the commands that are internal and those that are external.

Depending upon which kind of command you happen to choose then, DOS will either be able to carry it out immediately (an internal command), or else it will have to look into its disk filing cabinet for the (external) command program that tells it what to do. The practical significance of this is that the external command program must be on the disk when DOS goes looking for it. DOS can only carry out commands if it has access to the programs they represent. The internal commands are always on tap, but if you ask for an external command, its program disk must be in one of your disk drives in order for DOS to find it.

At first this may seem like a silly point since you expect to have your DOS diskette in a disk drive, but as you'll soon learn, using a computer isn't quite that straightforward. Unless you have a high-capacity, hard-disk system, you'll soon be using more command programs than will fit onto a single diskette. In fact, all of the parts of your DOS probably take up more than one diskette as it is. What do you do when you have more programs than you can keep on one diskette?

One very simple answer is to organize your diskettes functionally, so you combine all the parts that you need to carry out one kind of work. Later, I'll give you some advice about doing just that. For right now, though, what if DOS needs access to a program that isn't in one of your disk drives?

The obvious solution is to change diskettes. You take out one diskette, put in another, and you can have a whole new set of commands at your service. But DOS can't switch diskettes for you. If you ask for a command that isn't internal and isn't on your current diskettes, then DOS can't perform the command. It can, however, tell you something is wrong by displaying the message:

```
Bad command or filename
```

At first you might be confused by this rather unfeeling message, and that is part of the reason I'm discussing it. As you learn more about how external commands are stored on disk, you'll see that a command's name is the same as the name of a file on a disk, which explains the "or filename" part of the above message. The important thing to know is that when you see the message, DOS is telling you it couldn't find a command program that matched the command name you typed.

There are two reasons why DOS might not be able to find a command. One reason, which we've been discussing, is that the command program is on another diskette. The other reason, which you have to be prepared for, is much simpler: You typed the command name wrong. The first thing that you should do when you get the "Bad command" message is check what you typed as a command name—it may not be what you intended.

Common Command Notation

There is a standard format for asking DOS to carry out commands, a format usually called **command notation** or **syntax**, which governs the way we are supposed to enter commands. This section will explain the normal way you request DOS commands. Unfortunately there is a little too much variety in the way you can enter commands, and that can lead to some confusion about the best way to express commands. I'll try to clear all that up here.

First, all commands follow this basic format:

```
COMMAND-NAME   PARAMETERS-IF-ANY
```

For example, in the last chapter, you used this COPY command in duplicating your DOS diskette:

```
COPY   A:*.*   B:
```

The command name was "COPY" and two parameters were needed, the first indicating what to copy from ("A:*.*") and the second showing what to copy to ("B:"). That's the most basic part: A command begins with the name of the command, followed by whatever parameters are needed.

In addition, some kind of punctuation must be used to separate the command name and the parameters. In the examples so far, I've always used spaces, but DOS allows, in fact, sometimes requires, other punctuation marks, including commas, semicolons, and certain other symbols.

It is best, for various reasons, to use the space character, the comma, and the semicolon. You'll probably get the best results and have the fewest problems if you always use the blank space character to separate commands and parameters, except for one special circumstance, which I'll discuss next.

Most commands need only one or two parameters, but sometimes you may need to give DOS several parameters, which must be listed in a specific order. If you omit one or more of these parameters, you must tell DOS that you've deliberately left them out. I won't bother with the details right now, but here's an example of the type of command I'm talking about. It's called the MODE command, and you use the following format to tell DOS how to send or receive information through a connection to a modem or a serial printer:

```
MODE CONNECTION-NAME 1ST,2ND,3RD,4TH
```

Notice that the first through fourth parameters are separated by commas. DOS needs information about all four parameters, but for various reasons you may not need to enter all four. If, for example, you only needed to tell DOS about parameters 1, 3, and 4, your command would look like this:

```
MODE CONNECTION-NAME 1ST,,3RD,4TH
```

To tell DOS you're quite aware of parameter 2, you type the comma that holds its place in the list.

While most commands need only one or two parameters, some special command programs, such as compilers for programming languages, need a longer list of parameters, some of which may be left off. For this kind of command, there is a very useful convention: Each of the parameters is separated by a comma. If a parameter is being left off, then two commas appear in a row. When no more parameters follow (even if there might be more), a semicolon indicates the end of the list. Here is an example showing how this is done:

```
COMMAND 1st,2nd,,4th,,6th;
```

Notice that the third and fifth parameters don't appear, but the commas serve to hold their places, so that it is clear that the fourth parameter is the fourth parameter.

When you need to specify command parameters in this special way, do so. Otherwise, for simplicity, I recommend that you always use spaces to separate a command name from its parameters, and to separate the parameters from each other.

Setting the Switch

There is one more thing you need to know about how commands and their parameters are written. Some commands divide their parameters into two categories, regular parameters and those that are called **switches**. This short list gives you a simple way to understand what switches are:

- **COMMANDS** indicate what is to be done (for example, copy data).
- **PARAMETERS** indicate what the command is to act on (for example, what data to copy).
- **SWITCHES** indicate how the command is to be carried out (for example, should the copy be checked for correctness).

To make it easier to separate parameters (what to act on) from switches (how to carry out the action), DOS uses a special notation: The switch is preceded by a special character.

The standard switch identifier is a slash (/), and that's what all the programs that make up DOS itself use. Most other programs do, too. (Just to make life more complicated, though, let me warn you that some programs identify their switches with a hyphen, -, instead.) In this book, for consistency, I'll show the slash format, which is the normal DOS form.

You've already seen and used one example of a switch. In the last chapter, you used the /S switch when you used the FORMAT command.

Like /S, switches are usually very short and simple—typically just a slash and a single letter. The whole idea of a switch is to tell DOS to do or not do some variation on the basic operation. For example, the /S switch in the FORMAT command told it to include a copy of the operating system on the formatted diskette. Another example: the COPY command has a /V switch, which tells it to verify the copy, checking to see that the copy is accurate.

Files and File Names

Most DOS commands perform some operation on either an entire disk or on files stored on a disk, so most parameters are either a disk specification (telling the command which disk to do its operation on) or they are the names of some files.

I'll go over all the details of file names when we cover disks in more detail in Chapter 9, Understanding Disks. But since you're going to be seeing them a lot as we go over the DOS commands in the chapters in between, here is a quick summary that will give you some background and give you a head start when you come to Chapter 9.

Data on a disk is organized into **files**. For identification, each one has a *file name*. On any one disk, each file name must be unique so that files don't get confused. The name of a file actually has two parts called the **filename** proper and the **filename extension**.

The filename must be at least one character, and it can be as long as eight characters, but no longer. A filename can be made up of letters of the alphabet, digits, and some punctuation marks and special symbols (details in Chapter 9). You can't use a space character as part of a filename, nor can you use any of the characters that are used to punctuate a command and its parameters. You can use upper- or lowercase letters in filenames, but DOS treats them as if they were all uppercase. Here are some sample filenames:

```
FILENAME
12
A
ABC123
```

The extension to the filename is a short appendage added on after the filename. The two are separated by a period, so a filename and extension look like this: FILENAME.EXT. The extension is three characters at most, and it's optional. A file must have a filename part, but it doesn't have to have an extension part. If there is no extension part, drop the period that is used to separate the two parts.

The intended purpose of an extension is to indicate the category the filename falls into. It is an informal—not a mandatory—way of indicating what type the file is. In Chapter 9 you'll see some of the more common categories.

Here are some more examples of file names, with and without extensions, to give you more of an idea of what they can look like:

```
FILENAME.EXT   (this is as big as they can get)
A              (this is the minimum file name)
12345678       (numbers are OK)
NEW-DATA       (hyphens are OK)
NEW_DATA       (underscores are OK, too)
ADDRESS.LST    (this shows how a file name can indicate contents)
JULY.83        (another informative file name)
```

It is a little confusing to have a file's complete name called a file name, and part of that name be called a filename (with no space), but that is the terminology used with DOS, so we have to live with it.

Whenever you run across either term, slow down and be careful to see what is being referred to.

Wildcard Characters

There is a way to refer to more than one file at a time—through a mechanism known as **wildcards**, or (more officially) **global file-name characters**.

Wildcards give you a way of partly specifying a file name so that several files may match the specification. For example, in the last chapter you did a COPY command with a file specification of *.*, which meant any filename and any filename extension. If you had typed it as *.COM, that would mean any filename, but only if it had the extension COM.

There are actually two wildcard symbols: the asterisk (*), which you've seen and used, and the question mark (?), which you haven't encountered yet. Either or both can be used in many ways in file specifications, but we'll leave the details to Chapter 9. For now, just remember that you can use *.* as a way of saying any filename with any extension—or, in other words, all the files on a disk.

With this basic information under your belt, let's move on to look at some of the commands that DOS provides for us.

PART II

Getting Started with DOS Commands

4

ELEMENTARY COMMANDS

Introduction

In this chapter you'll begin learning the commands DOS gives you to work with and control your computer. I'll begin with the commands that are easiest to understand and the ones most commonly used, and work up to the more complicated ones in following chapters.

To make the commands (and DOS) easier to understand, I'll cover them by topic rather than in alphabetical order. I won't cover the precise details of how each command works. That's a subject that properly belongs to your computer's manual, particularly since some of these commands can vary a little from version to version. What I *will* do here is make sense of these commands for you, and give you tips and handy hints about how to get the most from them (and how to avoid problems with them, as well).

Two Simple Commands

Let's get started with the two simplest commands in DOS. They're called **CLS** and **VER**, and they're both handy and easy to use. All you do is type the command name and press the Enter key.

CLS

The CLS command stands for "clear the screen," and that's exactly what it does. It wipes the screen of everything on it and finishes up by displaying the DOS prompt in the top left-hand corner. You might wonder why you'd need a command to erase the screen. In practice, especially when you come to rely more and more on DOS, you'll find CLS can be useful in removing on-screen leftovers and distractions, and giving you the equivalent of a brand-new sheet of paper to work on. And, as you'll see in Chapter 7, Batch File Basics, you can use the CLS command as part of a batch-execution file, clearing the screen automatically so you can have DOS display something else.

If you're at your computer, here's a simple example you can try. First, start your computer with DOS (since all you want to do is clear the screen, just press Enter when DOS requests the date and time):

```
Current date is Tue 1-01-1980
Enter new date:
Current time is 0:00:12.34
Enter new time:

The IBM Personal Computer DOS
Version 3.20 (C) Copyright International Business Machines Corp 1981, 1986
                (C) Copyright Microsoft Corp 1981, 1986
A>
```

At the DOS prompt, type CLS and press Enter. This is what you get:

```
A>
```

Everything else is erased by the CLS command.

VER

Now, on to the VER command. As I mentioned, VER lets you find out what version of DOS you are using. If you've checked the start-up message on your computer, you already know about your own DOS. This command is helpful when, for example, you're using someone else's machine and want to find out what version of DOS is on that person's computer. (You may need this information, because some application programs will only work with certain versions of DOS.)

Like CLS, VER is easy to use. If your computer is running, try typing the command at the DOS prompt, like this:

```
A>VER
```

Press the Enter key, and you'll see a message like this one:

```
IBM Personal Computer DOS Version 3.20
```

Both VER and CLS are internal commands, so they are available at any time.

There is very little, if anything, you can do to make VER self-destruct. The same is true of CLS, but here's a tip for you. If you've been working with lists of files or file names or you've been creating files with DOS (you'll see how later), check what's on the screen before you use CLS to wipe it out. You may find you've erased something you wish you hadn't. I've done it.

The Calendar Commands

DOS keeps track of the date and the time of day. That's a very handy feature for all sorts of reasons, but one of the best is that every time you create or change some information on a disk, the disk data is marked with the current date and time. This marking can be extremely valuable to you in answering questions such as: "Which of these files did I work on last week?" or "Which of these diskettes has the latest changes to my report?" (You'll find out how to get these answers in Chapter 6, when we cover the DIR command.)

Just as with paper files, I've found that it's occasionally a lifesaver to know that all of my files are accurately stamped with the date and time, and there's hardly a day when I don't find it at least useful to see time stamps on my files.

Date and Time

To make it possible to enter or change the date and time, DOS has two special commands called, naturally, DATE and TIME. These commands work independently, so you can enter or change either one without affecting the other. By the way, when DOS starts up, it automatically invokes both DATE and TIME as part of its start-up procedures. You see these commands in action when DOS requests you to the enter the date and time.

DATE and TIME both operate in the same way, and both can be used in either of two ways. The first, which we might call interactive, occurs when you just enter the command name, with no parameters. Using DATE as an example, you would type:

```
DATE
```

As you've seen several times already in this book, DOS responds by telling you its current understanding of the date and asking for a new date, like this:

```
Current date is Tue 01-01-1980
Enter new date:
```

At that point, you can either type a new date or just press Enter to leave the date unchanged.

The other way to use the DATE and TIME commands is more direct. If you key in the command name, followed by the date or time, and press Enter, DOS will just change the date or time without displaying or requesting anything else. Here is an example of how we would use DATE and TIME this way:

```
DATE 7-4-1984
TIME 14:15
```

Here are some tips and notes on the DATE and TIME commands:

- When you type the date you can choose to punctuate it with either hyphens (-) or slashes (/). You punctuate the time with colons (:).
- You can leave leading zeros off the figures. So, for example, January can be entered as 1, rather than 01.
- When typing the date, you can leave off the century—the 19 in 1987.
- When typing the time, you can leave off the seconds, or both minutes and seconds, if you want.
- There isn't any normal way to have DOS display the current date or time without having it wait for a new value. (There is a trick you can use; you'll learn about that in Chapter 13 under the topic of "Introducing Redirection.")
- Under normal circumstances, if DOS is running when midnight passes, it automatically changes the date.
- DOS is smart enough to keep track of leap years.

The DATE and TIME commands are internal, so you can use them at any time, regardless of what you have on your disks.

The Clock-Calendar Option

I mentioned in Chapter 1 that some computer systems have special hardware functions to keep track of the date and time, even when the computer is turned off. This is standard equipment on the IBM/PC AT model and many of the other newer models, and it can be installed in other PCs in what's called a **clock-calendar option**.

These clock-calendars come with many of the most popular multifunction expansion boards for PCs and, combined with the right supporting programs, they can save you the trouble of having to enter the date and time every time you start up DOS. However, even if you have such equipment, you can still use the DATE and TIME commands to change DOS's record of the date and time whenever necessary.

And there you have it—a few gentle, but useful commands to get you started with DOS. You know how to clear the screen to get a "blank slate," you can find the version number of any copy of DOS, and you can check on or adjust DOS' knowledge of the date and time. Now let's move on to more interesting and valuable commands.

5

BASIC FILE COMMANDS

Introduction

I've made a point of emphasizing that most of the work DOS does is related to disks and the files on them. It's time to learn about the most fundamental and useful commands you can use with your disk files: the basic file operations. Just what are these things you'll want to do with files? Most of the time you'll want to: make duplicate copies of them, get rid of those you don't want anymore, display them, change their names, and compare them to see if two files are the same. All of these things are done with DOS, and all of the commands (except for the last, comparing files) are internal, so you can use them at any time. Let's begin with copying.

Copying Files

The COPY command starts out as something very simple—a tool to make copies of disk files. But it adds enough variations on the theme of copying that it ends up serving three distinct purposes.

The most straightforward type of copying just duplicates files from one disk to another. Here's an example that tells DOS to copy a (hypothetical) file named THISFILE from the disk in drive A to the disk in drive B:

```
COPY A:THISFILE B:
```

You did much the same thing, only with wildcard file names, when you duplicated your DOS diskette in Chapter 1. Then, you used the command:

```
COPY A:*.*   B:
```

to copy all the files (*.*) from the DOS diskette in drive A to the formatted diskette in drive B.

You can use both characters and wildcards in a file name. For example, you could copy all the files that begin with the letters XYZ like this:

```
COPY A:XYZ*.* B:
```

You can see there are many variations on this idea, but basically any COPY command in the form:

```
COPY [DRIVE:FILENAME] [DRIVE:]
```

results in the same thing: DOS duplicates the files onto a different disk, but under the same name as on the original disk. Since you haven't told DOS anything but the drive specification for the target, COPY uses the same file names.

You can, if you want, specify the names of the target files so that DOS not only copies them, but gives them different names from the originals. For example:

```
COPY  THISFILE  THATFILE
```

would make a copy of a file named THISFILE, and the copy would be named THATFILE.

Notice a big difference between this command and the one preceding it; it doesn't specify any drives (such as A: or B:). In this case, DOS uses its current default drive for both the source and the target. That means both copies, THISFILE and THATFILE, will be on the same disk. The names are different, so the two files can coexist on one disk with no problem.

The point to remember here (aside from how to copy) is this: If the copy is being made without any change of name, COPY requires that the source and target be on different disks because DOS won't let you have two files with the same name on the same disk. If the name is being changed on the copy, however, then the target file can be anywhere: either where the source is or, if you specify a different location, somewhere else.

For example, you could copy THISFILE from drive A to drive B and name it THATFILE at the same time by typing:

```
COPY A:THISFILE B:THATFILE
```

So far you've seen two of the three different uses of COPY: making duplicates on other disks, and making duplicates under a different name on either the same or a different disk. There is yet another use for COPY: combining the contents of several files into one. This combining operation is advanced and can be tricky, which means you shouldn't try it until you have become more experienced in using DOS. But you should know about this feature of COPY so when you need it, you can study it. Here is an example of how this use of COPY works.

Suppose you have two files, XX and YY, and you want to combine their contents into another file, ZZ. This copy command could do the trick:

```
COPY  XX+YY  ZZ
```

You should know that there are dangers and pitfalls in doing this kind of copying, and there are some special rules to follow. In particular, you need to make sure the files you're combining actually exist (if one doesn't, DOS won't stop to tell you there isn't any such file). You must also check whether the file you're copying to exists on the disk. If it does, the files you're combining will replace, not be added to, the information that's already there. When you need this use of the COPY command, be careful.

Basically, no matter what kind of copying you are doing, the COPY command will proceed whether or not there is already a file with the target name. If there isn't a file with the target name, then a new file will be created. If there is one, it will be overwritten, which could destroy some valuable data. There is no warning that an existing file is about to be destroyed, so be careful with all copies: This is one of the ways you can clobber your valuable data.

On the other hand, except when you combine files, COPY does require that the source files be there and that's natural enough. How can you make a copy of something that isn't there? COPY will let you know if it can't find the source file you claim you want copied by showing you the message "File not found."

Deleting Files with DEL and ERASE

If you can duplicate files (create new copies) with COPY, you'd expect that you can intentionally remove files as well, and you can. For that operation there is the DEL/ERASE command. This is one command, but with two different names: DEL, or delete, and ERASE, for erase. Either command name will cause DOS to throw a file away.

You can remove files one at a time or en masse, using wildcard file names. In the latter case, obviously there's a danger if you mistakenly tell DOS to remove all the files on a disk by using the wildcard filename *.*, meaning "all files." To protect you from that one possibility, DEL/ERASE will pause to ask if you are sure that's what you want to do. For example, if you type:

```
DEL *.*
```

DOS will ask:

```
Are you sure (Y/N)?
```

That's your only chance to back out. If you type Y and press Enter— all gone.

All other file deletion commands proceed without warning, however, so a command like this will proceed automatically:

```
DEL *.BAK
```

So will this:

```
ERASE THISFILE
```

and this:

```
ERASE MYFILES.*
```

If You Delete the Wrong File

Although DOS does not give you any way to recover files that have been erased, the data from erased files is, in fact, still on the disk. DOS doesn't literally go through the chore of wiping out every trace of a deleted file; instead, it just flags that file's space on the disk as "ready for occupancy" and writes over the old data as it goes through the process of storing new information.

Because the deleted information is still on disk then, it can sometimes be recovered by a clever "un-erase" program. If this kind of program is available for your computer, buying it could be one of the best investments you can make, because the program acts as an insurance policy for your data.

When I got my first personal computer there wasn't any such "un-erase" program available for it, so one of the first things I did was write one. That program saved the day for me many times, and I have a stack of letters from other people, thanking me for creating a tool that helped them rescue their data, too. As I said, if you possibly can, get yourself an "un-erase" program.

Erased data can be recovered with a little luck, but this applies only to data you have lost by mistakenly removing a file. You can also lose data by formatting a disk that contains information, and in this case, your data is gone for good. It cannot be recovered, because formatting (reformatting, rather) literally wipes a disk clean.

Reformatting is a handy way to provide yourself with a blank diskette, especially when your supply is running low, but if you're going to do this, take some precautions. You might try putting an X on the label of any diskette you no longer need, or you might store old diskettes in a separate box or drawer.

There are other ways to protect yourself here, too, but it's still a little early in the game to go into those details. You'll find more information on the dangers of erasing and formatting, and some tricks to safeguard yourself against these dangers, in Chapters 11 and 14. At this point, just keep these two rules in mind:

- Make sure you know what files you're deleting and why, before you actually remove them, especially if you are using wildcards to delete more than one file with a single DEL command.
- Make sure any diskette you reformat truly contains expendable information (the DIR command in Chapter 6 will help you out here).

Renaming Files with REN

Related to both copying and erasing files is a DOS command to change the name of a file. REN, short for rename, will change a file's name as long as the name isn't currently in use by another file on the same disk. Renaming is done like this:

```
REN OLD-NAME NEW-NAME
```

For example, if you had a file named DRAFT and you wanted to change the name to FINAL, the command would be:

```
REN DRAFT FINAL
```

Like other commands, you can use wildcards with REN to rename several files at once. For example, you could change every file with an extension of XXX to YYY, like this:

```
REN *.XXX *.YYY
```

or any variation on this idea.

Displaying Files with TYPE

So far you've seen how to copy, delete, and rename files. Suppose you're not quite sure what's in a file you're planning to copy/delete/rename, it would be nice to take a look and verify what's in it. Can you do so? Sometimes, with a command called TYPE. TYPE is a handy way to get a quick look at the contents of a file, because it writes a copy of a file onto the display screen of your computer. In fact, TYPE is really just a COPY command, with the target of the copy being your display screen instead of another file.

The file you want to see, however, must be something reasonable to look at. It has to contain display characters; it must be what is called a **text file**, or else what appears on your screen will be all or partly nonsensical. TYPE is done like this:

```
TYPE SOMEFILE.TXT
```

(You'll have to give DOS the full file name, including the extension if the file has one.)

One last thought on the TYPE command—if you tell DOS to display a file that is not a text file, you may be surprised to see and hear a string of indecipherable symbols and strange beeps. Don't worry, you haven't broken anything. Just let the command run its course, and remember not to use TYPE on that file again.

Comparing Copies of Files

When you make copies of files with the COPY command, you may want to confirm that the copy is exact. To be honest, there is little reason to check a copy you have just made; the copying process is extremely reliable and it is very unlikely that there will be any errors in copying, unless the copying procedure itself tells you there were problems. The main reason for comparing copies of files is to find out if the copies contain any discrepancies—small changes, perhaps, that you might have forgotten about.

COMP and DISKCOMP

There are two comparison commands, one called COMP that compares files individually, and one called DISKCOMP that compares entire diskettes (we'll cover it in the next chapter). The file comparison program checks the contents of files to make sure that they match.

Here is how file comparison is done. You provide the names of two files to be compared. If the two copies have the same name, but are on different disks, then you needn't specify the name of the second file. Just tell DOS where it is located by giving a drive specification. Here are two examples of how you would start a file comparison:

```
COMP    ORIGINAL   COPY
COMP    A:FILENAME B:
```

For instance, imagine you've just duplicated a very important file named CONTRACT in order to preserve the original, but make some changes to the copy. You've learned to have faith in DOS, but just to be on the safe side you want to know that the duplicate, named REVISION, is starting out as an exact copy of the original. That's when you would use the first of the two preceding examples:

```
COMP CONTRACT REVISION
```

Likewise, if you had copied CONTRACT from drive A to drive B, keeping the same file name, your command would be:

```
COMP A:CONTRACT B:
```

You can also use wildcard filenames to compare a group of files automatically. There are many of ways that can be handy; one of the handiest is in comparing all of the files on one disk with all the files on another, to see if they're the same. Using COMP, you can compare all the data between the two disks like this:

```
COMP A:*.* B:
```

As mentioned, when you compare files you usually have one of two things in mind: either you want to check that the files exactly match or you want to figure out what the differences are. Of the two, you're best off only checking to see whether the files are exact duplicates. You can also find out what the differences are, but the information may be useless to you. Here's why:

COMP *does* report any difference it finds between two files, but only in the most exasperatingly technical way. If it finds a difference, it reports both the location of the difference and the difference itself in **hexadecimal notation**, which is base-16 math. For most people, hex is just plain confusing. So in ordinary circumstances use COMP to tell you if the files it's comparing match exactly. If COMP does report differences, make your check the old-fashioned way: by comparing paper copies.

There's also one instance in which COMP will simply refuse to continue: If COMP finds that the files it's comparing are of different lengths, it will stop right there, without comparing any of the contents. If COMP finds 10 differences in the content, it won't try to hunt for a place where the files match up again, it will just stop. Next to smarter file comparison programs, our COMP is rigid and dumb. Still, it's part of DOS and it is good for finding out if two files match exactly, even if it's not very helpful in telling what the substance of any differences are.

6

BASIC DISK COMMANDS

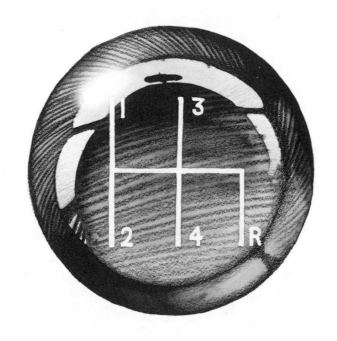

Introduction

In the last chapter we introduced ourselves to the most basic and useful commands DOS has to work with our files. Now its time to do the same thing for the commands that are most helpful in working with entire disks.

Checking Out Your Disks

DOS has two commands that let you find out what's on your disks. They're called called DIR and CHKDSK. DIR gives you a listing, called a **directory**, of the files stored on a disk. CHKDSK gives you a status report on the disk itself. Let's look at DIR first, since it's a command you'll probably use quite often.

What Is a Directory?

Like a telephone directory, a disk directory lets you look things up. In the case of a phone book, you look up names, addresses, and phone numbers. In the case of DOS, you can use a directory to check on several things: the names of the files on a disk, the size of each file, and the date and time each file was created or updated. Here's an example of what a DOS directory looks like:

```
     Volume in drive A is XYZ REPORT
     Directory of A:
FINAL    BAK    27520    6-25-87    5:13p
DRAFT    DOC    22144    6-22-87    4:47p
FINAL    DOC    27648    6-25-87    5:13p
DRAFT    BAK    21760    6-22-87    1:53p
MEMO     DOC      768    6-25-87    5:42p
     5 File(s)    261120 bytes free
```

The lines beginning with the words Volume and Directory are DOS's way of identifying the disk drive and directory you're looking at. As you can see here, your disks can have identifying names, known as **volume labels**, stored on them ("volume" is DOS's way of referring to a disk). These volume ID labels help you keep track of the many diskettes that you'll be using and are even handy with hard disk systems, too. In the next section of this chapter, you'll see how to put labels onto disks. For now, just keep in mind that the DIR command will report a disk's volume label, if there is one.

The directory listing itself begins below the Volume and Directory lines. It tells you there are five files on this disk—two named DRAFT, with the extensions DOC and BAK, two named FINAL, again with the extensions DOC and BAK, and one named MEMO.DOC. The last line of this display tells you how many files DOS counted on the disk and how much room you have left for storing more files. Now with that out of the way, let's look at the DIR command.

DIR

There are several ways you can use DIR. The most common way is to type in the command DIR with or without a drive specification. If you just type DIR, you see a directory of files on the disk in the default drive. If you type DIR with a drive specification, like this: DIR A :, you see a directory of files on the disk in the drive you specified.

In either case, this form of the command will ask DIR to list all of the files on a disk. As you saw in the earlier example, the list will include the filename, the filename extension, the size of the file in bytes (roughly, characters), and the date and time the file was created or last changed. Remember that, in the coverage of the DATE and TIME commands, I mentioned that files are marked with time stamps, and that is one good reason for giving DOS the date and time whenever you start up. The DIR command is your way to see the time stamp, as well as the size of each file on your disk, and the amount of space you have left for storing new files.

If you don't want to see a list of all of the files—if all you want is information on one—you can type that file's name as part of the DIR command, and DIR will report only on it. For example, if you just wanted to know when you wrote DRAFT.DOC, this command:

```
DIR DRAFT.DOC
```

would tell you.

Similarly, you can use wildcards to get information on more than one, but still not all files. For example, the command:

```
DIR *.BAK
```

would get directory information on all files that have an extension of BAK.

One of the things that DIR reports is the amount of space left free on a disk. So you may want to use the DIR command not to see a directory listing, but simply to find out how much space is available for use on a disk.

Specifics About DIR

A disk can have "hidden" files on it; usually if it does, they are secret parts of the DOS operating system (you'll learn more about that in the next section and in Chapter 9). The DIR command acts as though hidden files were not there at all, but CHKDSK, which we're coming to, tells you a little about them.

There is one peculiarity of the DIR command that you need to know about. Most DOS commands work with wildcard file specifications like *.*, which means "all files with any names." DIR works with wildcards as well, but it has one difference: DIR will assume a wildcard where you didn't type one. So, if you enter the command:

    DIR

it is treated just as if you had typed:

    DIR *.*

And if you put in a filename, with no extension, such as:

    DIR FILENAME

it will be treated as if you had typed a wildcard for the extension (DIR FILENAME.*). With our earlier sample directory, for instance, the command:

    DIR DRAFT

would cause DIR to report on two files, DRAFT.DOC and DRAFT.BAK.

This special feature of DIR is rather handy, but it has one real drawback: It is inconsistent with the rest of DOS. Consistency is important in anything as complex as DOS, because it reduces the number of rules you have to learn, and it increases your confidence that DOS will do what you think you are asking it to do. In this case, don't be worried if you find that DIR is acting a little different than all the other DOS commands. It isn't you misunderstanding things, it's just DIR doing things its own way.

Switches in DIR

There are two switches in the DIR command. One, /P, causes the command to pause after the screen fills. The other, /W, causes DIR to list the files in five columns across the width of the display screen. Both switches are intended to help you see long lists of files better. If you use the /W switch, however, the directory listing includes only the filename and extension of each file—not the size or time stamp. All that information won't fit into a five-column display. Here's what you would see for our sample disk:

```
Volume in drive A is XYZ REPORT
Directory of A:\

FINAL BAK DRAFT DOC FINAL DOC DRAFT BAK MEMO DOC
```

CHKDSK

While the DIR command shows us a list of the files on a disk, the CHKDSK, or check disk, command is intended to give us a status report on our disks. CHKDSK does two main things: first, it checks the disk over to see how much space there is and how much is in use, and to see if there is any discrepancy in the space usage. It then reports the total space on the disk, the amount of space in use, the number of files and, incidentally, whether there are any hidden files.

CHKDSK also does something else nice, that is completely unrelated to its check-your-disk function: It reports on the amount of memory available in your system. Just as you might use DIR just to find out about available space on disk, you couldt use CHKDSK just to see how much memory you have.

Here is an example of the type of report CHKDSK gives you (notice that like DIR, CHKDSK includes the disk's volume ID label):

```
Volume SAMPLE DISK created Jun 22, 1987 1:51p

362496 bytes total disk space
     0 bytes in 1 hidden files
101376 bytes in 5 user files
261120 bytes available on disk

655360 bytes total memory
305328 bytes free
```

(The 0 bytes in 1 hidden file may look peculiar, but it's fine with DOS. Don't concern yourself about it.)

Although CHKDSK tells you about discrepancies on disk, such problems actually are rare, and you may never encounter one. These discrepancies come up when things go wrong with the space allocation on a disk and, although it is a very interesting subject, it is one that is too technical for this book.

In addition to reporting on discrepancies, CHKDSK is also prepared to repair any logical damage in the use of space. If any space has been "lost," which is one of the possible discrepancies in the space usage, CHKDSK can recover it and also report or repair other kinds of mix-ups in the space. In the earliest versions of DOS, CHKDSK did this repair work automatically; but that can be a little dangerous. Starting with version 2.00, CHKDSK will repair the disk only if you give it permission with the "Fix" switch, /F.

This check, report, and repair operation is a valuable one, and it is a very good idea to do a routine CHKDSK on all of your disks occasionally. When you set up batch files, which are discovered in Chapter 7, it's a good idea to include CHKDSK in many of your batch file operations.

Volume Labels for Disk Identification

You've seen a few examples of DOS' reports on volume labels, so let's find out a little more about them.

VOL

If you just want to display the ID label on a disk volume, you don't need to go through the often time-consuming DIR or CHKDSK operation. There is a special command that does nothing but report the volume label on a disk. It's the VOL command, and you use it like this (include the drive specification if the disk is not in the current default drive):

```
VOL A:
```

The report it gives you is like the ones you've already seen:

```
Volume in drive A is XXXXXXXXXX
```

How do you go about putting a label on a disk in the first place? There are actually two ways to do it. If you're formatting a disk for use, the FORMAT command (which will be covered in in the next section) has a switch called /V that you can use to include a volume label. (Early versions of DOS don't have this feature.) On the other hand, if you have a disk that's already been formatted, you can use the LABEL command to add or change a volume label. In either case, the DOS displays requesting you to type a volume label looks exactly the same. For example, if you type:

```
FORMAT A: /V
```

DOS goes through its usual formatting procedure and at the end, displays this message:

```
Formatting. . .Format complete
Volume label (11 characters, ENTER for none)?
```

This, in DOS's terse language, means: "I'm through formatting this disk, so now type a volume label of up to 11 characters; if you've decided not to give this disk a label, press ENTER."

LABEL

Imagine you have a formatted disk, perhaps one on which you've stored a number of related files. You can't use the FORMAT command to give it a volume label, because formatting would destroy your data. In this case, you use the LABEL command, including a drive specification if necessary. The command looks like this:

```
LABEL A:
```

and LABEL's response looks like this:

```
Volume in drive A has no label

Volume label (11 characters, ENTER for none)?
```

Suppose your disk already has volume label, let's say it's called RE-PORT, and you want to change the label to XYZ REPORT. You type LABEL A: and the command responds:

```
Volume in drive A is REPORT

Volume label (11 characters, ENTER for none)?
```

Finally, if you want to remove a disk's volume label, replacing it with nothing, you again type LABEL A: and see the same display as before. This time, though, you press ENTER to signify that you don't want a volume label, and the command responds:

```
Delete current volume label (Y/N)?
```

If you press Y, the volume label is removed.

Basically, you use the VOL command to report on a volume label, and you use the LABEL command to set one on a formatted disk. Unfortunately, the command names themselves don't tell you which does which. There's no simple way to know that VOL just shows the volume label, while LABEL actually puts it on the disk, you'll just have to remember.

Now, on to the very important subject of preparing diskettes for use.

The Diskette Preparation Commands

Since DOS relies so heavily on the use of diskettes, it naturally has commands to prepare them for use. You took a short look at one of them, FORMAT, in Chapter 2. Now it's time for a closer look at the set up commands, FORMAT and SYS.

Keep in mind: From here through the end of this chapter, you'll be learning about commands that are primarily, if not entirely, used with diskettes—not hard disks. This distinction is particularly important where the FORMAT command is involved. Although the FORMAT command is needed to prepare a hard disk for use, it is unlikely that you'll need to format a hard disk more than once. In fact, unless you're willing to lose everything on your hard disk, you would be wise to think of the FORMAT command in terms of diskettes only. Going even further, I would advise you to double-check the FORMAT commands you type, making sure that you do not unwittingly tell DOS to format your hard disk (probably C:) instead of the diskette in another drive.

Format

As you saw in Chapter 2, the FORMAT command is used to do the most basic preparation of a diskette for use. It is the equivalent of drawing rules on a blank sheet of paper, to make it possible to later write evenly on the paper.

FORMAT actually does two important things with a diskette: It draws the electronic "rules" that make it possible for DOS to work with the diskette and it checks for any defects in the diskette. Because diskettes are so vulnerable, they may have damaged patches on them. But a diskette with a bad patch can still be used—the FORMAT command knows how to recognize these bad patches and put up a safety fence around them. When FORMAT finds bad patches, it reports them to you, indicating their size as well as the size of the usable part of the diskette. Once this done, the rest of the diskette is ready to use.

Whether or not you want to use a diskette with a bad patch is up to you. Obviously a bad patch takes up part of the space on a diskette, and it makes you wonder about the quality of the rest of the diskette. But bad patches are usually small and well-defined, so nothing is wrong with the rest of the diskette. If you need every bit of space that a diskette has to offer, or if you are unusually worried about risks to your data, then put aside any diskette that the FORMAT command tells you has bad patches. Normally, though, I would say that there is no problem with using a diskette with bad patches that are a small proportion of the diskette.

Usually, diskettes format without any bad patches. If you encounter them a lot, it is a sign of one of two things: Either you have a bad batch of diskettes, or the recording heads on your disk drives are dirty and should be cleaned. If you suspect that the problem is dirty heads, see your computer's manual for cleaning instructions.

When you format a diskette, you have the option of putting the DOS operating system on the diskette. Including DOS on many of your diskettes means you can start your system with any of them—you don't have to use just one special start-up diskette. This can be a real convenience, but having DOS on a diskette takes up some of the diskette's usable space.

I would recommend, for starters, that you include DOS on every diskette until you learn from your own experience which ones you do and don't want DOS stored on. At first, it is better to have DOS on all of your disks. Later you can be more discriminating—for example, putting DOS on all of your program diskettes but leaving it off your data diskettes. If you have formatted a diskette without a copy of DOS, then you cannot later add DOS to the diskette except by reformatting it (which would wipe out any data you had placed on the diskette). In general, it is better to include DOS in your formatting.

The System switch, /S, is used to tell FORMAT to include a copy of DOS on the diskette. Here's the command to format the diskette in drive B with a copy of DOS on it:

```
FORMAT B: /S
```

Here's an example of what DOS reports when the procedure is complete (depending on your version of DOS, the number of bytes used for the system may be different):

```
Formatting...Format complete
System transferred

   362496 bytes total disk space
    62464 bytes used by system
   300032 bytes available on disk
```

When the FORMAT command sets up a diskette as a system diskette, it places three files on the diskette. Two of these files are hidden, which means you can't ordinarily see them except through a CHKDSK command that reports on the number of hidden files on a diskette. The third file is not hidden, it can be seen like any other file, and is named COMMAND.COM. You'll see more about the two hidden files and the COMMAND.COM file when we move on to the SYS command.

Remember, too, that you can put a volume label on your diskettes when you format them. To do this, as well as transfer DOS to the diskette, you include both the /S and /V switches in your command:

```
FORMAT A: /S /V
```

Variations in Diskette Formats

Our PCs work with more than one diskette format, for example, single or double-sided diskettes. The FORMAT command is prepared to create diskettes in any of several formats. Normally you should let DOS decide which format to use, unless you know you need a special format that is used by another computer. New computers, and later versions of DOS, can create and use diskette formats that can't be read by some earlier versions. A PC AT, for instance, can use a 1.2-megabyte, high-capacity floppy disk that cannot be used by a PC with 360K disk drives.

The switches in the format command allow you to control which type of formatting is done. There are lots of combinations of formatting, and we'd get lost if I tried to explain them all. There are only three that matter, for most practical purposes, so I'll show you the format switches used to create each one.

First—and most important for us—is formatting with a copy of the DOS operating system, which you've already seen. You create this kind of disk by using the /S switch, like this:

```
FORMAT /S
```

Second, is the format that will give us the greatest possible storage space. This is a diskette formatted to the highest capacity that our diskette drives can manage, without a copy of DOS taking up any room. We create that kind of disk by leaving off all switches, like this:

```
FORMAT
```

Third and last, there is the "lowest common denominator" diskette. This is the diskette format that can be read by any model of PC, using any version of DOS, even the oldest PCs and the very first 1.00 DOS. This is the universal diskette format for IBM PCs. When we use it, we sacrifice storage capacity for universal use. Most software is distributed in this format, even though few PCs need this lowest common denominator. Technically this format is called single-sided eight-sector format, and you may occasionally hear those terms used.

We create this kind of diskette by using the switches "/1" (for single-sided) and "/8" (for eight-sector), like this:

```
FORMAT /1 /8
```

A Word of Warning   FORMAT is one of the most dangerous of all the commands in DOS because it can wipe out an entire diskette's worth of data at one go. If you format a diskette that has some valuable data on it, it is thoroughly gone and nothing will bring it back. Be very careful when you format diskettes—check that the diskette doesn't have something important on it before you wipe it off the face of the disk with FORMAT. On the other hand, if you have to destroy some confidential data and need to be sure that it can't be reconstructed, FORMAT is the right tool to use.

Transferring DOS with SYS

There are times when you may want to transfer a copy of the DOS operating system to a diskette that is already formatted to hold it. The SYS command is intended to solve this problem, but the key words here are "already formatted to hold it." The SYS command will copy DOS to a diskette, but it does not do so willy-nilly. You cannot, for example, format a diskette without DOS, store your data files on it, and then later decide to add DOS to the diskette so you can use it as a start-up diskette. In order for SYS to work, space has to have been set aside specifically for DOS to occupy. That doesn't happen with a regularly formatted diskette, thus if you try to add DOS to a data diskette, the quick and unequivocal response is:

```
No room for system on destination disk
```

There are, however, two reasons why you might need the SYS command. One is if you buy a program diskette that needs to have a copy of DOS on it. This is commonly done with copy protected programs (which we'll talk more about later in the book). Disks like that usually have space provided for DOS, but don't actually have DOS on the disk; so you have to transfer DOS to them.

The second reason why you might need to transfer DOS is when you get a new version of DOS. Like all other good programs, DOS is occasionally updated and upgraded. And when you have a new version of DOS, you need to transfer the new DOS to your old DOS diskettes.

The SYS command is designed to transfer the two hidden files that are part of DOS from one diskette to another. SYS does *not* transfer the third file that is part of DOS, the file COMMAND.COM. A complete transfer of the DOS operating system onto a diskette requires that you do two things: a SYS command to transfer the two hidden files, and a COPY command to copy the COMMAND.COM file. Whenever you read instructions about transferring DOS to a diskette, the instructions should mention both commands: SYS and COPY COMMAND.COM. (Refer back to Chapter 5 if you need a refresher on the COPY command.)

Copying and Comparing Disks

There is another way to set up a diskette for use besides the FORMAT command, and that is the DISKCOPY command.

DISKCOPY

DISKCOPY is a command that reads all the formatting and data from one diskette and copies it to another diskette, making a literal duplicate of the original in the process. Every file—indeed, every character in every file—will occupy exactly the same position on the copy that it occupies on the source diskette. To use DISKCOPY, you type the command name, followed by the drive specifications for the diskette you are copying from, then the diskette you are copying to. For example, if you have a data diskette in drive A and you want to make an exact duplicate of it in drive B, the command is:

```
DISKCOPY A: B:
```

DISKCOPY is a quick and efficient way to make copies of diskettes. It is so quick and efficient that you will find its use recommended to you over and over again. But there are some important problems with DISKCOPY, and so I recommend that you be very careful about using it. The preferred way to copy disk data is with the COPY command you've already learned about.

The major disadvantage of using DISKCOPY is that it does not allow for bad areas on your diskettes. If either the diskette you are copying from or the one you are copying to have unusable bad areas on them (the type of bad areas I mentioned that FORMAT detects), then DISKCOPY will not work properly. On the other hand, the COPY command, the preferred way to copy data, works nicely with bad patches on the diskettes.

Another advantage of COPY over DISKCOPY is that COPY can improve the use of space on a diskette, while DISKCOPY can't. This is an incidental and beneficial side-effect of how COPY happens to work.

Finally, DISKCOPY will wipe out anything that is on the target diskette, while COPY will merge new files with old to add information to a diskette.

There are some reasons not to use DISKCOPY, but there are still some good reasons to use it, too. For one thing, DISKCOPY is faster than COPY if the diskette is full of data. If there is only a little data on a diskette, COPY could be faster because it would copy only the data, while DISKCOPY would also faithfully copy all the unused diskette space, as well. Another reason for using DISKCOPY is to check a diskette for physical damage or for copy-protection. If you can DISKCOPY a diskette without any error messages, then the diskette is probably not damaged, and not copy-protected. This makes DISK-COPY a quick and easy way to check for these problems.

Confirming That a DISKCOPY Is Accurate

When you make copies of files or disks, you may need to confirm that the copy is accurate. In Chapter 5 you learned about the COMP command, which lets you compare files after you've used the COPY command to duplicate one or more files on another disk. As I mentioned then, there is little reason to check a copy you have just made—the copying process is extremely reliable, and it is very unlikely that there will be any errors in copying, unless the copying procedure itself tells you there were problems.

Where the COMP command lets you compare files, the DISK-COMP command lets you compare entire diskettes to see if they match exactly. DISKCOMP is primarily useful as a means of verifying the results of a DISKCOPY, because DISKCOMP will report two diskettes as being different even if they contain the same data and are functionally equivalent but differ in some minor way, such as the order the data is stored in.

If you have the slightest worry about whether two diskettes are identical, then by all means use DISKCOMP. If all you're interested in, however, is whether two diskettes contain the same files and you want to make sure the files bear the same time stamps, either compare directory listings for the two diskettes or use the COMP command with any specific files you need to verify.

The DISKCOMP command is easy to understand and use. To use it, you enter the command name, followed by the drive specifications of the two diskettes. Both diskettes are read from front to back and compared; any differences are reported. Here is a typical example of using disk comparison:

```
DISKCOMP  A:  B:
```

As DISKCOMP compares the two diskettes, it tells you the locations of any differences it finds with messages like this:

```
Compare error on side 0, track 7
Compare error on side 1, track 8
```

and so on. Like the report you get from COMP, which is in hexadecimal, the actual information may be meaningless to you, even one such message will tell you your diskettes are not identical.

7

BATCH FILE BASICS

Introduction

Batch-processing files are one of the most useful and powerful features of DOS, and in this chapter you'll take a look at them. First, you'll discover the simple idea of what a batch file is, and then get into some of the fancier tricks of using batch files. Finally, I'll finish the chapter with some suggestions and examples to help you begin to see batch files in terms of your own work and needs.

Before we really get into the subject, let's start with some philosophy—the philosophy of the black box. Roughly speaking, there are two ways of using a personal computer: expert and you-do-it. Experts know what they are doing (or think they do), and they usually enjoy being involved in the mechanics of how work gets done. Those of us with the you-do-it approach don't really know what's going on, and probably don't care—we want the results and don't want to get involved in the mechanics of how it's done.

For the you-do-its, computer operations need to work like what is called a **black box**. We don't need to see how the box gets its work done, as long as we are confident that it is doing the work correctly. Basically, it is very nice to have an expert's technical knowledge, but for most computer users, the more a computer can function as a trustworthy black box, the better for all concerned.

One of the features of DOS that can help make it work like a friendly black box is batch-file commands. My reason for explaining this so elaborately is to instill in you the idea that batch files are more than just a convenient, efficient, and safe way to direct the computer's operations. Batch files are also a key way of building black boxes to help make the use of your computer less technical. When you understand this, it can guide you into making the best possible use of batch files.

Introducing Batch Processing

The basic idea of batch processing is simple and ingenious: If you need the computer to perform a standard task, why should you have to key in the details? Let the computer find out what it is supposed to do by reading its commands from a file. With a batch file, DOS doesn't perform our commands extemporaneously, instead it reads from a script, leaving you free to do something else with your time.

There are some interesting details concerning what a batch file can do, but let's begin with the fundamentals. First of all, batch processing is always performed by a batch-processing file, which must have the filename extension of .BAT. The file must be a plain, unformatted text file (also called an **ASCII file**), which means it has to be a bare-bones, standard-characters-only type of file.

If you're unfamiliar with unformatted files, we'll be covering them in Chapter 9, Understanding Disks. For now, though, here's the important part to remember: You can create an unformatted or ASCII, file with any ordinary text editor, such as the EDLIN editor that comes with DOS. You can also use a word-processing program to create batch files, but you'll have to use your word processor's "unformatted" or "non-document" mode, so that the file comes out as plain unformatted text. (Your word processor's manual will explain how to do that.)

Inside a batch-processing file are ordinary DOS commands, just as you might enter them on the keyboard. There can be one or many commands in the file. You place each command on a separate line.

You put a batch file to work by giving DOS its file name as a command. This works exactly the same way that you use a program, you type in the name of the program, and DOS finds and starts the program for you. In the case of a batch file, DOS goes looking for the file and when it finds that the file has the extension BAT, it starts executing the commands held in that file.

How Batch Processing Works

The easiest way to understand this concept of batch processing is to actually see how it works. So let's take a look at a very simple batch file. Let's suppose you've created a file with the name D.BAT. Notice that the file name has the proper extension of BAT. Since the file name itself is D, then D is all that you need to type to invoke this batch-processing command. To start out on the right foot, let's make the contents of this batch-processing file something very simple: a single line that reads DIR (which, remember, is the name of the directory command that lists the contents of a disk). This is what your batch-processing file would look like. Here's the file name:

```
D.BAT
```

and this is what it contains:

```
DIR
```

Now, with this batch-processing file set up, what would happen if you keyed in the file name (the letter D) and pressed enter? DOS would first search for a file named D. When it found D, it would also find out that the file name's extension is BAT. Since BAT tells DOS to carry out the commands in the file, DOS would then start executing whatever DOS commands it finds in D. Since it would find only the command DIR, it would give you a directory listing.

This example is about as short and silly as you could imagine, and you might be thinking that it is a completely artificial example, with no practical value. Surprisingly, not, there is a use for batch-processing commands like this.

What this command does, in effect, is let you use D as an abbreviation for DIR. At first glance, that may not seem like a big deal, yet it cuts the keystrokes you have to type in half, from four to two (counting the enter key). This is one of the main purposes of batch files: to simplify the typing you have to do to get your computer to do some work for you. One of the best uses of batch files, then, is simply to provide convenient abbreviations of commands.

Let's expand our small batch file a little. Suppose you want DOS to switch from drive A to drive B before it shows the directory listing. D.BAT would have to contain two DOS commands: One to change drives, and another to display the directory. The file would look like this:

```
B:
DIR
```

Now we come to one of the rather clever things that DOS does when it works with batch files. It keeps track of where it is working in the file. So when the file has more than one command, DOS knows how to carry on. As it finishes carrying out each command, DOS returns to the batch file, reads past the commands it has already processed, then starts the next command. Thus, in our two-line batch file, DOS would read the first command, B: , carry it out, return to the file, bypass the first command, and carry out the second command, DIR.

You can see the most important reason why you would want to have batch-processing files. Even before we get into the advanced material, you know from this example that these files not only let you create an abbreviation for a command name—they let you group several commands into one functional unit.

Very often, you need to do several things to carry out a task you perform fairly often. For example, imagine you do a lot work with a spreadsheet program and a word processor. Some of your documents have the extension DOC (for document), and the others have the extension WK1 (for worksheet). Periodically, you make copies of these files onto archive diskettes and you check the directory of the copy to make sure everything's as it should be. The routine never varies:

```
COPY A:*.DOC B:
COPY A:*.WK1 B:
DIR B:
```

DOS can do it for you. You can put those commands in a batch file with a name like COPIES.BAT, and keep the batch file on each of your data diskettes. Whenever you need a copy, put your data diskette in drive A, a formatted diskette in drive B, and just type COPIES.

The most important reason then, for using batch files is to gather together, under one name, all the separate steps needed to perform a task. The reason for doing that is as much for uniformity and completeness as it is for convenience and ease. Regardless of the task, putting it in a batch file means that task will be carried out the same way, every time.

Very often you need to do several things to carry out one task. For example, to write the words you are reading, I used a batch file that has four steps: the first runs my text-editor program so I can type in these words; the second runs my spelling checker to check what I have written for speling erers; the third runs my editor again, so I can correct the errors; and finally, the fourth makes a backup copy of what I have written, putting the copy on another disk.

I could do each of these four steps separately every time I do any writing, but I chose to put them all into one batch-processing file.

That's done two very useful things for me. First, it has saved me the trouble of invoking each step by itself. Second, and more important, it has established a standard operating discipline for me. Each time I write, I check my spelling and I make a backup copy. Laziness or lack of time won't keep me from doing either of these two important tasks.

The most important reason, then, for using batch files is to gather together, under one name, all the separate steps needed to perform a task, and the reason for doing that is as much for uniformity and completeness as it is for convenience and ease.

Using Batch Files to Protect Data

There is one more key reason for using batch files, and that reason is safety. There are some maddeningly dangerous commands available to us in DOS, commands that can wipe out data in the blink of an eye. There are three such commands: DEL/ERASE, which discards data, COPY, which can overwrite good data with bad, and FORMAT, which can wipe out the entire contents of a disk beyond all hope of recovery. Batch files can reduce the danger of misusing these commands, not intentionally, of course, but everyone has "one of those days"—in a rush, perhaps your mind is half on something else. Here's an example.

Let's suppose you routinely delete a file called DATA.OLD, while preserving the file DATA.NEW. If you type in the command:

```
DEL DATA.OLD
```

each time, there is just a chance that one day, absent-mindedly, you will type NEW, rather than OLD. Wouldn't that put you in a pickle? But if you had a batch file with the DEL command in it, you won't have to worry about this kind of mistake. In fact, you might have a batch file that safely and reliably erased all sorts of files without a worry, because if you built the batch file correctly, then the commands would go right, each time; never a slip. You might even name the batch file something evocative and easy to remember, like

```
KILL-OLD.BAT.
```

A Special Batch File—AUTOEXEC.BAT

In the rest of this chapter you'll be looking at some DOS commands that are specially made for use in batch files. But before you get to them, let's pause to meet a special batch file, called AUTOEXEC.BAT.

When DOS starts up its operation, it's prepared to perform any start-up commands we want it to do. That can be very handy—those commands can be used to get DOS off to a running start. The mechanics of how this is done are very simple: When DOS starts up, it always checks to see if there is a batch file named AUTOEXEC.BAT on the disk it is starting up from. If there is an AUTOEXEC.BAT file available, DOS starts carrying out the commands in this file, just as if you had entered the command AUTOEXEC as your first instructions to DOS.

You can also enter the command AUTOEXEC, just like any other batch command, any time you want to. The one special thing about the AUTOEXEC.BAT file is that DOS will, if it finds such a file, automatically perform the commands in that file. This can be very helpful if there are any start-up operations you want to perform when you fire up your computer.

You can use AUTOEXEC.BAT to perform any beginning commands that you want, and it doesn't have to be long or involved. You can, for example, create an AUTOEXEC.BAT file just to start up the program you use the most. There are also more exotic uses for the AUTOEXEC command, but you'll see those in Chapter 20.

The First Two Commands—REM and PAUSE

Some commands built into DOS exist just to make batch-file processing better. Two of these are the REMark and PAUSE commands. REMark, as its name implies, is intended to let you put comments into a batch file. Such comments can be useful reminders of what is going on; they can say to anyone who reads them, "this is what I'm doing." When you include a remark, the line must begin with REM. If the remark is longer than one line, each succeeding line must also begin with REM. Here's a simple example:

```
REM DISPLAY DIRECTORY
DIR B:
```

Whenever DOS encounters REM in a batch file, it skips over the words in the remark and moves on to the next command it can carry out. (There's also another, clearer way to include remarks that DOS will display on screen; it's called the ECHO command, and we'll get to it in the next section.)

In the example, REM was followed by a DIR command. The DIR command might show us so many files in the directory that the REM-remark rolls right off the top of the screen. That could be a problem. Not in our example here, but if the REM-remark was something more important we wanted to make sure we could see on the screen, we would need a way of stopping things so that these comments can be seen. That is done with the PAUSE command, something like this:

```
REM DISPLAY DIRECTORY
PAUSE
.  .  .  .
   .  .  .  .
      .  .  .  .
```

Using Pause

What's this PAUSE command you see here? Technically speaking, PAUSE is just another form of the REM command. Instead of commenting on what's happening, however, it suspends the operation of the batch file until you press a key—any key—on the keyboard. You saw a type of PAUSE command in the /P switch of the DIR command, the switch that stops a directory listing after each screen-full and waits for you to press a key to continue.

The PAUSE command is good for two purposes. As in this example and the DIR command, it is helpful in keeping useful information from rolling off the screen. With a PAUSE command in a batch file, you have a chance to look at what is on the screen for as long as you want before the computer carries on its work.

The other use for this command is safety. If a command in a batch file can potentially do something that might endanger some of your data, then a PAUSE to check that everything is in order is a very good idea. This can be particularly valuable before a command that might ERASE or COPY over your data.

But if you use the PAUSE command in this way, what if you decide that you don't want things to carry on; how do you stop them? Simple: Press the BREAK key on your keyboard or type the equivalent of the

BREAK key, the Control-C key combination. (On some computers there is a special key for the break command, while on others it is just entered by holding down the Control key and pressing the C-key.) Either way, BREAK or Control-C will stop the operation of the batch file; it will not carry out whatever command it was going to. The PAUSE command gives you the opportunity to press the key at the right moments. You'll know that DOS is waiting because you'll see the message "Strike a key when ready . . ." on the screen.

Here is a dummy example of how PAUSE might be used for safety:

```
COPY DATA.NEW    DATA.OLD   make a safe-copy of our old data
PROCESS          DATA.NEW   use a program that creates new data
DIR              DATA.NEW   check the directory for info on new data
PAUSE If all is well, delete old data, otherwise, press BREAK
DEL              DATA.OLD   discard old data
```

This example is a little artificial, but the ideas are ones that you will probably want to use. Notice that DIR is used to take a quick look at the new data. It will show both the size and the time-stamp on the new data file, both of which ought to be enough to tell if the PRO-CESS program was successful in creating the new data. If everything looks good, we proceed from the PAUSE statement to clean things up by deleting the copy of the old data. If things aren't all well, then we break at the PAUSE, so that the old data isn't deleted, and we can try to fix whatever went wrong.

What you've seen so far makes batch files look very useful, but what you can do with them is even richer and more useful, as you'll see in the next section.

Making Batch Files More Attractive

Before we leave the subject of remarks, here's a handy and rather elegant tip to remember if you include a multiple-line remark in a batch file: Instead of beginning each line with REM, put the entire remark in a separate file and use the TYPE command to fetch and display it. Here is the kind of situation I mean. Suppose you have a remark like this (it's unlikely you'd include such a wordy one, but the idea should be clear):

```
REM THIS BATCH FILE COPIES FILES WITH THE EXTENSION NEW
REM AND GIVES THEM THE EXTENSION OLD
REM WHEN THE COPY IS FINISHED IT DISPLAYS A
REM DIRECTORY OF THE COPIES
. . . .
  . . . .
    . . . .
```

Rather than clutter up your batch file with these lines, you could put the entire remark in a file named, say, NOTES.REM and replace it with this in the main batch file:

```
TYPE NOTES.REM
PAUSE
. . . .
  . . . .
    . . . .
```

Using TYPE

The TYPE command, as we saw in Chapter 5, simply copies (or *types out*) onto the display screen the contents of any file you specify. That can be a very handy way of putting a series of comments on the screen. Using TYPE has two advantages over using a series of REMs: One is that REMs include the DOS prompt along with the comments they display and they also put a blank line between comments, which just uses up space on the screen; the other is that TYPE is usually faster, displaying the comments more briskly. On the other hand, there's a disadvantage to the TYPE approach as well, with TYPE you have another file (the one with the comments in it) to look after.

It's nice to have these two ways of showing comments, so you can make an intelligent choice between them. Shortly we'll see yet another way to make comments appear on the screen. First, though, we'll look at a way of improving the appearance of the screen when we're using batch files.

CLS Command

Suppose you create a batch file that shows a directory listing. As long as your batch file is properly constructed, DOS will display a directory, regardless of what else is on the screen at the time. With a short directory and an already cluttered screen, that could mean a lot of extraneous information to look at. But there's a way to make sure the screen is nice and clean before the DIR command is carried out: It's the CLS command. Here, for instance, is how you would use CLS in our earlier PAUSE example:

```
COPY DATA.NEW    DATA.OLD
PROCESS          DATA.NEW    this represents your working program
CLS                          get the screen ready
DIR              DATA.NEW    now display the directory
PAUSE
DEL              DATA.OLD
```

Now the directory would appear on a blank screen for easier reading.

Here's another point about batch files and your screen. When DOS is working its way through a batch file, it displays the commands it is executing, just as if you had typed them in. This is good and bad. It's good because it shows you exactly what is being done, bad because it clutters the screen with extraneous information. After all, one of the points of a batch file is to turn several commands into one unified operation. When you run a program, a listing of the program doesn't appear on your screen, so why should a listing of a batch file get displayed?

ECHO

This conflict is resolved by the ECHO command. ECHO is used to tell DOS to display (echo to the screen), or not display, each batch file command as it is executed. The ECHO command itself controls command echoing, like this:

```
ECHO ON     displays each command as DOS processes it
ECHO OFF    does not display each command
```

DOS's default is ECHO ON, so it displays each command it carries out. You can turn it off like this:

```
ECHO OFF
COPY DATA.NEW DATA.OLD
PROCESS DATA.NEW
CLS
DIR DATA.NEW
ECHO ON
PAUSE
DEL DATA.OLD
```

Any commands performed between the OFF and ON will not appear on the screen. That is, the command itself won't appear. If the command program generates any display output, as the DIR command does, that will continue to show on the screen.

One of the things that ECHO OFF will suppress is the display of comments from the ordinary batch file commands REM and PAUSE, but we might want some comments to appear on the screen. To make that possible, there is a third option to the ECHO command, besides ON and OFF. If the command name ECHO is followed by anything other than ON or OFF, then what follows ECHO is displayed as a comment on the screen. The command is entered like this:

```
ECHO MESSAGE
```

and it works with any message that doesn't begin with ON or OFF. In our preceding example, for instance, it would help to remind people that pressing the Break key will stop the DATA.NEW files from being erased. You can do it like this:

```
ECHO OFF
COPY DATA.NEW DATA.OLD
PROCESS DATA.NEW
CLS
DIR DATA.NEW
ECHO Press Break to cancel deletion of DATA.OLD or
PAUSE
DEL DATA.OLD
```

The word or at the end of the ECHO message is there to work with DOS's PAUSE message. The display will look like this:

```
Press Break to cancel deletion of DATA.OLD or
Strike a key when ready...
```

ECHO's messages appear whether command echoing is on or off, and it has one real advantage over the REM command. When we use the REM command, the REM itself appears on the screen, which doesn't do anything to clarify the message. With the "ECHO message" command, only the message appears, which is cleaner and clearer.

Slightly More Advanced Batch Processing

You'll remember that I mentioned I used a batch file to help me write this chapter. The name of the file might be WRITE.BAT, and, simplifying things a bit, the contents of that batch file might be like this:

```
EDIT CHAPTER.7
SPELL CHAPTER.7
EDIT CHAPTER.7
SAVE CHAPTER.7
```

But there is something drastically wrong with this batch file: It only works for Chapter 7. I would need to change it to work on any other chapter, which would be a remarkable waste of time. The solution? Parameters. When I invoke the batch file, instead of just entering the batch command: WRITE I would give a parameter, indicating what chapter I wanted to work on:

```
WRITE 11
```

Meanwhile, inside the batch file WRITE.BAT, everywhere the chapter number was needed, the batch file would have a special symbol, "%1", which would tell DOS to substitute the parameter that I had entered. So my batch file would look something like this:

```
EDIT CHAPTER.%1
SPELL CHAPTER.%1
EDIT CHAPTER.%1
SAVE CHAPTER.%1
```

There can be more than one parameter, so a digit is used after the percent sign (%), to indicate which parameter is used. %1 is used for the first parameter after the command name, %2 for the second, and so on, for up to nine parameters. (If you need anywhere near that many, you're probably making things much too complicated.) Parameter number zero, %0, is used to get the name of the batch command, but there isn't much point in that.

Other Features of Batch Processing

There are additional things to know about batch files in general, before we go onto the extra features of DOS's batch processing. Inside a batch file are commands, which can be program names, or the names of other batch files. If the command is a program, then when that program is done, we can carry on with the batch file. But if the command is the name of a batch file, then control never comes back to the original batch file. In technical terms this means that batch files are **chained** but not **nested**. If batch file A invokes batch file B, when B is done, things stop; they don't carry on where A left off. (In the next chapter you'll see that there is a special way to make batch files work like that.)

One of the batch commands that could be in a batch file is the file's own name. A batch file can invoke itself, starting an endless repetition of the same work done over and over again. This can be very useful when you have to repeat some operation. The **Break key**, commonly called Control-C, can be used to break out of this endless repetition. Putting a PAUSE command just before the repetition starts can be a good idea.

It is also possible for a program to control its own destiny, by writing out the contents of a batch file that will be executed when the program is done. This is a very clever mechanism that makes it possible to use the full rich logical capabilities of a programming language to decide what commands are to be carried out next. The way this is done is like this: We create a batch file, let's call it A, which runs our program; following the program, our A batch file tells DOS to carry out a batch file named B. But the program that is run by the A batch file itself creates the file B.BAT, thus the program decides what is to be done when it finishes. The program in the A batch file creates whatever exact instructions are to be performed in the B batch file.

If you go in for this sort of trick, test your work carefully, and beware of certain traps. For example, it is much safer for a program to create the next batch file that will be executed than to try to change the batch file currently being performed.

That gives us basics of batch files. Now we're ready to investigate some of the more advanced features and also explore some batch file tricks—both in the next chapter.

8

MORE ON BATCH FILES

Introduction

So far you've seen examples of batch files that proceed in an orderly, linear way: step to step to step. But at the end of Chapter 7, I also mentioned that you can control the way batch files are carried out—have them repeat sets of commands and so on. Now let's find out how to open the door to more batch-file magic—in a sense, teaching batch files how to make decisions.

Advanced Batch Commands

One of the enrichments DOS provides is a logical capability within batch commands. This means that batch command files can react to developing situations, in a scaled-down version of the kind of logic that can be used in a computer program. Four batch commands are related to this logic capability: SHIFT, GOTO, IF, and FOR. The full scope of these commands is really an advanced topic beyond the range of this book, but I'll give you a sketch of what these commands can do.

The SHIFT Command

Let's start with the SHIFT command. If you have a batch file that uses several of the % replacement parameters, the SHIFT command lets you move the parameters over, one by one, to make it easier to process them. When a SHIFT is done, all the values have been moved over one place, so the parameter symbol %1 has the value that had been %2, and %2 has the value that used to belong to %3.

The advantage of the SHIFT command is that one batch file can be used to work with a number of files fairly easily. The process first works with one filename taken from the %1 parameter, and then SHIFTs the list over to deal with the next filename, and SHIFTs again if there is a third filename. The real use of the SHIFT command comes when you use it with the GOTO and IF commands, which we'll get to next. But to help you understand what SHIFT does, let's create an artificial example.

Suppose you want to create a batch file that will COPY a list of files; let's say, for simplicity, that you want to be able to give it a list of any three file names, and have it copy them from drive A to drive B. If the name of the batch file is 3COPY, and your file names are X, Y, and Z, you can copy the files by just entering the name of the batch file, followed by the three filenames as parameters, like this:

```
3COPY X Y Z
```

Here is what your 3COPY batch file might look like, using the SHIFT command:

```
COPY      A:%1 B:      this copies the first file, X
SHIFT                  this shifts Y into position as %1
COPY      A:%1 B:      this copies Y
SHIFT                  this shifts Z into position as %1
COPY      A:%1 B:      this copies Z
```

Since each shift command moves the parameters over, the second and third COPY commands find the filenames Y and Z in the first parameter, or %1, location.

Obviously, this example is a little artificial, since you could have just used %2 and %3 in the second and third COPY commands. But this example sets the stage for something more complex, where the SHIFT makes more sense.

GOTO

Our 3COPY batch file will copy exactly three files, no more. What if you would like it to copy more files, without limit? In that case, you can set up a loop that will SHIFT and COPY forever. To do that, you use the GOTO command, which makes the batch command loop around in circles. This time let's look at an example before the explanation:

```
:ONWARD
COPY A:%1 B:
SHIFT
GOTO ONWARD
```

The first line you see here, ":ONWARD" is a **label**, which is needed so that the command can loop around in circles. The label begins with a colon to identify it, and it can have any symbolic name you want to use. I chose ONWARD, but you could have used any other short name, such as AGAIN, or CYCLE. The label, by the way, must be on a line by itself, just as you see it here.

Following the ONWARD label are our familiar COPY and SHIFT commands; the COPY does the work, and the SHIFT command moves the % parameters over one place, ready for the next COPY command, then comes a new command, GOTO. The GOTO command tells DOS to find the label that follows the GOTO command name, and to pick up processing from there. Since the line says GOTO ONWARD, DOS will go back up to the ONWARD label and continue through the COPY and SHIFT commands again.

What you have here is a **loop**, something that will make DOS go around in circles. Each time around, another file will be copied, and then the parameter list will be shifted over one. As it's done in this example, this looping could go on forever—there's nothing to stop it. Naturally at some point you would run out of filenames to copy, but the batch-processing file would continue looping forever—with the COPY command complaining that you weren't giving it any names to copy.

The IF Command

To keep the batch file loop from going on forever, you can use the IF command. The IF command will test some logical condition, and then if the condition is true, it will carry out one command. One of the things you can have the IF statement test for is whether a file name exists. So you might precede your GOTO ONWARD statement with this:

```
IF EXIST %1
GOTO ONWARD
```

This IF statement will test whether there is a file with the name given by the parameter %1. If there is such a file, everything will loop around to the ONWARD label, and you'll continue merrily along. But, if you've run out of file names, then the IF won't loop back, and the batch file will end.

More About GOTO and IF

There is more to the GOTO and the IF than you have seen so far. For example, our GOTO skipped to a label that came before it in the batch file, but it could just as easily have gone to a label that came after the GOTO statement. There's a big difference in what happens: Skipping to an earlier point in the file will set up a loop, while skipping forward to a later point in the file will bypass any commands in between. Depending upon your needs, either direction of GOTO will work.

The IF statement can test for two conditions other than the existence of a file. One is to check whether any program has reported trouble by signaling an **error code** to DOS. We test for these like this:

```
IF ERRORLEVEL 1 GOTO SOMEWHERE
```

The other kind of condition is a **string comparison**, which we can use to test for some particular parameter value. For example:

```
IF %1==FINISH GOTO SOMEWHERE
```

For all three kinds of IF conditions, there is a corresponding IF NOT condition.

There are more complicated details to the IF command than I can go into here—it becomes a quite advanced subject, when you look at everything that IF can do. When you are ready for all the variations, check your computer's DOS manual for the details.

There is one more advanced batch-processing command that gives you another way to repeat commands: the FOR statement.

FOR

FOR lets you create a list, for example, a list of file names, and then repeat a command with each of the names in the list. It involves a symbolic variable marked with two percent signs like this: %%. That variable is then set to each of the items in the list, in turn. Here is an example:

```
FOR %%NAME IN (A,B,C,D,E) DO COPY A:%%NAME B:
```

In the example, the COPY statement will be repeated, with each of the names in the list—A,B,C,D,E—substituted for the symbolic variable %%NAME. In effect, this FOR command is translated into five separate COPY commands:

```
COPY  A:A  B:
COPY  A:B  B:
COPY  A:C  B:
COPY  A:D  B:
COPY  A:E  B:
```

If you are ingenious, you can create some very clever batch-processing files using the FOR command. It is also quite easy to create a mess with it, since the whole process is rather tricky.

All of the advanced batch-processing commands you have seen here have their uses, but they certainly aren't for beginners. There is also some question about how really useful they might be for advanced users, when everything is considered. A lot depends upon how much taste you have for trying complicated tricks. If it suits you, don't let me discourage you at all from trying it—just be careful.

Nesting Batch Files with COMMAND

Now's the time for you to learn one of the most interesting and useful tricks that you can perform with batch files: **nesting**.

Although many of us make rather casual use of batch files, if you become a dedicated batch file user, you may get to the point where you find that practically everything you do with your computer is wrapped up in a batch file. Since batch files are designed to combine several commands into one unit, you may get to the point where the operations you want to combine together are also batch files. At that point, we're **nesting**, invoking one batch file inside of another one.

Unfortunately, DOS doesn't cooperate with us here. If one batch file invokes another by including the name of the second batch file as a command in the first, then DOS will merrily branch off from the first batch file to the second one (so far, so good). But when the second batch file is finished, DOS won't return batch to the first one—it will just stop batch file operations, and wait for our next manual command. This happens because DOS doesn't keep track of how it jumped from one batch file to another, and since it didn't keep track of how it jumped over, it can't jump back.

We could deal with this problem in a very crude and simple way—by copying the contents of the second batch file into the first one. If we did that of course we wouldn't actually be invoking the second batch file from the first, we'd just be incorporating the contents of the second into the first. That's a crude and clumsy way of accomplishing what we want, because it means we might have to make numerous copies of a secondary batch file and then try to keep track of them whenever we need to make any revisions to the operations in the secondary batch file. Quite a mess.

Luckily, there is a special trick that allows us to actually nest our batch files so they work properly. This is done by what's called a **secondary command processor**. Let's imagine we have a batch file something like this:

```
PROGRAM1
BATCH
PROGRAM2
```

where "BATCH" represents a batch file operation we want to insert between our two programs, PROGRAM1 and PROGRAM2. If we do things just as they are here, DOS will never return from the BATCH file and PROGRAM2 won't get run. But suppose we do this:

```
PROGRAM1
COMMAND /C BATCH
PROGRAM2
```

Now, in the second line, our direction to DOS is to run the program named COMMAND, which is DOS's command processor, the part of DOS that knows how to carry out batch files. Further, we told COMMAND something quite special, with the /C switch we gave it.

This /C switch—the **continue switch**—tells the COMMAND program to carry out the name of the command we give it (in this case, the batch file command BATCH) and then continue. Meaning it will jump back into the original batch file and can continue processing. This special facility of DOS's command processor allows us to nest our batch files as much as we'd like to, a very handy feature. If you plan to use it, experiment a bit until you're familiar with just how it works, and then put it to work for you. (DOS version 3.3 adds a new CALL xxx command that does essentially the same thing as command /C xxx.)

Suggestions and Examples of Batch File Tricks

In this section I'm going to show you some examples and tricks in using batch files. Let me warn you right away that some of the examples are a bit complicated, and it's possible you might get lost as you go over them. Don't worry if that happens. Just back off from them for a while, and keep your own use of batch files simple and straightforward. Later, when you are ready and willing to tackle some of the messier tricks, you can come back here.

At the beginning of Chapter 7, I mentioned the philosophy of using batch files to make computers function like friendly black boxes. The key element in making batch files work this way is to write them in a style that makes them work as smoothly and as unobtrusively as possible.

Several features of DOS help make this type of unobtrusive operation possible. One is the ECHO command, which lets you suppress the display of the commands that are being carried out. Another is the redirection of output, which you'll see in detail in Chapter 13. Sometimes, for example, you need to include a command in a batch file, but you really don't want to subject the computer user to whatever output the command displays. A prime example of this is the CHKDSK command, which can clean up messy file allocation left over from some programs. If you want to use CHKDSK, but you also want to hide its report from the screen, the output can be redirected like this:

```
CHKDSK >NUL.
```

Notice that you send the output of CHKDSK to a **null device**—a device that doesn't exist. The result is that the output is thrown away. This is a handy way to get rid of extraneous display output.

On the other hand, you might decide it's better not to throw the information away completely. If something has gone wrong, you might want to come back and look over the results. In that case, you might prefer to use a little catch-all file to store this information, like this:

```
CHKDSK >CATCH.ALL
```

Using REM and PAUSE with Batch Files

Two of the most useful things you can put into batch files are remarks and pauses, using the REM and PAUSE commands. It is surprisingly easy to lose track of exactly what you are doing. That sounds really dumb, but it's true—especially if you are doing the same thing over and over again. If you are, working your way through a list of files, it's quite easy to lose your place in the list. This problem can be solved by using the REM command to show you the parameters your batch file is working with. Example? All my batch files that run my text editor end with this REM:

```
REM Was editing the file named %1
```

And, of course, the parameter %1 shows me the file name.

The same thing can be done with the PAUSE command, but PAUSE has some extra advantages. If you are running something lengthy and automatic through a batch file, PAUSE can be used to suspend the operation, then you can see the current screen display and decide whether or not to proceed with the rest of the batch file. If you don't want things to proceed, remember that the break key will shut down the batch-file command.

Pausing for approval to continue is a very important part of any batch file that does anything potentially dangerous. For example, you might have a series of programs that deliberately leave their work files on disk, so that you can recover the data if anything goes wrong. In a batch file like this, you could have the last command of the batch file ERASE the files, and then you could put a PAUSE just before the ERASE, giving you a chance to check that everything was all right before the files were destroyed.

On the subject of the ERASE command, if you use ERASE/DEL in a batch file, it's a good idea to put a DIR command right before it, so that you see a list of the files that are about to be erased. This is a nice safety feature, since it keeps you in the know.

Using CHKDSK and DIR

There are some commands in DOS that are very useful to use but are a nuisance to type in. With batch files, you can use them liberally with no effort at all, since the batch file does all the work for you. One of the most important is the check disk command, CHKDSK. CHKDSK is useful to put in your batch commands for two reasons. First, it lets you know how much working space is left on your disk, and it is useful to see that often, so you get early warning about running out of space. CHKDSK also inspects the disk for some logical damage (meaning scrambled data but not physical damage) on the diskette. It's a good thing to do that frequently, even though the scrambling isn't a common occurrence.

It is also quite handy to add the DIR command to most of your batch files. You can put in a specific command (indicating what files you want to know about), to see things like the file size and the files' date and time stamp. Here are some examples:

```
DIR %1
DIR *.BAS
```

/W Switch and /P Switch

You can also use the show-me-everything form of the DIR command, just to see what's on the disk you are using. If you usually have a lot of files, the /W switch (Wide), which is an option of the DIR command, will list them across the screen, thus they take up fewer lines. For example: If you need to pause while scrolling, use the /P switch instead.

```
DIR
DIR *.*
DIR *.* /W
DIR /P
```

Piping

With piping, you can get a directory listing sorted, so that file names appear in alphabetic order, which makes for easier reading. With a long listing, you can also stop the display after each screen-full. This is done with a pipeline, combining DIR, SORT and MORE:

```
DIR | SORT | MORE
```

The BAA Batch File

There is also a very simple, but very handy batch file I call BAA, because of the way it works with the default disk drive. Probably the most common set up for PC-family computers is two floppy disk drives, A and B. The most common and efficient way to use those drives is to dedicate drive A to holding programs, and drive B to holding data on which the programs work.

Since it is usually more convenient for a program to use data from the default disk drive, the BAA batch file is designed to temporarily switch the default to drive B, execute the program (from drive A), then switch the default back. The batch file would look like this for a program named XXX:

```
B:          (switch the default to B)
A:XXX       (run XXX from drive A, but use B as the default data drive)
A:          (switch the default back to A, ready for the next task)
```

You would set up one of these batch files for each program you wanted to use it for. The natural name to give the batch file would be a handy abbreviation of the name of the program. (You can't give the batch file the same name as the program, since DOS looks for programs before it looks for batch files: If both a program file and a batch file have the same name—but different filename extensions—when you entered the name as a command, DOS would directly execute the program, and bypass your batch file.)

On the other hand, if you would prefer to use the name of the program as the command name you use to activate a batch file like the BAA batch file, then you can use the RENAME command to change the program file to an alias and then use the original name for your batch file.

Before we finish with the BAA batch file, you should note that you can also easily set up a generic BAA file that uses a parameter to specify the program name. In this case, the BAA batch file would look like this:

```
B:
A:%1
A:
```

You could do this if you wanted to, but the main point of batch files, and of computers in general, is to make your work simpler and easier.

It makes more sense to set up a separate batch file, tailored to the needs of each particular program that you run. In fact, it is likely that each program's batch execution file will have more in it than the BAA file shown above; what else will be in there depends upon what you need to help you best use your programs.

The Chaining Trick

Closely related to the BAA batch file is a trick you can use to make it easier and more convenient to make backup copies of your data. Since the most common operating style for computers with two diskette drives is to use the A drive for programs (and batch files) and to use the B drive for data that the programs work on, how do you make backup copies of that data? The only sensible way to do it is to leave the data diskette where it is in drive B, and replace the program diskette in drive A with the diskette you use to back up the data in drive B. There are two convenient ways to use batch files to supervise this backup copying: one is under manual control, and the other is fully automatic.

The manual-control way of making backup copies is to place a batch file on the backup diskette. The only task of this batch file is to copy from B to A like this:

```
COPY    B:*.*    A:*.*
```

This is the straightforward backup operation, and you might give it a command name of SAVE or just S for short. When the computer is being used by someone who knows when a backup copy of the data is needed, then this simple method is best.

There is also a more elaborate method, which adds an element of foolproofing to the backup operation. This is the fully automatic backup procedure. This method makes use of **batch-file chaining**, so as an added advantage you have an opportunity to see how chaining is done. Let's set the stage with a little explanation of what we want to do, so you can better understand the chaining trick.

For the manual backup method, remember that the knowledgeable computer user removed a program diskette from drive A, replaced it with a backup diskette, entered the command SAVE, then switched back to the program diskette. But our user had to know what steps to follow. To make the backup operation as foolproof as you can, so even the rawest novice can do the backup, you need a batch file to lead the person by the hand through the steps to be done. That's what I'll explain here.

The first part of this scheme, the first link in the chain, is the BAA batch file already being used on the program diskette in drive A:

```
B:
A:XXX
A:
```

The point of this operation is to back up new data after the end of a program operation, so we assume our computer user is using a program and that the BAA batch file is used to run the program.

Now, at the end of the batch file, we place a command to switch over to another batch file that is located on the data diskette in drive B, which will be the second link in our chain of batch files. That batch file has to have a command name (which is the filename, minus the .BAT extension), so let's call it AUTOSAVE. The last line in the BAA batch file on the program diskette will switch control over to AUTOSAVE, like this:

```
B:
A:XXX
A:
B:AUTOSAVE
```

Notice the "B:" part, which is important. The third line of the BAA batch file switched the default to drive A, so we have to specifically tell DOS to look to drive B for the AUTOSAVE command.

Why are we chaining to another batch file? Why don't we just continue on using the batch file in drive A for whatever we need to do? For one simple reason: We're about to remove the program diskette from drive A, and DOS wouldn't be able to find the instructions inside the batch file. We temporarily switch our base of operations, the location of our batch file, over to drive B. This is the heart of our chaining trick.

What will be inside this AUTOSAVE batch file? Two things: one is the working part, a COPY command to copy the data from the master data diskette in drive B to the backup diskette in drive A. The other thing that will be in the AUTOSAVE batch file is the foolproofing, in the form of simple instructions telling the computer user of what to do; this part we do with PAUSE commands. So our AUTOSAVE batch file looks like this:

```
PAUSE  Place the data backup diskette in drive A
COPY   B:*.* A:*.*
PAUSE  Replace the program diskette in drive A
```

To match your particular needs, the comments in the two PAUSE statements can be more specific; they can use your terminology for the particular diskettes to be used with drive A. For example, they could say "accounting data backup" and "accounting program," or whatever is appropriate.

What happens after the second PAUSE statement in this AUTOSAVE command file? Since the default drive is A, DOS gives the prompt for drive A, and our computer user at the keyboard can enter the next command. On the other hand, we could add a third link to this chain of batch files, by putting the name of a batch command as the fourth and last line of AUTOSAVE. DOS would then take off and execute that batch file, and things would be even more automatic.

If we wanted to, the name of this command on the last line of AUTOSAVE could be a parameter (like %1), so that the command line that invoked AUTOSAVE would also indicate what was supposed to be done when AUTOSAVE was completed. With this trick of passing the name of the next command as a parameter to AUTOSAVE, you could have one universal form of AUTOSAVE batch file that you could use with every one of your program and data diskettes. If you wanted to, you could write a custom AUTOSAVE batch file for each different use—or you could use the universal form with its parameter. You can use whichever technique better suits your operation.

This example of chaining batch files for the purpose of backing up data should give you an idea of how command chaining can be used to add more automation to your computer operations. Commands can be chained from diskette to diskette (as you saw in setting up AUTOSAVE), or they can work on the same diskette. There is less reason to chain commands when you are not switching diskettes, since any command that you chain on the same diskette could be just included in one command file, but that's a matter of taste and style. Some people prefer to do lengthy operations as a chain of commands, and others prefer to use one large command file, the result is the same. But where batch-file chaining really pays off is in allowing you to switch diskettes and still keep operating under the automatic control of batch files.

Besides all the handy things that you can put inside of batch files, there are some very useful things you can do outside of them—that is, how you name and organize them.

The A-B-C Trick

One of the handiest of these things is what I call the A-B-C trick. Many of the things you do with your computer follow a logical series of steps. For example, if you are writing programs, the first step might be to use your text editor to do the writing, while the second and third steps would be compiling the program and then testing it. For each of these steps you'd set up a batch file to supervise it. You could give each of these steps meaningful names like EDIT, COMPILE, and TEST.

Another example is in writing a letter or a report. The first step is composing the letter, the second is to check its spelling, and the third step is to re-edit it for corrections. Here, your batch files might be called WRITE, SPELL, and EDIT.

It is a very good idea to give batch files simple meaningful command names. On the other hand, for convenience, we could just as easily name these steps A, B, and C, or 1, 2, and 3. There are two advantages to the A-B-C trick: The command names are shorter and quicker to key in, and it is easier to combine them and remember the names of the combinations. There is a logical progression to the steps you go through, and your batch files can simply number the steps 1, 2, 3 or letter them A, B, C. Thus, if your edit step is named A, and your compile step is named B, then a batch file to do both an edit and compile would be named AB, which can be easy to remember and key in.

There is one obvious disadvantage to the A-B-C trick: You have to remember that A means EDIT (or whatever), and so forth. This can be confusing to your co-workers, or even to yourself. But if you won't have any trouble keeping track of the meaning of the steps, then A-B-C is a good way to go.

To show you how far you can take this and how useful it can become, take a look at what I do when I write Pascal programs. There are actually five separate steps to creating a Pascal program: edit, first stage compile, second stage compile, link edit, and then test run the completed program.

I have separate batch files for each step (which I happen to call 1 through 5 because it suits me), and then lots of different combination batch files. Depending upon the kind of program I'm writing, it makes sense to use different combinations of the five steps. Sometimes I do step one by itself, and at other times I combine steps one and two. Other combinations are handy at other times. By having a batch file for each step by itself, and as many combinations as I find useful, I'm in full control of what is going on when I write these programs, and its all quick and convenient for me. The same idea can be applied to any multistep operation that you do. The more complicated the steps, the greater the advantage in setting up A-B-C type batch files to supervise them.

There is one further handy thing you can do with A-B-C, and that is to create parallel batch files for tasks that are similar in general, but different in detail. To use the example of programming again, I happen to write programs in three languages—Pascal, assembly, and BASIC. For each of them, I have the same setup of batch command names. So, for me, editing a program is always done with the command named one, and the compile or assemble is always begun with the command named two. What the command "one" actually does is different in each case, but what it means to me is always the same: It means let me use my text editor to write a program.

The same thing applies to writing a letter or to writing this chapter. Everywhere, the first step, which I always call one, is to use my editor to compose something—a letter, a program, or a part of this book. The next step after that is step two, and it's quite different depending upon what I'm doing—for writing, step two is a spelling check, while for programming, step two runs a compiler or assembler. But as I use them, these numbered batch-processing steps make perfect sense, since they follow the natural progression of whatever work I am doing.

Batch File Versions

Another handy trick with batch files is to have different versions lying around waiting. Why would you want to do that? Let me use my programming as an example again. Sometimes I do my programming work on ordinary diskettes; other times it is handy for me to move everything onto an electronic disk. Finally, when I work on my biggest programs, I need to use both an electronic disk and ordinary diskettes. So I keep three versions of my main programming batch files. Now there are two ways to handle this, and I think one of them is a really nifty trick.

The first way is to have all three versions active at once, under slightly different names. For example, my step one, named "1", could have its diskette version named "1D", and the electronic disk version named "1E". While this puts them all on tap at once, it means that I have to remember which version I'm using and keep entering that form of the command name, that's clumsy and prone to error. The second way uses a foxy trick to solve the problem.

The trick is to keep all three versions around under the same command name, but with an alias for a filename extension. My electronic version of the "1" command would be in a file named 1.ELE. Now, as you know, batch files have to have the extension BAT; so this ELE file can't be used as it is, but it can be moved into place very easily. With a simple COPY command, all ELE batch files can be activated:

```
COPY *.ELE *.BAT
```

does the trick. Thus, each of my three versions of my batch files is kept with its own distinct extension name. Then each set is activated by an appropriate COPY command, which makes it the current working version, and overrides whatever version was working before. I don't have to use any different command names — the names stay the same, but different versions take effect. Naturally I don't type in the COPY commands, another series of batch files does that for me.

Since the real magic of using batch-processing files comes from tailoring them to your own needs, my suggestions and examples can only scratch the surface of the possibilities, and can only hint at some of the things that you can accomplish on your own through the creative use of batch files. There is almost nothing in the use of DOS that will reward your efforts like the rewards of speed, convenience, and safety you can gain by making full use of batch files.

PART III

Deeper into Disks

9

UNDERSTANDING DISKS

Introduction

Now that's you've gotten a handful of the most useful DOS commands under your belt, it's time to look inside the workings of your disks. Understanding them is the key to knowing the whys, hows, and wherefores of the DOS commands, particularly the more advanced disk commands you'll encounter in this part of the book. This chapter is mostly about understanding disks, but you will learn about one special command, called RECOVER, that deals with scrambled disks.

What's on a Disk

Let's begin by briefly pulling together everything we've covered about disks. A storage disk is used to hold data that you need to preserve. Like a filing cabinet, a disk is a safe place to keep information, and it has a large, but limited, capacity. And, just as a filing cabinet has its contents organized into file folders, a disk has its data organized into files.

The files on a diskette are distinct, and each file contains its own particular data. The files are identified by their filenames. On any one disk, each filename must be unique, but on two separate disks you can have separate files with the same name. Since files are identified by their filenames, it is a very good idea to make sure that every file on every disk has a completely unique name, except when there is some good reason to re-use the same name. For example, if a file on one disk exists solely as a safeguarded copy of a file on another disk, that is a good reason for having a duplicate filename. Even then, it could be a good idea to give the files different names in order to distinguish the original from the copy.

Most of the space on a disk is devoted to storing data, but some of the space is used by DOS for bookkeeping purposes, such as maintaining a directory of the files on a disk. In the directory, DOS keeps its record of everything that it needs to know about the disk's files, including notes to itself about how to find their contents. Most of this information is of little use to us, but there are three things about a file that DOS will let us know.

The first is the filename itself, including the filename extension. The second is the size of the file, and the third is the time stamp that shows when the file was most recently changed. If a file has not been changed since it was created, the time stamp shows when it was created. These time stamps give both the date and the time, except in the very first release of DOS. (If you're using that version, 1.00, you're a pioneer indeed!)

Time Stamps

There are several special things to know about time stamps. First, if a copy is made of a file, the copy gets the same time stamp as the original. Second, there is no way to tell if a time stamp is the original time the file was created, or the time the file was later changed. Third, although time stamps are displayed to the minute, they are actually calculated to within two seconds of the exact time. When necessary, advanced programming techniques can be used to find the complete time stamp.

These time stamps on files can be very useful in safely controlling your data. Looking at the time stamp can answer such questions as:

- Which of these files was I working on yesterday?
- Is my backup copy up-to-date with my master copy?

Because of this, it is important to make sure that your system always knows the correct date and time. If your personal computer needs to have you enter the time when it is turned on, I urge you to never be too lazy to key in the right date and time. The benefit of having the right time stamps on your files can be enormous. Sometimes it can be as valuable as an insurance policy.

If your computer has a clock/calendar feature that automatically keeps track of the time when it is turned off, you are fortunate indeed. As I've mentioned elsewhere, clock/calendar hardware is a popular feature of multifunction expansion boards for the PC family, and the IBM AT model comes with a clock/calendar as standard equipment. Since the time stamp on files is quite valuable, this is a good feature to have in your computer.

Other Parts of Disk Storage

Including the directory, there are actually three parts of overhead (unavailable storage space) on a disk. Since you may occasionally come across mention of them, it is worth knowing what they are.

The first is called the **boot record**, and it contains a very short program used to help start up the DOS operating system from the disk. Each disk has a boot record on it, whether or not the disk contains the rest of DOS. (If a disk has all of DOS on it, it is a system disk, which we'll come to in a moment.)

After the boot record, the next bit of overhead on the disk is a table DOS uses to keep track of the available space on the disk; this table is called the **File Allocation Table**, or just **FAT** for short. The FAT records where each file is located, so it is something like an index to the disk. It also keeps a record of the part of the disk's space that isn't in use. When the CHKDSK command reports on how much space is available on a disk, the information comes from the disk's FAT.

The third and last part of the overhead on a disk is the directory, which lists all of the files on the disk. We've already discussed the directory since its contents are so important to us.

Altogether, the three overhead parts of a disk, the boot record, the FAT, and the directory, take up very little of the space on a disk—typically only about 2% of the total. The rest of the space is used to store data.

The overhead I talked about here is overhead that is intrinsic to the disk itself—the disk's own necessary overhead. There is also a potential overhead you can choose to live with, but can reduce the amount of disk space available: DOS. When you format a disk, remember that you have a choice of including DOS on the disk. With DOS on it, the disk is called a **system-formatted disk** or for short, a **system disk**.

A system disk has the advantage that you can always start your computer system with it. On the other hand, having DOS on your disks uses up some of the space you might need for your own use. The amount of overhead for DOS varies according to the disk capacity and the version of DOS. It can be as low as 8% or as high as 25%. A typical figure is 12%. The space devoted to having DOS on your disks may, or may not, be important to you. Start out by putting DOS on all your disks, and then later deciding what is best.

All about File Names

Files have file names, and the better you understand them, the less likely you are to make a mess of them. First, the simple mechanics. File names have two parts, the filename itself and the filename extension. A filename can be up to eight characters long. Some examples are:

```
A
LONGNAME
1234
AB__34
```

The filename extension is just that—an extension to the file name. An extension can be up to three characters long. While a filename must have at least one character in it, the extension can be nothing at all. When a filename has an extension, the two parts are connected by a period between them. Here are some sample filenames with extensions:

```
JANUARY.85
PROGRAM.BAS
CHAPTER.2-3
1985-12.25
```

There are some rules about what is a proper filename. The filename and the extension can be made up from any combination of the allowed characters, which consist of:

the letters of the alphabet, A through Z
the digits 0 through 9
the punctuation characters: $ & # @ ! % ' ^ ( ) -

You can use any of these symbols in any combination, but you can't use blanks. It seems like a terrible idea to use the more exotic symbols, but some of these symbols work very nicely as a form of punctuation in a file name. For example: JAN__MAY

You'll notice that a few common (and some uncommon) symbols aren't allowed in filenames and extensions. They're reserved for other uses. Table 9.1 shows the symbols and their uses.

Table 9.1 Symbols and Their Uses

Symbol	Use
* and ?	reserved for wildcards
.	used to separate filename and extension
:	used to identify drives and devices
\	used for paths
/	used for switches
< and >	used for data redirection
, and ;	used to punctuate parameter lists
=	used to punctuate parameter lists
+	used to punctuate parameter lists
I	used for piping
[and]	reserved
"	reserved

Only capital letters are actually used in filenames. DOS, in a friendly way, lets us type in filenames in lowercase if we want, but it automatically converts lowercase to upper. This is why you'll find that DOS always lists files with their names all in uppercase letters.

You may discover that there are some trick ways to sneak illegal filenames past DOS. For example, it is possible to create a file that has a blank space in the middle of its name (like "AA BB.CCC"), or to create a file that has a lowercase name. Don't play that dangerous game; you are almost certain to regret it.

Names for Devices

One of the nice things DOS does to make life convenient and easy is that it lets us refer to parts of the computer, such as the printer, with simple names that are the same as filenames. These are called **device names**, because they refer to devices, or parts, of the computer. In order to be able to do this DOS has to reserve these names for their special uses, so there is a short list of names you can't use as your own filenames. The exact list may vary from computer to computer. Here is the usual list of names with what they are used for.

Table 9.2 Device Names

Name	Meaning
NUL	A null or empty file; if a program tries to read from NUL, it finds an empty file; data written to NUL is thrown away. This empty, or null, device can come in handy at times.
CON	The user console; refers to both the keyboard (input data) and the screen (output data).
USER	Under some circumstances, this is an alternative version of CON; USER can't always be used as a device name, but CON can. (Unless you know that USER will work, stick with CON.)
AUX	The communications line, or asynchronous communications port.
COM1	The first of several possible communications lines; COM2 and COM3 are used to specify the others. COM1 is the same thing as AUX.
PRN	The printer device.
LPT1	The first of several possible printers; LPT2 and LPT3 are used to specify the others. LPT1 is the same thing as PRN.

With the exception of these special device names, you are free to give your files any names you wish, within the grammatical rules for filenames (one to eight characters, and so forth). It is almost the same with filename extensions, but not quite. We'll cover that in the next section.

There are three more things to know about filenames, which we'll cover in the next sections and in the last part of this chapter: what filename extensions are really about, what wildcards are in filenames, and some special advanced DOS items, such as disk labels, and paths.

The Importance of Filename Extensions

You can give your files filename extensions as freely and arbitrarily as you can give them filenames. In fact more freely, since there are reserved filenames, but there are no reserved filename extensions. Extensions like COM and BAT are reserved in the sense that they represent certain types of files, but you can use them—if you know when it's appropriate.

There is then, a distinct purpose for filename extensions: They indicate the category and classification of files. Unfortunately, the importance and usefulness of filename extensions isn't emphasized much, and many users of DOS don't fully understand them. In this section let's see what filename extensions are all about.

Filename extensions are intended to classify and categorize files so that their purpose can be quickly and simply identified. The assignment of standard filename extensions is rather casual, and it is not explained fully anywhere that I know of, which leads to confusion about them.

There are two basic types of filename extensions: those that you assign and those that are used by programs—all sorts of programs, from DOS to applications to programming languages. In DOS, the main extensions you'll encounter are **COM**, which refers to the parts of DOS you usually use, and **BAT**, which refers to batch-processing files.

In the applications arena, there are many different extensions you may encounter, because these programs use extensions of their own for identifying their support files. Microsoft Word, for example, uses DOC for document files, PRD for printer-description files, and BAK for its automatic backup copies. Lotus 1-2-3 uses WKS or WK1 for spreadsheet files, PIC for graphs, and PRN for unformatted, or ASCII, files. It also uses FNT for display character fonts and XLT for modules to translate between program data formats—for example, from 1-2-3 to Symphony. d-BASE III uses, among others, DBF for databases defined with the Create command, DBT for files containing database text, FRM for reports, LBL for labels, and so on.

Here are the main standard uses of filename extensions:

- Executable program files have extensions of EXE or COM; there are two formats for program files, (which we'll go into in the next section), so there are two filename extensions to distinguish them.

- Batch execution files have the extension BAT.

- Lotus 1-2-3 uses WKS, WK1 and WRK for its main data files (worksheets) and PIC for graph printing (picture) files.

- dBASE uses quite a list of extensions, including DBF, DBT, NDX, FRM, LBL, PRG, FMT, MEM, and TXT.

- When a program creates printer-type output, but the output is stored in a file, LST is the customary extension. If there is more than one listing file being created at a time, other extensions may be used. Compilers typically use COD for assembly-like object code listings, and the linker uses MAP for the map of the contents of a program. When practical, LST is the best extension to use for printer-type files.

- Editors and word processors use some standard extensions. When the old version of an edited file is preserved for safety reasons, it is given the extension BAK (for BAcK-up copy). DOC is very commonly used by word processors for text files. Some word processors prefer to use TXT as the extension for the edited data. FMT may be used to hold the editing format.

- When a program uses a data file in its own format, DAT is often the extension.

- When a program needs a temporary work file, $$$ is most often used as the extension; occasionally TMP is used instead. The program fully intends to delete these temporary work files before finishing. If you ever find a file lying around with an extension of $$$ or TMP, that's a very good sign that something has gone wrong—you ought to take the time to figure out what it was.

- Programming languages make use of several standard filenames. For source code, a different extension is used for each language: ASM for assembly, BAS for BASIC, COB for COBOL, FOR for FORTRAN and PAS for Pascal. For object code, in any language, OBJ is the extension. For library routines, the extension is LIB. When BASIC uses BLOAD-format files, BLD is the customary extension.

Table 9.3 is a list of the most common filename extensions in alphabetical order.

Table 9.3 Filename Extensions

Extension	Meaning
$$$	temporary work file
ASM	assembly source
BAK	text file backup copy
BAS	BASIC source code
BAT	batch-processing file
BLD	BLOAD format for BASIC
CAL	spreadsheet calculation file
COB	COBOL source code
COD	object-code listing, from compilers
COM	executable programs, in memory-image format
DAT	data files, in general
DBF	used by dBASE
DBT	used by dBASE
DIF	data interchange files, as from a spreadsheet
DOC	word-processing document
EXE	executable programs, in relocation format
FMT	used by dBASE
FMT	word-processor format specification
FOR	FORTRAN source code
FRM	used by dBASE
FW	Framework
FW2	Framework Version II
LBL	used by dBASE
LIB	library routines, for compilers
LST	printable listing files, in general
MAP	program maps from the linker
MEM	used by dBASE
NDX	used by dBASE
OBJ	program object code, from compilers
OVL	program overlay or module (read into memory when needed)
PAS	Pascal source file
PGM	program overlay or module (read into memory when needed)
PRG	used by dBASE
TMP	temporary work file
TXT	text files, for word processors
WK1	Lotus worksheet for 1-2-3, Version 2
WKS	Lotus worksheet for 1-2-3, Version 1
WRK	Lotus worksheet for Symphony

The more closely you follow the pattern of these extension names, the more easily your files will smoothly fit into the broad use of your computer. This is one of the many ways that you can safeguard the effective operation of your computer.

Wildcards and Their Use

Connected with the subject of filenames is the use of **wildcards**, or generic file names. A wildcard is a non-specific part of a file specification that can be used to match more than one particular file.

Every file has a specific, unambiguous filename (and extension), but you can often refer to more than one file at a time by using wildcards in a file specification.

There are two forms of wildcard—the question mark (?) and the asterisk (*). When a question mark is used in a file specification, for example:

```
THISNAM?
```

then it will match with any letter in that one particular position of the filename. So THISNAM? would match with any of these files:

```
THISNAME
THISNAM1
THISNAM$
THISNAM
```

This works as long as all of the rest of the positions of the filename match exactly. Wildcards, as you might expect, can be used in both the filename and extension parts of the complete name.

The asterisk form of the wildcard is just a shorthand for several question marks. While a question mark is wild for the single character position that it occupies in a filename, an asterisk is wild from that position to the end of the filename, or the end of the extension. An asterisk acts as if there were as many question marks as there are positions left in the filename or in the extension. An asterisk in the filename "stops" at the end of the filename, not at the end of the extension. If you use the question mark form then you can be specific about the following positions in the name; with an asterisk you can't; if you try it, anything after the asterisk will be ignored, without warning.

Either of these uses of wildcards:

```
*.*
????????.???
```

would match any filename and extension. Note that they mean exactly the same thing, since an asterisk (*) is just shorthand for a series of question marks.

These wildcard specifications are mainly used with four commands, the DIR directory listing, the DEL/ERASE file erase command, the REN/RENAME file name change command, and the COPY command. They also have a special copy-and-concatenate use with the COPY command, as I mentioned in the section on combining files with COPY in Chapter 5. (If **concatenate** is a new word to you, it means to fit the two files together into one.)

Other than the commands just mentioned (DIR, DEL/ERASE, REN/RENAME and COPY), most programs that require a file specification will not successfully use a name with a wildcard, even if the wildcard specification ends up matching only one single file.

There are advanced programming techniques that make it easy for a program to make good use of wildcards, and DOS provides some special services to programs just for that purpose. It's a good thing for programs to make use of these services, so they can accept filenames with wildcard specification. But not all programs do so, and you shouldn't be disappointed if one of yours doesn't recognize wildcards. Finally, before we leave this discussion, here's a one-word piece of advice: Beware.

The use of wildcards can be very dangerous. Many a DOS user has accidentally misused wildcards and erased files that weren't supposed to be erased; and giving a wildcard to a program that doesn't expect it can lead to other mishaps.

Disk File Formats and What They Mean to You

It can help to understand what your disk data is like—how it is structured, what it looks like, and how it is stored. In this section, we'll take a look at disk file formats.

First, how is data stored on disks? The scheme is simple and efficient. As DOS sees it, the storage space for data on a disk is made up of fixed-size chunks of space, called **sectors**. The size of the sectors may vary from one type of disk to another, but within one disk, the sectors are all the same size—typically 512 or 1,024 bytes. If a disk has too many sectors for DOS to conveniently keep track of them one by one, then sectors are combined into logical units called **clusters** of sectors.

DOS manages the space on a disk by allocating sectors, or clusters of sectors, to any files that need them. One sector at a time or in clusters, space on a disk is allocated to files in uniform, fixed amounts. As a typical example, a single-sided 5¼-inch diskette might have its space allocated as individual 512-byte sectors, while a double-sided diskette might use two-sector clusters, so that its space is allocated two sectors at a time, which would be 1,024 bytes for each cluster.

Actually, while this is interesting to learn about, you don't need to know this information at all, and that is one of the beauties of DOS's way of storing data on disks. DOS reads and writes disk data in fixed-size sectors, and allocates this space one or more sectors at a time. We and our programs don't see these fixed-size sectors at all, instead, DOS lets us store our data in any size that is convenient to us.

DOS worries about fitting our data into the fixed-size sectors, and does it so efficiently and so quietly that we never have to concern ourselves about the mechanics of how the data is stored. Shoehorning our data into fixed-size sectors is work for DOS and not for us nor our programs. This is a very good thing, because it makes a clean division of labor: DOS worries about where and how to store our data, and all our programs have to worry about is how to use the data.

There are usually four file formats that are used to store our data on disks—three special formats and one sort of a catch-all format.

COM and EXE Formats

Two of the three special formats are used to store executable programs. The formats are known by their standard filename extensions—COM and EXE. COM files are used to hold programs that are completely ready-to-execute; this is a **memory-image format**, which means that what's on disk is identical to what is in the computer's memory when the program is executed. The EXE format is more sophisticated; EXE programs require some last minute fix-up work to be done as they are loaded from disk into memory. This fix-up mostly involves placing the program into the right part of memory, and letting the program know where it has been placed. The EXE format is mostly used for the more complicated type of program that is produced by compilers. Because of the extra overhead, EXE format programs are bulkier when they are stored on disk; but inside the computer's memory, they can be just as compact as COM-type programs.

There is nothing about these two special program file formats that is of much practical consequence to you. In fact, the main thing worth knowing about COM and EXE program files is just their filename extensions. By looking for COM and EXE files, you can see which are the executable programs on a disk.

BASIC Formats

The BASIC programming language is an exception to many rules, and that's also true when it comes to program files. If you have BASIC programs that are run with the BASIC interpreter, then those programs are stored in files with the extension BAS. You may think of these as executable programs and from your point of view, they are, but from DOS's point of view a BASIC program in a BAS file is just data that the BASIC interpreter reads in order to find out what to do. This is a technical point, but one worth knowing. As DOS and the computer see it, the BASIC interpreter is a true program, and a BASIC BAS file is just data. That is why the BASIC interpreter is stored in a COM file—because it's a true program.

ASCII Format

The other special file format—one that will be of particular interest to you—is the **ASCII text file format**. This is the format that is used to store your text data, such as correspondence, reports, and the source code form of programs.

There are various terms used to talk about this file format—sometimes it is called a text file, or an ASCII file. I usually call it an ASCII text file. ASCII text files use a format that is very flexible and is adapted to serve many purposes. It is probably the most widely used format for computer data; it is certainly universal to small personal computers.

The acronym ASCII refers to the code scheme computers use to recognize the letters, numbers, and symbols that make up a file of written text. ASCII is short for the American Standard Code for Information Interchange, and it's the standard code used for computer characters. In lay terms, the letters ASCII mean written material, as the computer sees it.

An ASCII text file consists mostly of a stream of written information: the alphabet letters, numbers, and punctuation that make up the types of things we write. What you are reading in this book is typical of the contents of an ASCII text file and, in fact, these very words are stored on a disk in an ASCII text file on my computer.

Besides the words, or text, an ASCII text file also contains some formatting information that helps make the text more useful. At the end of an ASCII text file is an end-of-file format marker. (This is the ASCII character number 26, which is sometimes called Control-Z.)

Within an ASCII text file itself, the text is broken into lines by two **formatting characters** at the end of each line; these two characters are known as **carriage return** (ASCII character 13) and **line feed** (ASCII 10). This is all the formatting that is normally placed in an ASCII text file—carriage return and line feed at the end of each line, and end-of-file at, naturally, the end of the file. ASCII text files don't normally have any more format punctuation in them, there aren't normally paragraph or page markings. But in the definition of ASCII there are formatting characters, which can be used for this kind of marking, and more besides.

I've been mentioning some special characters by their ASCII codes, for example ASCII 13 is the carriage return character. Everything inside a computer works like a number, and so every character has a numeric code, whether it's a letter of the alphabet, like capital A, which is ASCII 65 or it's a special character, like end-of-file, which is ASCII 26. If you know, or will be learning, the BASIC language, BASIC refers to these numeric character codes like this: CHR$(26).

The type of programs that are known as **editors** or **text editors** all work with ASCII text files. DOS itself comes with a simple but powerful text editor called EDLIN (we'll take a close look at EDLIN in Chapter 18). Word processors, too, usually work with ordinary ASCII text files. However, sophisticated word processors, such as WordPerfect, DisplayWrite, and Microsoft Word, need more complex formatting information than ordinary ASCII can easily accommodate, therefore they augment some, and bend the rules some, to get the kind of data that they need. As a consequence, word-processing text files are a little different than ordinary vanilla-flavored ASCII text files. Yet, underneath the trappings of a word-processing file, there is a simple ASCII text file.

What's particularly interesting and important about ASCII text files is that they are the most common and interchangeable of all file formats. This means that if you have one program tool using ASCII text files, then you can expect to be able to move data from it to other programs using ASCII, with a minimum of fuss and difficulty. This transportability can be a tremendous advantage in flexibility. Because of this, it can work greatly to your advantage to have as much data in ASCII format as possible—or to have the ability to convert files to ASCII format, as many word processors do.

The upshot is, if you are programming, or having programs designed for you, consider using the ASCII text file format, even if it is not the most convenient for your programs. In the long run, the benefits can be considerable.

General Data Files

After these three special file formats—COM program files, EXE program files, and ASCII text files—we come to the catch-all format of the general data file. Unless a file has a special format, it consists simply of data stored on a disk. Usually data files are made up of fixed length parts called **records**. The records can be as short as a single byte, or as long as you like. To read or write such a data file, a program tells DOS the basic information about the file, such as what the record size is; and DOS does the work of finding where each record is, in what part of what disk sector.

There is one special thing worth knowing about files that are made up of fixed-length records. Since the records are all of the same size, a simple arithmetic formula can be used to calculate where each record is stored. This means that it is possible for a fixed-length record file to be accessed randomly, skipping arbitrarily from one record to another. A fixed-length record file can be processed either sequentially, one record in order after another, or by random skips. This is one tremendous advantage over an ASCII text file, which must be read and written sequentially, from front to back in proper order.

When you think about files, and consider what can be done with them, you should keep in mind the special random access capability that a fixed-length record file has.

Diskettes and Other Storage Formats

There are more creatures in the disk forest than you or I might imagine, and just when you think you've seen them all, up pops another. So it is with disk storage, for whatever computer you have that uses DOS, you probably know the particular options that are available for disk storage. But it's worthwhile to know a little about the full range of disk storage formats.

There are three main types of the disk storage, with lots of variations and a few hybrids thrown in for variety. The three main types are diskettes, hard disks, and electronic disks.

Diskettes

Diskettes have been the most common form of disk storage for small personal computers, although they are rapidly being supplanted by newer, more advanced storage media. The most common kind of diskette is whimsically called a **floppy**. Floppies get their nickname because they are made of a flexible plastic and can be easily and harmlessly bent. A classic floppy comes in a black, square-shaped protective cover. In the cover is a hub opening where the diskette is grabbed and spun in the disk drive, and another slotted opening where the diskette surface is read and written on magnetically.

The original floppies were eight inches in diameter. Later, $5\frac{1}{4}$-inch mini-floppies were developed, and they have been the most common size used in personal computers. Pretty much with the advent of the Apple Macintosh, however, another kind appeared: the $3\frac{1}{2}$-inch micro-floppy diskette. This type of diskette comes in a relatively hard plastic shell, although it's just as floppy as the others on the inside. Originally used on lap-sized DOS-based computers such as the Toshiba T-3100 and the IBM Convertible because of their small size, these $3\frac{1}{2}$-inch floppies are coming into more widespread use, although tradition and existing equipment will probably keep $5\frac{1}{4}$-inch diskettes in business for quite a long time.

There are lots of variations in diskettes besides their size. They can be recorded on one or both sides, and the recording density can be in what is called single, double, or quadruple density, which are recorded at 24, 48, or 96 tracks-per-inch density. One of the most common forms of diskette, especially for modern personal computers, is double-density soft-sectored. Every possible variation is used on some computer, somewhere.

Typically, a diskette holds somewhere from 160,000 bytes to 1,200,000 bytes of data or more, but the full range of capacities is much wider than that, given all of the formats that are available.

Hard Disks

Hard disks are a higher-capacity storage medium than floppies. Hard disks are made of a rigid platter coated with magnetic record-ing material. Usually they make use of a technology that was first code-named Winchester, so hard disks are also called **Winchester disks**. Their capacity is dramatically higher than floppies. The mini-mum capacity of a hard disk is around 5 million bytes, and some can hold as much as 50 million bytes. A true Winchester disk is com-pletely sealed against the outside air and dust and isn't removable— you can't change these disks like you can swap floppies. But then, with the high storage capacity, there is less need to. There is, how-ever, also a variety of hard disk that has a removable cartridge that can be taken in and out of the disk drive, just like a floppy.

Electronic or RAM Disk

The third completely different format of disk storage is the elec-tronic disk, or **RAM disk**. An electronic disk isn't disk storage at all, but a combination of memory and computer program that produces a simulation of a disk-storage device in **random access memory (RAM)**. The point of using an electronic disk is to adapt the speed of electronic memory to the operating standards of disk storage. With an electronic disk, numerous programs and their associated data can be moved from conventional disk to electronic disk, then used at much higher speed than would be possible on a true disk device. Elec-tronic disk operations are perhaps ten times faster than floppy disks, and twice as fast as hard disks, which can be an enormous advantage. There are, however, special problems and considerations in using electronic disks.

Risky File Recovery Using RECOVER

Now we come back to DOS, and to a powerful, but dangerous, file-recovery program called RECOVER.

There are many ways that your disk data can be lost or damaged, and the whole subject of file recovery is a very important one, beyond what we can do here. DOS does not provide much in the way of file protection and file recovery, but there is one command, RECOVER, that does two limited kinds of file recovery.

If part of a disk has been damaged so that a file can be partially read and partially not, the RECOVER command will remove the unreadable part so that you can use the rest. Depending upon the kind of file it is, the recovered portion may or may not be usable. Generally this kind of file recovery only works with text files, which contain written material. To use RECOVER in this way, you enter the command followed by the name of the file it is to check for readable and unreadable parts.

The other kind of file recovery done by RECOVER is completely different. Unfortunately, it is easy to confuse the two, and this is where the danger lies. In this second kind of file recovery, RECOVER assumes that the entire directory of the disk is damaged and nonsensical. It throws away the entire directory and replaces it with a new one, which contains the data it found on the disk, organized into files as well as possible. But the new directory contains files with arbitrary names that RECOVER gives them—it is then your job to figure out what is what, as best you can.

To use RECOVER in this way, you enter the command without specifying any filename. But remember that this form of RECOVER wipes out your entire directory. Be careful—and attentive—if you use it. It can be *extremely* dangerous, as too many sad folks have discovered. In fact, you might want to completely avoid the use of the RECOVER command, for safety's sake.

10

HARD DISK SET UP

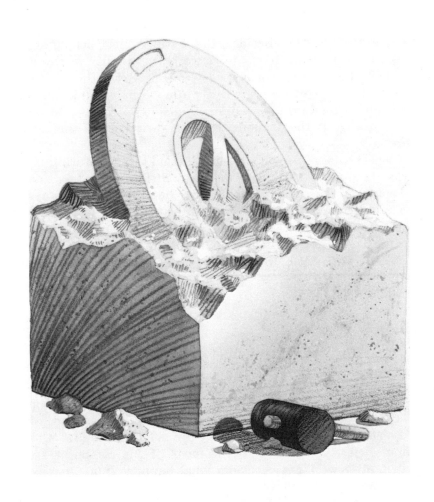

Introduction

Personal computers have traditionally used floppy diskettes for storage, but today most serious PC users prefer, if they can, to take advantage of the special capabilities of hard disks. In this chapter you'll find out about the special needs of hard-disk storage, but before we get into the details, let's cover a little background information.

First of all, the practical use of a computer centers around its storage. That may not seem sensible—after all, computing power is what you use a computer for. Besides, the features most people are most interested in are more likely to concern the quality of the display screen (can it do graphics or is it easy to look at?) or the printer (how fast is it? can it print italics?). But while we may think most about our machine's computing speed, or its display formats and printing quality, storage is the element that the entire use of the computer centers around.

Widespread use of personal computers and their operating systems, such as DOS, was based upon the floppy diskette—and for good reason. Diskettes are cheap, reliable, and flexible in more ways than one. Their technical flexibility made it easy for all sorts of computers to use them. Their flexibility of use, easy for put in and take out, easy to store, easy to mail, greatly enhanced how practical it was to get things done with a small computer. But floppy diskettes have two severe disadvantages: slow speed and small storage capacity. Let's look a little at each.

Computing Speed

A computer consists of a collection of components all working together. Each part has a particular speed at which it can accomplish its own task. In a rough sort of way, the separate speeds of the different parts can be compared, so that we can get an idea of whether they are appropriately balanced. If the parts of the computer are well matched, all is well. Let's consider what happens if one part is made much faster or much slower.

Suppose that one part of our computer takes up exactly 10% of the total time needed to get some work done. If we replace that part with one that is ten times faster, then the new part will get the same job done in only 1% of the old time—and our whole computer will run 9% faster. One part is improved 10 times, but the whole is improved less than 10%. If we now replace that part with one that's 10 times slower than the original, the one part now takes 100% of the original time just to do that one part of the work. The whole computer now runs 90% slower, almost halving its effective speed, thanks to just one slow component.

The moral here is that there is little advantage in having one part of the computer that's disproportionately fast, but there is a huge disadvantage in having one part that's disproportionately slow. The question is one of balance, and of bottlenecks. If one part is slow relative to the rest of the computer, it becomes a bottleneck that can cripple the entire computer.

Time Trials

In most personal computers, floppy diskettes are the greatest bottleneck in overall performance. This statement is not absolutely true, but is generally true. How true it might be for you depends upon two things: first, the relative balance of speed in the parts of your computer and second, the relative balance of how your work utilizes the computer's parts. If you and I had identical computers, but you used your disks hardly at all, they wouldn't be a bottleneck for you. But if I use mine very heavily, mine are certain to be a bottleneck for me, so there are no absolutes here. For most users of most personal computers, though, the disks are clearly the bottleneck, the limiting factor in the entire computer's working speed.

Let's look at some representative numbers, so that you can see what I'm talking about. The computer this book was written on uses both floppy diskettes and a hard disk for storage. In my own practical speed trials, I found that the hard disk was five to ten times faster than the floppy diskettes. But these speed tests were for purely disk operations, not for the whole computer. What did they mean in practice? Is there a bottleneck? To find out, I tested one of the most time-consuming things I do with my computer: I checked something that I wrote for spelling errors.

I knew that my spelling checker did lots of computing and a fair amount of disk work, but I didn't know about balance; I didn't know where the bottlenecks were for that particular computer task. I chose a large chunk of text for the spelling check, and used each of the three possible storage media: floppy diskette, hard disk, and electronic disk.

Using the floppy diskette, the operation took about three minutes. Then I tried the hard disk, which, for disk work alone, is five times faster. When I used the hard disk for spelling checking, the time was down to about two minutes. A dramatic improvement—a full third off the time. Then I tested further to see if, even with a hard disk, the disk speed was still a bottleneck. I did that with a RAM disk, using the computer's electronic memory (RAM) as a storage disk. But even though a RAM disk works many times faster than a hard disk, using it to check spelling only saved another six seconds; proof that my hard disk was fast enough for this job, and no bottleneck at this task.

My own speed trials dramatically demonstrated both sides of the speed question . Up to a certain point, a faster disk can help you, but beyond that speed is not the problem. Your own speed needs or problems are uniquely yours, but typically they will be similar to mine. For most users of personal computers, ordinary floppy diskettes are somewhat of a bottleneck, and anything that promises to be several times faster will eliminate that bottleneck.

Holding Capacity

Let's look at the other side of storage: capacity. There are many formats used in disk storage, and so there are many different storage capacities for different disks. The diskettes used in the PC family range in capacity from a low of 160,000 bytes for the PC's "lowest common denominator," the single-sided 8-sector diskette, to a high of 1.2 million bytes for the AT model's special high-capacity diskettes.

There are three problems you encounter when you use diskettes that won't hold all of your data. First, there is the nuisance of shuffling diskettes, putting in one set for one kind of work, and another set for other work. Not only is this inconvenient, but the physical handling of the diskettes greatly increases the danger of damage to our data. Second, you may want to have more data on tap than will fit into our diskette drives at one time—it is hard to correlate the information on three diskettes, when you have only two diskette drives. Third, diskettes set a low limit on how big your biggest single file can be, since no file can be bigger than the disk that holds it.

Hard Disks

Hard-disk systems solve all three problems. They eliminate diskette shuffling, allow the simultaneous use of large amounts of data, and they allow single files to grow quite large, indeed.

If you don't have a hard disk, you may be wondering how much you might need one, or what size you should get. (After all, if you get one that is too small, you again have the problems you faced in the diskette world.) If you can estimate your data storage needs, fine, if not, here is my suggested rule of thumb.

For a computer in personal use, or professional use without large amounts of data, a hard disk with a storage capacity of 10 million bytes capacity is likely to be enough. For a professional user, or for a business with moderate amounts of records, 20 million bytes might be right. For extensive business records, a large research data base, or anything similar, 30 or more might be needed. (I have a 40-megabyte disk in mine, and I've never regretted having so much.) If you are choosing a hard disk, it is safer to get larger, rather than smaller. If you know that you can add more later, then you can safely start small.

Organizing Your Hard Disk

Whether your hard disk holds 10 million bytes or 50, basically what you have is a whole lot of storage space into which you can toss programs and data with gay abandon. The problem is, if you don't do anything to organize those millions of bytes' worth of files, you might as well have tossed all that information into a black hole. How are you going to find it again?

We'll leave the details of organizing your files to the next chapter, because that's where you'll find out about some commands that help you treat a hard disk like a giant filing cabinet. But right now, in terms of the things we'll look at in this chapter, a small introduction is needed.

Basically, you can treat a hard disk as if it were a huge warehouse with movable partitions inside: You divide and subdivide, until all your files (things in storage) are neatly organized and easily accessible. This analogy of a warehouse is fairly useful, in fact (and a little different from the traditional hard disk equals file cabinet analogy).

Overall, think of your hard disk as the warehouse building. Big and roomy, but potentially chaotic if things aren't organized correctly. In your warehouse, you have one main area—let's call it receiving—where everything gets checked in and out. On your hard disk, this "receiving area" is a special directory called the **root directory**.

Moving out from the receiving area, you can separate this from that in your warehouse by putting up partitions; on your hard disk, you can do that same thing by creating electronic partitions called **directories**. Likewise, in your warehouse, you can divide a partitioned area into smaller areas holding related goods. Same with your hard disk, only the smaller partitions are called **subdirectories**. And, warehouse or directory, you can divide and divide again, until things (**files**) are stored just where you want them.

Finally, to finish up our warehouse analogy, when you don't need a partitioned area anymore, you can remove the walls or shelves and stick new things in the same storage space—again, same with hard disks.

That is the idea behind organizing a hard disk. You, instead of DOS, decide which directories need to be created and what they should be named, you divide directories into smaller units, or subdirectories, and you tell DOS which directory/subdirectory to store your files in.

With this general introduction to the needs for and uses of hard disks finished (and electronic disks, since a lot of what I've discussed about speed and storage capacity applies to them, too) let's move on to the special things you need to know about each.

Key Hard-Disk Commands

Having a high-capacity hard-disk system on your computer adds extra power and capabilities to your system. It also calls for some special servicing, and to meet that need, DOS provides four special programs tailored to the needs of hard disks (although, except for FDISK, they work on diskettes as well). The programs are FDISK,

BACKUP, RESTORE, and ATTRIB. We'll begin with the one that's entirely tailored for hard disks, FDISK.

FDISK

FDISK is geared to one simple matter: dividing your hard disk into separate sections, called **partitions**. (These are not, by the way, the same thing as directories or subdirectories. To carry out our earlier analogy, they're more like separate warehouse buildings.) There are two main reasons why you might need to partition your hard disk.

The first, and most practical one for most people, is that DOS can only work with so much space at one time. There's a practical limit of 32 megabytes in the working disk size. But what if you have a larger disk, like the 40-megabyte disk in my machine, or the 70- and 120-megabyte monster disks that come in some computers? The solution is to carve a big disk up into smaller chunks that DOS can work with, by partitioning the disk.

The second reason, which doesn't apply to most PC users but could apply to you, is that DOS isn't the only operating system in use on PCs. There are others. If you are going to be using two different operating systems, say DOS and something else, perhaps a version of the famous Unix system, then each operating system needs a separate part of the disk it can call its own. Partitioning a disk can solve this problem as well.

FDISK's job is to create and manage partitions on a hard disk. If you know or think you might be using another operating system in addition to DOS, you can set aside part of your hard disk with FDISK.

Having DOS coexist with another operating system is not the only task for which you need FDISK. Another, and more important point, is that when you first set up a hard disk on your personal computer, you'll need to use FDISK to establish the DOS partition on that disk. Even if you only use DOS on your hard disk, you'll still need to use FDISK at first, simply to mark the disk as being entirely devoted to DOS.

The use of FDISK is remarkably simple, and I won't go over the details here. What I will do instead is summarize the most common operation: setting up a hard disk for the first time.

Setting Up a Hard Disk

When you first set up your hard disk, you need to start your computer with a diskette copy of DOS, and then invoke the FDISK program:

```
FDISK
```

FDISK will present you with a menu of options. If you're uncertain which one to pick, choose the "display partition data" option, and see what you have. If the command reports that there already is a DOS partition on the hard disk, then you probably want to let it be. (Very often, the dealer from whom you purchase your equipment will set up your hard disk for you, before delivery. Because of that, lots of PC hard disk users never even learn about FDISK or know that their disks couldn't be used until they are set up with FDISK.)

If there is no DOS partition, go back to the menu and choose the "create DOS partition" option. You'll be asked if you want to devote the entire disk to DOS. Under normal circumstances (in other words, if you're not planning on using more than one operating system) you will.

After you create your DOS partition, you'll need to reboot your computer, and then use the FORMAT command to format the DOS partition and place a copy of the DOS system there (using the /S option of FORMAT).

Once all that is done, which seems like more steps than it should be, but that's the way it is, your hard disk will be ready to use, and you'll be able to start up DOS from the hard disk without having to use a floppy diskette copy of DOS.

One word of caution, before we finish with FDISK: Once you've created a DOS partition and started using it, you should be careful to not destroy it by using FDISK again. If you tell FDISK to change the DOS partition, you'll probably lose everything that's stored on the disk. If that's not what you want, the result could be disaster—equivalent to reformatting your hard disk, so take care with FDISK.

Protecting Your Data

Once you start using a hard disk system, you're sure to load it up with lots and lots of data, that's what a hard disk is for. How do you safeguard that data? For one thing, you should make periodic backup copies of the data on your hard disk, and that's where the commands BACKUP and RESTORE come in.

BACKUP

BACKUP is designed to copy your data from a hard disk to as many floppies as are needed to hold them. Starting with the three-series of DOS, you can also use the same techniques that BACKUP provides to copy from any type of disk to any other and you can even back up your floppies onto a hard disk. While it's nice to be able to transfer data in any direction, the main use for the BACKUP command is to put copies of your hard disk data onto floppy diskettes for safekeeping.

BACKUP provides you with several options that make it easier to control how you copy your data and what data you copy. Starting with the big picture, if you want to copy the entire contents of a hard disk (we'll assume it's drive C) onto floppy disks (assume they're placed in drive A), then you use the BACKUP command like this:

```
BACKUP C:\ A: /S
```

Here are the key ingredients of that command: the parameter C:\ instructs BACKUP to start from the root directory (that's the main directory—the receiving area in our warehouse analogy) of drive C. The /S switch tells BACKUP to copy all the subdirectories as well as what's in the root directory. By starting at the root directory, and including any subdirectories, you've told BACKUP to copy everything that's on the disk.

If you wanted to, you could back up just the contents of a particular directory or subdirectory. You would do this by telling DOS how to get to the directory you want to back up. This route you specify is called the **directory pathname**, and it's your way of telling DOS,

"Go to directory X, then find subdirectory Y and back up all the files you find there." Using this form of the command, you would specify a subdirectory this way:

```
BACKUP C:\X\Y
```

If you also included the /S option:

```
BACKUP C:\X\Y /S
```

you would include any additional subdirectories within the directory you chose.

BACKUP is clever enough to work with as many floppy diskettes as are needed to copy the files we've asked it to, and even to spread files across more than one diskette when it's necessary.

You'll find when you back up the contents of a hard disk that it's a time-consuming process that takes lots of diskettes—typically 20 or more. Fortunately, there are some shortcuts that can reduce the time and quantity of diskettes involved in the process.

BACKUP Shortcuts

Once you've backed up all of a disk, you really don't need to copy it all for a while, just periodically copying any files that you've added or changed should be enough. DOS keeps a record of which files have been changed and have not been backed up, and BACKUP is smart enough to recognize them if you ask it to. This is done with the /M switch, which tells BACKUP to only copy the files you've changed since the last backup.

What I do with my hard disk, and what I recommend that you do, is periodically make a complete copy of your hard disk, however of-ten you think is wise. I think once a month is a good idea, but I have to admit it's usually several months till I get around to the chore. Then, between these complete backups, make "incremental" back-ups, copying only the files that have been changed in the meantime. You should do this much more often—daily, or at the very least, weekly.

If you follow these suggestions, you'll find that your backing up procedures will be very practical and not that tedious.

As a reminder, here are the two commands to use to backup files:

```
BACKUP C:\ A:          (for a full backup)
BACKUP C:\ A: /M       (for an incremental backup)
```

Other Switches in BACKUP

There are two more switches in BACKUP you ought to know about. One is the Date option, /D. Like the /M (meaning back up only Modified files) option, the date option lets you select which files will be backed up, but the selection is based on the date (the date stamp that indicates when they were last changed) being on or after a date you give to BACKUP. This lets us choose to back up recent materials, without regard to whether they have been backed up before or not (which the /M option uses). That's a handy alternative. Here's the command form using the /D switch:

```
BACKUP C:\ /D:MM-DD-YY    (for the entire disk)
BACKUP C:\DIRECTORY\SUBDIRECTORY /D:MM-DD-YY     (for a directory or subdirectory)
```

The other thing that you need to know about BACKUP is that it will completely take over a diskette and wipe out any existing files on the target diskette, unless you tell it to be more civilized. This is done with the /A switch, which tells BACKUP to add its backup files to whatever else is on the target diskette. Without the /A option, BACKUP will clear out whatever is already on the target disk. Here's that command form:

```
BACKUP C:\ /A    (for the entire disk)
BACKUP C:\DIRECTORY\SUBDIRECTORY /A     (for a directory or subdirectory)
```

Restoring Data to the Hard Disk

Naturally, there is a RESTORE command to match BACKUP. RESTORE reverses the backup operation, and has the same sort of features. There is one practical inconvenience that you should be aware of. More often than you might think, an occasion arises when you want to restore a copy of a file that's been backed up, but you want to place in a different directory—probably so you can work on it separately from the original copy. Unfortunately, RESTORE will only restore files to exactly the same directories from which they were backed up. Keep this in mind when you selectively restore files.

If you do need to put a file into a different directory, about the only way to do so is by using the COPY command.

11
WORKING WITH SUBDIRECTORIES

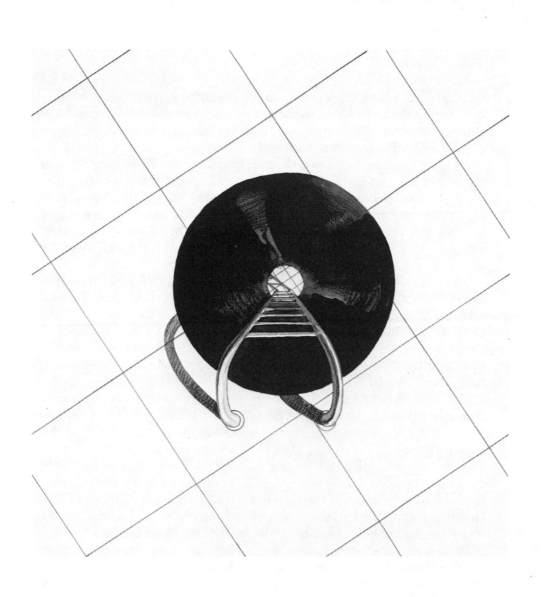

Introduction

Disks, especially hard disks, can be used in a rich and complex way in DOS, thanks to the concept of subdirectories and paths, which you encountered briefly in the last chapter. Let's take a closer look at directories and see them in relation to what you now know about disks.

All disks, whether floppy or hard, have a fixed-size directory of files. This is called the **root** or **main directory**. This isn't the only directory a disk can have, though. The disk's root directory can have subdirectories under it, and each of those can also have any mixture of files and subdirectories under it.

As they are stored on the disk, subdirectories are files, just like any other you keep on the disk. But DOS marks subdirectories specially, so it can treat them as part of the directory structure. Thus, subdirectories are unique hybrids—plain files in the way they are stored on disk, but very special files in terms of what they are and what they contain. This has some interesting and important consequences for us.

First, a subdirectory can grow in size, just as any file is allowed to grow. This is a major difference between the root directory and a subdirectory. The root directory is fixed in its location and size, thus there is a definite upper limit to the number of entries it can hold. A subdirectory, on the other hand, is limited only by the space on the disk and there is no arbitrary limit to the number of entries it can hold.

The second practical consequence of a subdirectory being stored like any other file is not as advantageous. DOS has to hunt around the disk for a subdirectory, and it takes longer to get to it. A disk's root directory is always located at the very beginning of the disk, next to the table (FAT) that keeps track of the available and used space on the disk. When you tell DOS to process a file with an entry in the root directory, all the information DOS needs to find the file— the directory entry and the storage location where it can find the file itself—is placed close together, where DOS can find it quickly.

With a subdirectory, it's another matter. Suppose you have a set of subdirectories like this (we always begin with the root directory, because everything else comes under it):

```
Root
    Subdirectory AA
        Subdirectory BB
            MYFILE
```

To work with MYFILE, which is kept in subdirectory BB, DOS first has to hunt through the path of subdirectories that leads to the file. The path here is Root to AA to BB to MYFILE. Each subdirectory is stored on the disk some distance away from the space table (officially known as the FAT, for File Allocation Table). Tracing through the directory path, and going back and forth from each directory to the table and back again adds a lot of overhead to the work that DOS must do. If a disk is fast (as most hard-disk systems are) and if the path is short, as I recommend that you keep all your paths, then there isn't much problem. But with a slow diskette device or with complicated paths, the extra work can slow your computer down considerably.

Tree-Structured Directories

As I've mentioned, each of your disks has a root directory, to which you can add other directories. Each new directory branches out from its parent directory, and each one in turn can have any number of other subdirectories under it. This type of branching is referred to as a hierarchical, or **tree-structured**, directory system.

It is possible to have directories branching out from directories without limit, creating a complex tree structure. You may be tempted to make use of this capability to give a thorough logical structure to your files. The idea is appealing: You create master directories for a major subject area, and subdirectories under it for more details. For example, you might want to create a directory for all accounting data, with subdirectories for each accounting year. Or you might want to create a master directory for each person who uses the computer, with subject-matter directories under them. There are all sorts of possibilities.

In practice, though, tree structures like these are a terrible idea. The main reason is that your computer has to do much more disk work to trace its way through complex directories, and disk access is usually the slowest part of your computer's operation. A secondary reason is that the more complicated a subdirectory system is, the harder it is to keep track of. It's harder to find necessary data, and, especially important, it's more unlikely that you'll discard unneeded data. There are nearly a thousand files on the hard disk of the computer system this book is being written with, and I'm often finding some neglected file that is cluttering up my disk space. If I had a complex tree structure, the problem would be much worse.

When Do You Need a Subdirectory?

Subdirectories are really only intended for use with the fast speed and huge capacity of a hard disk system. Unless you have a lot of files on a disk, there is little need for organizing them into isolated groups by putting them in subdirectories. More important, the extra overhead of work that subdirectories require can cripple the operation of slower, diskette-type storage. Subdirectories are practical only with the fast speed of a hard disk system, which works about five or ten times faster than an ordinary diskette system.

As a general rule, you only need subdirectories if you have a multi-million-byte-capacity hard disk system. Also, you can only afford the extra overhead of subdirectories if you have a hard disk. Otherwise, you should not use them.

From my own practical experience, I would recommend that you create as many subdirectories as you need, but make your tree structure the simplest possible: Place all your subdirectories onto the disk's root directory. Unless you have a really good reason to do so, don't create branches off of any other directory than the root.

Judging when you should create a directory at all is another question. There are advantages and disadvantages to creating lots of small directories. With many directories containing only a few files each, it is easier to keep track of the files that belong in one particular category. But it is more difficult to use files in different directories at the same time, so it can become inconvenient if you have your files split into lots of directories. Also, the more subdirectories you have, the harder it becomes to manage the totality of your files.

The way you create and use your subdirectories will depend upon your needs and your own taste. Let me recommend what I have found works very well for me. First, as I mentioned, I have only one level of tree. All of my subdirectories branch off my disk's root directory; there are no further subdirectories. When I created my tree I asked myself what subdirectories I really needed. The answer: I needed subdirectories to help keep track of my data, but not to keep track of my programs. So I placed all of my programs, including all of the DOS programs and other programs that I have written or bought, in the root directory. There, they are easily accessible and can serve each of the subdirectories, but they don't clutter up the directories where I keep data.

Paths to a Directory

With the potential complexity of a branching tree-structured directory, you need a way to to find and control where you are, and you need a way to indicate what part of the tree you are interested in. You need a notation, a way of specifying a location in the tree.

How you (and DOS) find your way to a particular subdirectory on a disk is referred to as **a path**. A path is the route that traces the way from a disk's root directory, out to some point in the branching directory tree. The description of the path is called the **pathname**.

Let's take our earlier example, in which we have the subdirectories AA and BB leading to a file named MYFILE. At the top of the heap is the disk which, of course, has a root directory. The root directory has a subdirectory named AA, and it in turn has a subdirectory named BB. Finally, in subdirectory BB is the file we want to refer to, MYFILE. To find the way to MYFILE, we need describe the path something like this.

- Starting with the ROOT, find its subdirectory named AA;
- next find AA's subdirectory named BB;
- then find BB's file named MYFILE.

Pathnames can be written like this, but all the lengthy words can be replaced with a short and simple reverse-slash (\); so our verbose path description shortens down to this:

```
\AA\BB\MYFILE
```

Notice you don't have to say anything about starting from the root— the first slash indicates that. If a pathname begins with a reverse slash, that tells DOS, "start the path from the root."

With this way of writing a pathname, we can tell DOS where in any disk's directory tree we want to work. And vice-versa: DOS can tell us where things are.

With the "hooks" on which we can hang subdirectories and pathnames out of the way, let's see how to go about setting up and managing directories.

Creating a Directory with MKDIR

To create a new directory, you use the make directory command, which is typed either as MKDIR or as MD. For example, you would add a directory named LETTERS to the root directory with this command:

```
MD LETTERS
```

When a directory is created, it is empty except for two terse reference entries, a single dot (.) and a double dot (..), which DOS uses as markers to tell it where it is and where it came from. For example, a directory listing of our LETTERS example would show entries like these:

```
Directory of C:\LETTERS

 .        <DIR>    6-25-87 11:25a
 ..       <DIR>    6-25-87 11:25a
```

After a directory has been created, then files (or other directories) can be placed in it. All of the names in one directory—names of files, or names of subdirectories—must be unique within that directory, but the same names can be used in other directories.

If you want to add a subdirectory to another directory, include the path to the new directory in your command. For example, you would create the subdirectory A_M under LETTERS with this command (you'll see another way to do this when we get to the Change Directory command):

```
MD \LETTERS\A_M
```

and if you requested a directory listing, DOS would show you something like this:

```
Directory of C:\LETTERS

.       <DIR>    6-25-87 11:25a
..      <DIR>    6-25-87 11:25a
A_M     <DIR>    6-25-87 11:32a
```

Using RMDIR to Remove a Directory

If you can make directories, you should be able to remove them as well, and this is what the RMDIR, or RD, command is for. It's as easy to use as MKDIR, but to avoid leaving any files or subdirectories without a home, RMDIR will not work unless the directory is empty. If you try to delete a directory that contains any files or subdirectories, DOS displays the informative message:

```
Invalid path, not directory,
or directory not empty
```

If you see this message, take a look (with the DIR command) at the files in the directory. If you want to keep what's there, use the COPY and DELETE commands to move the files to another directory. If you want to keep a subdirectory, think twice about whether you really want to remove the directory at all.

Using the TREE Command to Find Branches

Since a disk can have numerous subdirectories branching out from the root directory, you need a way of finding out what all the branches of the tree are. The TREE command does this for you. TREE will display a list of all the branches of the directory tree for any disk. Here's the type of display you see with the TREE command:

```
DIRECTORY PATH LISTING FOR VOLUME (name of your volume)
Path: \CLIENTS
Subdirectories: LETTERS
Path: \LETTERS
Subdirectories: None
```

As you can see, DOS works its way down (or out) along each branch of your directory tree, telling you the pathname and the name of any subdirectories that branch off from there.

Changing Direction with CHDIR

If you are going to be working with various files in a subdirectory, such as our sample \AA\BB directory, it would be a nuisance to have to keep typing \AA\BB in front of the name of each file. More than likely, you'd make a typing error at some point. To solve this problem, DOS keeps track of what it calls the **current directory**. If you refer to just a filename, without specifying the path to get to it, DOS assumes that the file is in the current directory.

You can control which directory DOS assumes is the current directory, and you do it with the change-current-directory command, CHDIR (which can be abbreviated CD). For example, to make \A\B your current directory, you would enter the command:

```
CHDIR \AA\BB
```

If you wanted to change back to the root directory, you would only have to type:

```
CHDIR \
```

because the backslash is DOS's shorthand for the root directory.

Then, too, if you ever forget which directory you're in, the command:

```
CHDIR
```

with no parameters tells DOS to let you know. For example, if you type CHDIR while you're in the BB subdirectory, DOS displays:

```
\AA\BB
```

to let you know where you are.

Furthermore, if you want to create a directory underneath another directory, you can use the CHDIR and MKDIR commands like this:

```
CHDIR \AA
```
 (to make subdirectory A the current directory)

and this:

```
MKDIR NEWDIR
```

to create the subdirectory NEWDIR underneath subdirectory A.

Finally, to make things even easier, DOS keeps track of a separate current directory for each disk device it has. If you have an A-drive and a B-drive, you could set the current directories for them, independently, like this:

```
CHDIR  A:\DIR1\DIR2
CHDIR  B:\OTHER1
```

Then, whenever you referred to the A-drive, DOS would look in the \DIR1\DIR2 directory, while for any use of drive B, DOS would look in its \OTHER1 directory. If you did a global copy command, like this:

```
COPY  A:*.*  B:
```

the files from the \DIR1\DIR2 directory in drive A would be copied to the directory \OTHER1 in drive B. No other files and no other directories would be affected.

Pathfinding Shortcuts

If you type a pathname starting with a slash, you are telling DOS to start tracing the path from the root, but there are other ways to work around directory trees. If you don't precede the pathname with a slash, then the pathfinding begins right where you are, at whatever happens to be the current directory. Thus, this pathname tells DOS to start with the root:

```
\AA\BB\MYFILE
```

while this pathname tells DOS to start wherever the current directory is:

```
AA\BB\MYFILE
```

There are also two special trick names to help you work your way around paths. They are the single (.) and double (..) dots mentioned earlier. These special names are used to refer to the current directory (.) and the directory, called the **parent directory**, that is one level above the current directory (..). For example, if you were in the AA directory and wanted a directory listing, you could type:

```
DIR  .\BB
```

instead of:

```
DIR  \AA\BB
```

It might seem silly to you, at first glance, to have a . entry that just refers to the same directory that you're already in. Why have a directory name that basically means "do nothing—don't shift to another directory?" The reason emerges when you start thinking about some of the complex ways that you can use directories in batch files, which were covered in Chapters 7 and 8.

If you can specify a directory name in the middle of a path, like this: \DIRECTORY\ then you also ought to be able to substitute nothing in place of the name DIRECTORY; that's just what the period (.) will do for you, like this: \.\ Without the period, you'd have something like this: \\. And those two slashes would confuse DOS no end.

The parent-name, two periods (..), is used if you ever want to trace your way backward from the current directory. Let's switch back to our first example:

```
CHDIR  \AA\BB
```

You're now in the \A\B directory. But suppose you want to find a file named MEMO that's in the \AA directory—the parent of the current directory? You can find your way to it like this:

```
..\MEMO
```

This business of using .. to refer to the parent directory can be used for all kinds of sophisticated tricks. But bear in mind that they would be tricks and as such, any command that uses them is likely to be tricky and error prone. It's nice to know what the two periods mean, but you'd be well advised to steer clear of the whole business. After all, if you had a complex pathname that traced its way forward and back, like this:

```
..\..\AA\BB\..\CC\FILE
```

you'd have to think your way up and down the directory tree and very likely would misunderstand or misremember it. There's really no reason to introduce unnecessary complications.

Paths, Programs, and Data

There is one more very interesting thing to consider about finding your way along the paths through the trees, and that is how you find programs and how you find data.

When programs and data are stored on disk, they are no different from one another—they are just disk files which contain one kind of information or another. Yet DOS uses a different method for finding programs than it does for finding data. This seems puzzling at first, but there is a good reason for it, and it turns out to be very handy.

When you tell DOS to go looking for a data file, it looks only in one place: the current directory. (If you specify a pathname with the filename, then DOS looks along the path you specify, rather than in the current directory, but it is still looking in only one place.) This is true whether you specify a particular drive to look on, or use DOS's default disk drive.

Each drive has its own current directory (which is the root directory, unless you've changed to a subdirectory with the CHDIR command). This is also true whether you are using a DOS command, such as COPY to refer to a data file, or whether a program you are using asks DOS to find a data file for it. If DOS is asked to find a data file, then it looks in only one directory—the current directory, or the directory in the pathname given with the filename.

For programs it is different; when you enter a command to DOS, you are telling DOS to find a program with that name and then to execute the program. The command program might be internal to DOS, as was discussed in Chapter 2 or it might be external, which means the program to carry out that command is located on disk storage.

When DOS goes looking for a program file to carry out a command, it does not look only in the current directory. Instead, if DOS doesn't find it in the current directory, it will search in as many other places as you have told it to. How do you tell DOS to do this extended search for command program files?—with the PATH command.

The PATH Command

As you'll see, the PATH command has a slightly misleading name. From the way we've been looking at it, you might think the PATH command is like the yellow brick road in the Wizard of Oz: a way to point DOS in one particular direction. That's true, as far as data files are concerned. DOS will follow a path you give it and, if it doesn't find the data file you want, it will tell you File not found, period.

But with programs, PATH also describes a list of paths DOS should search for command program files. Instead of pointing DOS down the straight and narrow, PATH now tells DOS, "if you don't find a program along this path, go along that one...and that, and that." Here, PATH is a command to set the extended program search paths.

Remember, however, that the search always begins in the current directory. If the program file isn't found there, then the search goes on where the PATH command says it should. Directories in the PATH command are separated by semicolons, like this:

```
PATH \PROGS;\OTHER\PROGS;\
```

In this example, the PATH command would lead the search for a program file into four directories, in this order:

- the current directory (automatic—regardless of the PATH);
- the PROGS directory, under the root (\PROGS);
- the PROGS directory, under the OTHER directory, under the root (\OTHER\PROGS);
- finally, to the root itself (\).

One of the most remarkable things about the PATH command is that the search paths can be located on different disks. Even if you don't use subdirectories, you can make good use of the PATH command to have it automatically search from disk to disk, looking for the right program. For example, if you had four disk drives, A, B, C, and D, the command:

```
PATH A:;B:;C:;D:
```

would tell DOS to search them all.

If you want to discontinue the extended program search, this command deactivates it:

```
PATH ;
```

After that, only the current directory will be searched for command programs.

Why would you want to use the PATH command? There are two reasons, one if you use subdirectories, and one if you don't. If your computer has diskettes only, and not a high-capacity hard-disk system, then you are sure to have more programs than you can fit onto one diskette. You may have two different diskettes loaded into your diskette drives, each one with programs on it. If you use the PATH command to search both diskettes, then you don't have to bother indicating which programs are on which diskette—DOS will automatically go looking for them.

On the other hand, if you have a hard-disk system, you are probably using subdirectories, and you probably have programs scattered around in various directories. Even if you follow my advice and try to keep all of your programs in the root directory, there will still be times when you need to have some programs (or batch files) in other directories. If you set the PATH command to search through all of the directories where you keep programs, then each and every one of your programs will be on tap for you, regardless of which directory it is buried in.

There is one rather obvious practical note you need to keep in mind about using the PATH search command: the more directories DOS has to search through, the longer it takes to find a command program. To speed things up, put the most frequently used program directories at the top of the list.

The PROMPT Command

Next we come to a command that can help enormously in keeping track of where you are in your directory structure: the PROMPT command.

When DOS is ready for a command, it shows a prompt, which is normally the default drive, followed by a greater-than symbol, like this: A>. But you can change the prompt to nearly anything, including a display of the current time and date with the PROMPT command.

The format and rules for setting a prompt are complicated and quite specific, so you should see your computer's DOS manual if you want to use this command. If you feel playful, there are all sorts of fancy things that you can get into (as your DOS manual will show you).

In a moment I'll show you one of the more exotic prompts you can set up, but before we get into that I want to show you the one—and only, in my opinion—really useful prompt command. This is a variation on the standard system prompt that shows you not only the default drive (A>), but also the default directory path as well.

If you make use of subdirectories on your disks, even just a few subdirectories, it's easy to lose track of where you are and what the current directory is. But there is a version of the PROMPT command that will change the DOS command prompt so it always tells you what the current directory is. It's done like this:

```
PROMPT $P$G
```

This prompt command changes the command prompt to show the current path (that's what "$P" asks for) followed by the familiar greater-than symbol, ">" (which is what the "$G" part of the command asks for). Suppose, for example, you change the prompt as I indicated and you have two subdirectories, LETTERS and AC-COUNTS, on your C drive. If you are working in the LETTERS subdirectory, your prompt will now look like this:

```
C:\LETTERS>
```

If you change to the ACCOUNTS subdirectory, your prompt will change to:

```
C:\ACCOUNTS>
```

Try this PROMPT command, and you'll find it quite helpful. It is, in fact, so useful that I feel blind without it. If, as sometimes happens, I must use someone else's computer, the first thing I do is change the prompt so I can tell where I am.

Now for the fun: Try either of these two PROMPT commands, and see what happens:

```
PROMPT $V $T $D $P $G
PROMPT I await your command, Oh Master $g
```

To change back to DOS's normal prompt, type PROMPT all by itself. To change back to the drive plus directory prompt I recommended, type PROMPT PG (with no spaces between the dollar signs and letters).

12

ADVANCED DISK COMMANDS

Introduction

In your everyday work with disks, especially hard disks and sub-directories, you'll probably need no more than the DOS commands you've encountered so far. I would guess that somewhere in the neighborhood of 80 to 90 percent of all your work with disks will involve four basic commands: FORMAT, COPY, DIR, and DELETE. If you use a hard disk, you'll expand your repertoire with the commands in the last chapter, particularly MKDIR, CHDIR, RMDIR, and PATH.

But there's more to DOS, a lot more. So in this chapter, let's finish up our work with disks by covering some of DOS's advanced disk-management commands. We'll begin with a look at a way to check up on DOS.

Double-Checking Your Disk with VERIFY

When DOS is writing information to disk, it normally accepts the disk drive's report that all went well. This is generally okay because disk drives are quite reliable. If you wish, you can ask DOS to check, or verify, all data that is written to disk. This is controlled with the VERIFY command, which can set verification on or off. DOS normally does not verify. If you are concerned, you can set verification on, but it will add considerably to the time it takes to use the disks.

Because our computers and their disk drives are so reliable, I personally don't recommend using the verify option, but I'm glad it's there for anyone who feels they need it. When most people first learn about the verification option, they assume that it's something more thorough than it really is. You'd be inclined to think that verifying the data that's been written to disk means reading it back and comparing it with the original—that's *not* what VERIFY does. VERIFY simply has the disk drive perform a routine that tests for **recording errors**. Every disk has a self-check mechanism built in that can detect lost bits. So, the verify operation checks that the data is recorded correctly (i.e., no lost bits). It doesn't actually check that the correct data is there. Verification isn't quite as thorough a test as you might think, but it is a reasonably good test for errors.

You can turn verification on an off at will with the VERIFY command. Turn it on like this,

```
VERIFY ON
```

and turn it off like this,

```
VERIFY OFF
```

Being able to turn it on and off like that can be handy, because you may not want to have verification in action all the time, but you might want to turn it on for some critical operations. By putting these VERIFY ON and OFF commands in a batch file, you can easily control when verification is done. DOS defaults to having verification off.

Masking Your Disks

DOS includes several commands that can help you fool a program into thinking that one drive or directory is a different drive or directory. While such pretenses may strike you as electronic sophistry, they are actually both necessary and realistic in certain circumstances, as you'll see.

Pretending One Drive Is Another

Some programs have to have things their way. This causes a very special problem that arises when we try to match old-fashioned programs with new computer concepts. Here is the problem: Many older programs for personal computers were written in the days when PCs just used small-capacity floppy disks for storage. In those days, the standard way of operating a PC was to have two diskette drives, A and B, and to use them in a certain way: the program diskette in drive A, and the data diskette in drive B.

Now, there is nothing wrong with that style of operating. Lots of today's computers have two floppy drives, A and B, used in the way I just described. The problem is that more and more computers have a large hard disk to work with, usually as drive C. But some programs were written so that they could only work in one way: with the program disk in drive A, and the data disk in drive B (or whatever). This creates a problem when you try to adapt such programs to work a hard disk. The ASSIGN command is designed to help.

The ASSIGN Command

ASSIGN instructs DOS to reroute requests for one disk drive to another, essentially "pretending" that drive X is really drive Y. For example, if you assign both drives A and B to your hard disk drive C, then any program that insists on asking for drives A and B will have DOS, in a sneaky end-run maneuver, actually refer the requests to the hard drive C. That lets DOS outfox some single-minded programs, and helps you a lot.

To have all this happen, you issue the assign command in this form:

```
ASSIGN OLDDRIVE=NEWDRIVE
```

You can assign several drives at the same time if you want, too. Thus, for example, if you want to assign drives A and B to your hard drive, C, the command is:

```
ASSIGN A=C B=C
```

When you want to undo the assignment, as you certainly will, so that program references to A and B go where they were originally intended, just issue the ASSIGN command with no parameters, like this:

```
ASSIGN
```

Now, the reason—it's an important one—that you will want to un-assign drives is this: ASSIGN can be very dangerous, because it will redirect destructive operations as well as constructive ones. Commands like DEL *.* or FORMAT can be redirected by ASSIGN, so you could end up erasing data or reformatting a disk you didn't mean to.

To avoid this problem, I strongly recommend that you follow these rules when, and if, you use ASSIGN:

1) Use it only when you really need it; don't use it routinely.

2) Use ASSIGN only in batch files, and have those batch files automatically reset the assignments as soon as you're done with them.

Following these rules should avoid most problems with ASSIGN.

Pretending a Subdirectory Is a Disk Drive

We come next to a more sophisticated variation of the ASSIGN command. It's called SUBST (for Substitute), and it lets you make a subdirectory appear to be a separate drive. Why would you want to do this?

Well, first of all, some programs refuse to admit that subdirectories are the legitimate offspring of the root directory of a disk. They will not work with a subdirectory, and that can cause problems for you if you've got your hard disk neatly organized into a bunch of different subdirectories. The solution is the SUBST command.

Then, too, there's you. If you've divided and subdivided your directories to create a many-splendored tree, your pathnames can become long and somewhat unwieldy, and unless you're a good typist, they can become prone to typing errors. Again, the solution (other than pruning your tree) is the SUBST command.

In both cases, you can tell DOS to treat a subdirectory as if it were a disk drive. The basic form of this command is:

```
SUBST DRIVE: \PATHNAME
```

For example, if your word processor won't work with your subdirectory named LETTERS, you can type:

```
SUBST B: \LETTERS
```

and make it treat the subdirectory as if it were drive B.

Likewise, if you've created a directory system with a pathname like this:

```
\CLIENTS\LETTERS\A_M\DAVIES\MARCH
```

you can type:

```
SUBST B: \CLIENTS\LETTERS\A_M\DAVIES\MARCH
```

and make the drive letter B act as a shorthand substitute for this lengthy pathname.

When you're finished with the substitution, be sure to turn it off with the command:

```
SUBST DRIVE: /D
```

Don't forget, and don't take the SUBST command as a license to build a towering tree of directories. It isn't, and you shouldn't treat it that way. Like ASSIGN, it's best used sparingly, and only when necessary—meaning with programs that cannot work with subdirectories. There are the same types of pitfalls here as there are with ASSIGN, and you're really much better off using SUBST as a way of making a closed-minded program work for you. And, again, it's best to use SUBST as part of a batch file that turns the command on at the beginning and turns it off at the end. That way, you guard yourself and your valuable data against the forgetfulness that afflicts us all at times.

Pretending a Disk Is a Subdirectory

Finally, you can pretend that a disk in a disk drive is really a subdirectory of a directory you're working with. This is the opposite of the idea behind SUBST, and the command you use is called JOIN. There's no really compelling reason to use JOIN, although it can be convenient, especially if you want to gather several diskettes together and work with them and a subdirectory in a unified way.

To use the JOIN command, type it in the form:

```
JOIN DRIVE: DRIVE:\PATHNAME
```

If, for example, you have a data disk in drive A and you want access to that data while you're working with the files in a subdirectory called CLIENTS, you would type:

```
JOIN A: C:\CLIENTS
```

When you're finished, you undo the marriage with the command:

```
JOIN A: /D
```

Once again, my advice is not to use this command willy-nilly. It's a special-purpose command, best left to those situations when you really need it (for example, when you're using a disk that you cannot, or should not, copy to another drive). And, like ASSIGN and SUBST, use JOIN as part of a batch file that will automatically turn off the command when you're through.

Using ASSIGN, SUBST, and JOIN

I've emphasized several times the importance of not using AS-SIGN, SUBST, and JOIN as everyday commands that you think will be handy shortcuts to a little bit of disk-swapping or extra typing. These operations are all a little screwy and potentially confusing. (It's easy to forget what you've assigned, joined, or substituted—and where.) In fact, the only really strong reason to use them at all is when a program can't work with subdirectories in which case you use SUBST. But the fact is, programs that can't handle subdirectories are quite old-fashioned now and getting more and more obsolete, so there's less and less need to find your way around such problems.

Also, these operations are intended only for alternate ways of accessing data files. They are definitely not for hard-core disk operations such as formatting or deleting files. Such operations can have frustrating, if not disastrous, results when they're carried out with with these "masquerade" commands in effect. ASSIGN, SUBST, and JOIN are useful, but as I mentioned, they should be used sparingly and with a full understanding of what they do. It's also very important not to leave them active when you're finished with them. As a safeguard, you should only use them in batch files that do three things: activate them, use them, and end by deactivating them.

Special Kinds of Copying

We've learned how to copy files with the COPY command, and we've already learned about one special file-copying command, the SYS command that will transfer DOS's two special hidden files onto a system disk. Now it's time for us to learn about two more specialized file-copying commands, REPLACE and XCOPY.

The REPLACE Command

The REPLACE command is designed to help automate a problem that you'll encounter more and more as your use of the PC grows: updating copies of files. As a simple and important example of why you might need the REPLACE command, consider what happens when a new version of DOS comes out (as they do periodically). Once you've gotten really organized with your computer, you've probably spread around the various files that make up DOS. If you have a hard disk, you may have put the miscellaneous DOS programs (CHKDSK, FORMAT, etc) in a program directory (such as \PROGS\DOS), but the command interpreter COMMAND.COM and some other parts of DOS are likely to be in your root directory. You may have intentionally or accidentally made duplicate copies of some DOS files. Now you have a new version of DOS and you need to replace each old DOS program file, wherever it is lurking, with the new one. How do you do that easily and conveniently? With the REPLACE command.

REPLACE performs this task of tracking down files with matching names and copying new versions on top of them. It also performs some related tasks whose use will be obvious as we explain them.

The command form for REPLACE is like this:

```
REPLACE   source-files   target-path
```

The **source-files** is the specification for the *new* files that you want to put into place; it's a *file* specification, since it says what you want to install. Often enough that'll be just *.* or A:*.* to bring over all the files from a new diskette. The **target-path** says where you want the files to go; it's a **path** specification, since it says where (not what) to make the replacement. Here is an example:

```
REPLACE A:*.* C:\
```

A simple replace command will just replace the files in one directory (the target-path), but we probably want REPLACE to track down files in whatever directory they are. To do this we use the /S (or subdirectories) switch that tells REPLACE to hunt in all subdirectories of the path we specified. Our example probably should be like this, with the switch added:

```
REPLACE A:*.* C:\ /S
```

Sometimes we may not want to actually replace any files we have, we may just want to bring in new ones we don't already have copies of. For that REPLACE has a /A (for Add) switch. With /A, REPLACE will copy over only files that are completely new to the target directory. (If you're wondering about copying files that are not new but *newer*—meaning with a more recent date—we'll come to that with the next command, XCOPY). The /A switch, by the way, can't be used with the /S switch.

There are also some other handy switches for the REPLACE command. /P, the (Pause) switch, pauses for Yes–No confirmation before copying any file. There is also a /R switch to allow replacing read-only files. Finally, the /W (Wait) switch pauses (waits) before beginning to search for source files, so you can use REPLACE with a single diskette drive (and two diskettes) if you wish to.

That's the story on REPLACE. Now we're ready for another fancy variation on copying, one that is even more powerful.

XCOPY

XCOPY, like REPLACE, is another "power copier." But what distinguishes it? Before we plunge into the details of the command, we need to know the concept behind it—so we can easily understand it's features. While REPLACE is a power copier that's oriented toward *updating*, XCOPY is oriented toward the backup and transfer of files. If you keep that in mind, then the features of XCOPY will make sense to you.

(By the way, I guess we're supposed to pronounce XCOPY as "Cross Copy". At least, that helps us understand what it's about as a useful command.)

XCOPY will copy groups of files including (and here's the key part) a whole tree structure of files. Note that while REPLACE will track down multiple copies of the same filename in a *target* tree (and replace all the copies) the *source* of REPLACE's files is a single directory (typically a diskette that is being used to update a hard disk). But with XCOPY the *source* of copying can be all the files in a directory tree and XCOPY will duplicate that directory tree on the *target* disk.

The basic form for XCOPY is like this:

XCOPY *source   target*

where the "source" and "target" specifications can be either file specifications indicating which files we want to cross-copy or directory path specifications indicating all the files in the source directory and corresponding filenames in the target directory. All the various rules for the copy command (wildcard file names, target names different than source names, etc.) also apply here, as you might expect.

XCOPY gets interesting not its simplest basic form, but in what its option switches can do for us. Let's take a look at them.

Option Switches

The key option switch and the most important one is the /S (Subdirectory) switch that tells XCOPY to perform its copying magic on any subdirectories under the source directory. XCOPY will make sure that there are corresponding subdirectories on the target—using them if they exist, creating them if they don't.

Note that while XCOPY will duplicate a subdirectory structure for us, the tree structure above where we're cross copying doesn't have to be the same. For example, our source could be all the directories under a directory called \ACCOUNTS\CURRENT while our target might be something called \DATA\LASTMNTH. This example should suggest one of the most important reasons for using XCOPY: It can be easily used to do things like preserving a copy of data that will be changing.

There's a supplement to the /S switch that deals with the problem of empty directories. If we use XCOPY with just the /S switch, it will copy only where there are files, thus it won't create any empty directories on the target area. But if we need to have an *exact* duplicate of our source (including empty directories, which are ready to accept files) XCOPY can do that for us, too, if we give it the /E (Empty) switch. This feature—of creating copies of empty directories—can be an important one because we may be copying the data of programs that will create files in those directories and expect the directories to be here, empty or not.

Other switches for the XCOPY command echo things we've already seen with other commands. Like the BACKUP command, XCOPY can use an /M switch, which copies only files that have been modified (this is noted by the file's archive bit being set). As it is with the BACKUP command, if we use the /M switch, XCOPY will reset the archive bits that it acts on. On the other hand, if we use the /A (Archive) switch, XCOPY will copy the same, but won't reset any archive bits, so that the fact that these files have been changed is still recorded. Likewise, the /D (Date) switch will only copy files dated on or after a given date.

As with the REPLACE command, there are /P (Pause) and /W (Wait) switches to give you more control over the progress of the cross copying. And finally, as with the COPY command, there is a /V (Verify) switch, in which the copies are verify checked to see if they are recorded correctly.

It might appear to you that the XCOPY command is a lot like the BACKUP command, but there are several key differences. Both commands can be used to make archival backup copies of our files, but the BACKUP command is *entirely* oriented to archiving. The copy it makes can't be directly used because each copied file has reference information added to it, which changes its size and content (when these files are copied back with the RESTORE command, of course, the changes are undone). Further, BACKUP doesn't re-create the source's directory structure (that's done when the backed-up files are restored). But XCOPY does give us an exact copy of the files, unmodified, and it also duplicates the directory structure that the files reside in. We'd use BACKUP to make a purely archival copy—particularly one that has to fit onto smaller media, say from a big hard disk onto littler floppies. You'd use XCOPY to make a full working copy of files in the context of their directories.

Now that we've looked at these advanced disk commands, we're ready to move onto our next topic, something called **piping**.

PART IV

Special Items

13

PIPELINE TRICKS

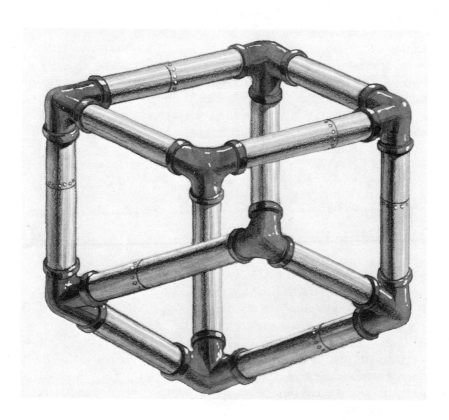

Introduction

In this chapter you're going to learn about a pair of interesting facilities in DOS known as **redirection** and **pipes**. These two features are interrelated and allow you to do some quite useful and fascinating stunts, as you'll see, besides; they're fun.

The idea of redirection is one of the most interesting parts of DOS, and basically what it does is enable you to act like a railroad engineer, switching trains from one track to another. Let's start at the beginning.

First, it's easy to see that DOS directs information to certain predictable places. Leaving disk commands and whatnot aside, think of what happens when you type a DOS command. Suppose you type the command DIR. DOS takes your keystrokes and mulls over them somewhere inside your computer. But, when it carries out your DIR command, it automatically directs the results of that command to the screen. It's like a train going from station A to station B, with no switches in between. In DOS's terminology, the information moves from one of its standard input devices (here, the keyboard) to one of its standard output devices (the screen).

Introducing Redirection

Suppose you didn't want to see the directory listing; what if you wanted to print it instead. Could you do it? Sure, by telling DOS to shunt that listing off to your printer, instead of the screen. In effect, you move your train to a different track, so that it goes somewhere else. That's the idea of redirection: Send my information someplace other than its usual destination. And, given DOS's usual linguistic economy, you redirect your information with either of two small symbols: >, meaning send data from here to there, and <, meaning send it from there to here.

The redirection symbols are used like this: If we want to change a program's routine output (which would normally appear on the screen) so that instead of going to the screen, it goes into a file (which we'll name OUTFILE), we'd do it like this:

```
PROG > OUTFILE
```

On the other hand, if we wanted to change a program's input, so that instead of coming from the keyboard it comes from a file (for example INFILE), we'd do that like this:

```
PROG < INFILE
```

And, as you might expect, we can do both at the same time:

```
PROG > OUTFILE < INFILE
```

Before you get too excited about the prospects of using a command like this, it's important for you to know that it only works for a limited variety of information. We can only redirect a program's output when it's very garden-variety line-by-line output that would normally appear on the screen. This means that we can't redirect file data (that's not screen output) and we can't redirect, say, the screen display for 1-2-3 (that's not garden-variety line-by-line output). Likewise, for input we can only redirect input that would be coming from the keyboard and used by the program in a standard way. In short, only certain kinds of very plain input and output can be redirected, and then only if the program that's working with them is designed to allow DOS to do this redirection. You can't necessarily tell in advance when redirection will work for you—when you want to do it, you have to experiment with the programs you want to use it on to see if it will or not.

Since DOS is an operating system—a program designed to support your work-oriented programs—redirection isn't some wonderful way to send data steaming off to every corner of your computer system. In fact, redirection works with only certain kinds of data, meaning the output of DOS commands. Thus, it's primary use is within DOS or with programs designed to take advantage of the situation. But where you can use it, redirection is handy and often fascinating to watch.

For example, I mentioned that you can send a directory listing to your printer instead of to the screen. The command is simple:

```
DIR > PRN
```

(PRN is DOS's name for your printer.) The result is that nothing appears on your screen, but your printer immediately begins spewing out the directory listing you requested. Likewise, you can send a directory to a disk file with the command:

```
DIR > FILENAME
```

A Redirection Example

For a nifty example of how redirection can be used to your advantage, let's consider something both handy and annoying about DOS's DATE and TIME commands. DATE and TIME were basically designed for us to interactively set the computer's record of today's date and the current time. These commands also do something useful in simply showing us the today's date and the current time. But if we want to use these commands only to show the current date and time, we have to respond to DOS's prompt for us to enter a new setting (which we do by just pressing the *Enter* key, which tells DOS to leave the old date or time setting unchanged). That makes it not a very convenient way to show the current settings.

Redirection to the rescue! We can use redirection of input to hand that *Enter* key to the TIME or DATE program, so it won't have to wait for our response. Here's how we do it. First, we create an "input" file that contains nothing but an empty line, the equivalent of the Enter key pressed by itself. (To do this, we use EDLIN, discussed in Chapter 18, or our word processing program, or an editor, or whatever other way we'd use to create, say, a batch processing file). Let's call that empty file EMPTY. Then we give DOS a command like this:

```
TIME < EMPTY
```

In this command, TIME gets the Enter-key response it wants from the EMPTY file and doesn't have to wait for us to give a live response on the keyboard.

Under the right circumstances—and you'll have to experiment thoughtfully to find them—you can use this technique to prepare "canned responses" to programs in advance. This can save you both time and mistakes (since the canned responses will be correct each time).

If you decide to make use of > and < for redirection, you're likely to find, as I did, that redirecting output is a fairly safe and routine operation, while redirecting input can be much trickier (consider what happens when program needs an input response that you didn't antic- ipate). Still, if you are both careful and adventuresome, you can both have fun with redirection and make quite productive use of it as well.

From Redirection to Pipelines

If you can use redirection to send information off to somewhere other than its usual destination, can you also send it on a longer trip? Perhaps even have that information processed along the way? Yes, you can.

Programs use data, so it is natural that the output of one program might be needed as the input to another program. DOS provides a handy way of making this automatic. Before you see how DOS does this for you, let's consider how you could accomplish this with what you already have.

If you have a program named ONE, which creates data that is needed by another program named TWO, you could use > and < and a working file name, to pass the data like this:

```
ONE >WORK
TWO <WORK
```

The first program would write its data into WORK and the second would read back from it.

This is the basic idea that DOS accomplishes with **pipelines**. A pipeline is just an automatic way of doing what we did with ONE, TWO, and the file WORK. In a pipeline, DOS takes care of creating the work-file to pass data through. To create a pipeline, you just write the program names on the same command line, separated by a verti- cal bar, (l), which is the signal for a pipeline. Here, then is how you would pipeline the programs ONE and TWO:

```
ONE  l  TWO
```

If you want to, you can informally think of the data as passing di- rectly between the two programs, but actually it is stored temporarily in a file that DOS creates especially for this purpose. The first pro- gram writes out all of its data and ends operation before the second program begins working and reads the first part of the data. When the whole operation is done, DOS removes the temporary files used to pass pipeline data so they do not clutter up our disks. The whole process goes on quietly, behind the scenes, without needing any attention from you.

A pipeline can have as many programs in it as you want it to, for example:

```
ONE | TWO | THREE | FOUR | FIVE
```

There is an obvious difference between the programs at the beginning, middle, and end of a pipeline. Unless there is something unusual going on, the first program in a pipeline would be generating data. The ones in the middle would do something with the data, but still pass it on; this kind of program is called a *filter*. The last program in a pipeline could be a consumer of data, to balance the generator on the other end. Usually though, the last program of a pipeline is a filter, just like any of the ones in the middle. If the last program is a filter, then it passes the finished result to DOS's standard output device, and it will appear on our display screens.

DOS's Filter Programs

This leaves the subject of filters still a little mysterious. To understand them better, lets take a look at the filters that DOS provides us with. There are three main ones, called SORT, FIND, and MORE.

SORT

Each of these three programs is a classic example of a filter—they read from standard input, do something with the data, then pass it on to standard output. SORT is quite obvious, it sorts the data that is passed to it. SORT treats each line of data as a separate entity, and so it is the order of the lines of data that SORT rearranges. Normally SORT arranges the lines in first to last order, but a switch, /R, will make the sort work in reverse order. Another switch, /+n (where n is a number), will make the sort start on the nth column of each line. A common example of the use of SORT, and of the use of the + switch, is with the DIR directory command.

Using SORT with DIR

DIR will list files in more or less arbitrary order. But if you combine it with SORT, you can get the directory listing in order by filename, or by the filename extension, or by the size of the file. This pipeline will sort the files into order by name:

```
DIR | SORT
```

By using the /+n switch to shift the sorting over to the column where the file size is displayed, you can get the list in order by size:

```
DIR | SORT /+14
```

MORE

When you have information displayed on the screen, there is often more than can fit onto the screen at one time, and some of it may roll off the top of the screen before you get a chance to study it. The MORE filter is designed to display only as many lines of information as will fit onto your computer's screen, and then wait for a keystroke to indicate that you are ready to see more. Naturally MORE is only used at the end of a pipeline—it wouldn't make much sense to use it anywhere else. So, for a long (30-line directory), you could type:

```
DIR | MORE
```

Or, you can combine SORT and MORE. For example:

```
DIR | SORT /+14 | MORE
```

FIND

The FIND filter is used to identify the lines of data that have, or don't have, some particular data on them. To use FIND, you must specify what you are looking for, enclosed in double-quotes. FIND filters out the lines that don't contain what you are looking for, and only passes on the lines that do. Here is an example, where you use FIND in combination with the MORE filter to look for error messages:

```
TEST | FIND "error" | MORE
```

As you might expect, FIND has some switches: the /V switch reverses the search so that lines with the specified information are filtered out and the others are passed through. The /N switch adds in the relative line numbers (which can help you know where the data was found). The /C switch gives a count of the lines found, without passing any other data on.

Using SORT, MORE, and FIND

While these three filter commands, SORT, MORE, and FIND are intended to be used inside pipelines, they each can be used by themselves. For example, we can use SORT together with ordinary > < redirection to sort the contents of one file and place it in another:

```
SORT <FILE.OLD >FILE.NEW
```

Similarly, MORE can be used like the TYPE command, but with automatic pauses when the screen fills.

While DOS provides us with three handy filters, SORT, MORE, and FIND, these aren't the only filters we can have. Remember, any reasonable program that reads from standard input and writes to standard output can be used as a filter. If you have any ideas for useful filters, you can write programs to carry out your ideas, and then make use of them in your pipelines.

14

SPECIAL COMMANDS

Introduction

So far, you've seen many of commands that let you use DOS to do work of one kind or another. There are also four special DOS commands that let you control the way your computer or your programs operate. Each of these commands has its own particular uses, and that's what we'll look at here. We'll begin with the MODE command.

Controlling Devices with MODE

MODE is a command with quite a few faces to it, but they all add up to variations on the same concept: controlling some of our hardware devices. In particular, MODE is used to control the printer (the **parallel port**), asynchronous communications (the **serial port** or the **RS232 port**), and the **display screen.**

Screen Modes

Let's begin with the display screen options. If you have a Color Graphics Adapter (CGA) for your display screen, MODE gives you a way of selecting which of four modes it works in. If you have *both* a CGA and a monochrome adapter, MODE gives you a way of switching back and forth between them. Let's start with the four CGA modes: A CGA display board can operate either in color or black and white; and it can operate with regular characters, 80 across the screen, or fat characters that fit 40 across the screen. Taken together those two choices give us the four different modes a CGA can work in. The MODE command lets us select from the four options like this:

```
MODE BW40  (for black and white, 40-column mode)
MODE BW80
MODE CO40
MODE CO80
```

There is also a variation that sets just the width, but not the black-and-white vs. color option:

```
MODE 40
MODE 80
```

But oddly enough there's no similar option just to select between BW and CO.

We should discuss why you might want to do any of this mode switching. First you can forget about the 40-column mode. It was designed in the early days of the PC in case anyone used a TV set as a display monitor for the computer. (Television, at least old-fashioned low-resolution ones can't show 80 columns of data legibly, but 40 columns works reasonably well on a set.) If you're doing that, you're not taking your PC very seriously. Second, as you may know, just because you have a *color* display adapter in your computer doesn't mean you have to hook it up to a color display screen; you might have a black/green/amber-and-white screen connected. In that case, it helps to let DOS and your programs know you really don't have colors on the screen—*that's* why the BW versions of the MODE exist.

If you do set your computer to the black-and-white mode, some programs will recognize this as a signal from you that they should create their screen information without relying on color, which can be very helpful. That, in fact, was one of the intended uses of the MODE command, for us to inform all our programs if we wanted color used or not. Unfortunately, many programs do not follow this convention and they ignore the MODE color setting.

As I mentioned before, if you have both a monochrome display screen and a CGA you can use the MODE command to switch DOS's primary operation from one to the other. To switch to the monochrome screen, use this command:

```
MODE MONO
```

To switch the other way, use any of the previous MODE commands, such as MODE CO80 or MODE BW80.

In addition, there are some variations on the MODE 40/80/BW40/BW80/CO40/CO80 commands that allow you to shift the display information either to the left or right. This feature is available because some display screens may not center the data correctly, but the MODE command is able to issue shifting commands that will move things around. To do this, we issue either of these commands (where the "x" stands for either nothing or one of the 40/80 . . . CO80 options):

```
MODE x,R
MODE x,L
```

The R and L options, of course, shift the screen left and right a couple of character positions each time. If you add a ",T" test option, like this,

```
MODE ,L,T
```

then the MODE command will also display a test pattern, and you can judge if you've shifted enough and go into an interactive mode that allows you to repeat the shifting until it has gone as far as you would like.

Those are the numerous variations on the screen-controlling MODE command. Next we'll see what it can do for the printer.

Printer MODEs

There are three different kinds of printer controls you can issue with the MODE command. First, if you have one of the very basic varieties of printers, such as the IBM PC Printer or the IBM Graphics Printer, or any of the Epson FX / MX series of printers, you can use this MODE command to set the print width selecting either 80 or 132 characters per line and set the print height selecting either 6 or 8 lines per inch. It can be done independent of any of the three possible printer interfaces, which are identified as LPT1, LPT2 and LPT3. The command is done like this:

```
MODE LPT1:80,6
MODE LPT3;132,8
```

or any of the obvious permutations and variations on the command. You don't have to specify both width and height, you can set only one, like this:

```
MODE LPT1:,6
MODE LPT2:80
```

There's an additional parameter we can add to the end of this command, adding a P to the end of the command like this:

```
MODE LPT1:,,P
```

This P option will keep the software control of the printer from "timing out" if the printer takes too long to respond to a command. DOS is smart enough to recognize when the printer is taking too long to do something, which might indicate that the printer is turned off or is otherwise not on the job. This is accomplished by setting a time limit for response to a command; going beyond that time limit is called a **timeout**. If you find, however, that DOS is reporting printer timeouts when the printer is working just fine (but perhaps a little slowly), then you may want to set this P option to prevent timeouts.

There's one more print MODE command you need to know about. As you may know, there are printers that connect to your computer's **serial ports** as well as those that connect to the more standard printer or **parallel port**. If you have such a printer, you'll need to make sure that the printer output is routed to the right port, a COM port instead of an LPT port. Some programs aren't prepared to do that—so DOS can perform the task of rerouting from LPT to COM for us. It's done like this:

```
MODE LPT1:=COM1
```

Or any variation on this, using any of the three LPT ports 1 2 and 3 and either of the two COM ports 1 or 2. After this command, any program that sends its output through DOS to the first printer, LPT1, will find the results pass out through the first communications port COM1. This will work as long as the printer data goes through DOS, but if the program bypasses DOS, then it won't work.

Finally, we need to examine the MODE commands that can be used to control the serial or communications ports this last printer MODE command uses.

Serial MODEs

The serial ports (also known as **communications** or **RS-232 ports**) on our computers were designed as a general-purpose channel for two machines to talk to each other. Although the most common use of a serial port is to connect our computers to a telephone line, these serial ports are also used for printers, to connect a mouse, to interface with scientific and lab equipment, and zillions of other uses. In fact, the RS-232 connection is widely used as a standard interface between many different kinds of machines that have nothing to do with our PCs.

As a consequence, the serial connection was designed to be as flexible as possible, which in turn means that it can be adjusted in quite a few ways to adopt to changing needs. These adjustments—the serial port parameters—can be made under software control and often the job of setting them is taken care of for us by the programs that work with the serial port. But we also need to be able to set these communications parameters ourselves, and that is what the final variation on the MODE command is able to do for us.

There are four communications parameters that can be set with MODE: the speed, the parity, the data bits, and the stop bits. The speed is measured in **baud** or bits per second; the possible choices are 110 baud, 150, 300, 600, 1,200, 2,400, or 9,600, but most of these speeds are never used on our PCs. The commonly used speeds are 300 or 1,200 for telephone communication (although 2,400 is gaining wider use) and 9,600 for dealing with devices like laser printers, which can take data as fast as we can dish it out. Incidentally, it typically takes 10 bits, overhead included, to transmit a byte or character of information, so if you divide the baud rate by 10, you get the approximate characters-per-second transmission rate.

For the other parameters, the **parity** (which is used for error checking) can be set to odd (O), even (E), or none (N). The **data bits** (the number of significant bits per character) can be either 7 or 8. As you know, PC computers use 8 bits for each character, but since the most commonly used characters (letters of the alphabet, etc.) all begin with a 0 bit, sometimes only seven bits are transmitted through the serial port. The final parameter, called the **stop bits**, can be set to 1 or 2. While the speed (the baud rate) has an obvious meaning and use to us, these three other parameters are more technical and less directly meaningful to us. For two pieces of computer equipment to talk to each other, they must agree on the setting of these parameters so that the "lingo" matches.

The MODE command is used to set these four parameters like this:

```
MODE   line, speed, parity, databits, stopbits
```

for example:

```
MODE COM1:,300,N,8,1
MODE COM2:,1200,E,7,1
```

In addition to these four standard communications parameters, there is an extra one that we can add to the end of this version of the MODE command, when it is used to connect with a printer. This is a P option, which works just like the P option for the MODE LPT command, to prevent the printer from "timing out."

MODE and Memory-Resident Programs

Some of the uses of the mode command require it to leave an active part of itself in your computer's memory. This is what's called a **memory-resident program**, which is the topic for the next chapter. After you read the next chapter, you'll have a better understanding of what that's all about. For now I want to note, so you have a record of it, that the versions of this command that leave a resident portion behind are the LPTx = COMx, LPTx, , P, and R and L options for the screen.

Controlling Interruptions with BREAK

There are times you may need to interrupt the operation of a program—because you don't need it anymore, because you told it to do something you'd now like to stop, or because it's just running wild.

Short of turning off your computer and turning it back on, there's no foolproof way to interrupt a program. There is one standard and accepted way you can often use to break into a program's operation, and that's the **Break key** (usually labeled Break on your keyboard) or its equivalent (the Control-C key combination).

There is no guarantee that pressing the break key will effectively work to interrupt your computer every time, but many programs co-operate in recognizing this shut-down signal. DOS does as well, and DOS goes even further by giving partial control over when and how the break key can take effect.

This is accomplished with a feature of DOS known as the **break switch**. If the break switch is not active, DOS will only recognize your pressing the break key if it is actively doing I/O work. For example, when it's writing information onto your display screen, which concerns only when DOS recognizes and acts on the break key. Many more sophisticated programs independently recognize the break key and either act on it or, for good safety reasons, ignore it.

On the other hand, if the break switch is active, DOS does its best to recognize the break key whenever you press it, and does its best to act on the key and force any program that's running to recognize it.

There are two ways you can set the break switch so you have fairly good control over how it works. One, which we'll get to in Chapter 19, allows you to tell DOS what the default setting of the switch should be: on or off. The other, our topic here, is the BREAK command, which explicitly turns the switch on or off.

You use the BREAK command in three ways. If you type:

```
BREAK
```

DOS tells you whether the break switch is currently on or off with a message like this:

```
BREAK is on
```

If you type the command like this:

```
BREAK ON
```

you set the switch on, telling DOS to use every opportunity to recognize when you've pressed the break key. Alternatively, if you type:

```
BREAK OFF
```

this does the opposite, setting the switch off so that DOS only recognizes a break action when it's doing standard I/O operations.

As I mentioned, setting this break switch with the BREAK command only gives you a limited degree of control over whether the computer can be interrupted. Whether it's on or off, other circumstances may override DOS's ability to respond to the switch. Still, at least this command gives you some control.

Remote Control with CTTY

As handy as it is to work with a personal computer in person, there are also times when it might be nice to operate a computer by remote control—say, by calling it up on the telephone, issuing commands, and getting responses back.

DOS actually makes this possible through a command called CTTY. When you're working with DOS, it is accepting input from you through the computer's keyboard and it's showing you the results on the display screen. DOS doesn't necessarily have to work with those two devices; instead, it is possible for DOS to redirect its attention to a telephone line, for example, that's hooked to another PC. When this is the case, DOS can get its keyboard-type input from the phone line, and can put its screen-type output into the phone line.

The CTTY command makes this work by letting you tell DOS what device to pay attention to. For example, with a command like:

```
CTTY COM1
```

you can tell DOS to look to the first serial port (COM1) for its operations. If that serial port is hooked to a modem that's dialed up to another PC computer—you can control your PC remotely.

Before you get too excited about the possibilities, here comes the "however." To make all this work takes more than just the CTTY command that comes with DOS. It also means that your computer has to be set up the right way, that you have the necessary remote connection (through a modem and a telephone line, or whatever), and that the program you're running is designed to take input and send output through a standard DOS means that can be redirected by this CTTY instruction. This last part can't be done with many of the most important programs, such as Lotus 1-2-3 or ordinary word processors. These programs (naturally enough) aren't designed to be used remotely. But, with the right kind of software, which might be something you've had specially prepared for your needs, you can operate your PC remotely, through the facilities of CTTY.

Passing Information with SET

Sometimes a program needs to be told how you want it to operate. For example, you might have a reference program that needs to be told where on disk, you've stored the data files it uses. It would be a nuisance to have to tell the program where to look for data files each time you use it. To solve this, and similar problems, DOS gives you the SET command.

For the most part you don't have to worry about using SET. It's only needed when you have some software that knows how to benefit from it. When you do need SET, the documentation for the program will explain what you have to do. For your own information, however, here's some background on the SET command and what it does.

The DOS Environment

To begin with, DOS creates a common information source for all your programs to use. This source is called the **environment**. Inside the environment, DOS records information in a series of equations, each beginning with a name, followed by an equal sign, followed by some value. For example, some of the information that's stored in my own computer's environment will show you what an **environment equation** looks like:

```
COMSPEC=C:\COMMAND.COM
FF=c:\data\common
PROMPT=$p$g
```

Given these equations, any program looking for information can scan through the environment, looking for a name that identifies the information intended for it. In my case, one of the IBM-written programs I use is called File-Facility (FF for short). It looks for the equation in the environment that begins FF=, which happens to be the second equation in my list. When File-Facility finds that equation, it can latch onto the information that's been left for it. Here, as is often the case, the information is a disk directory pathname, which tells File-Facility where to look for some data files.

The environment is intended to be a general-purpose way to leave information for the use of programs that you run. In order for it to work, though, you have to be able to place these equations into the DOS environment, and you ought to be able to see what they are. The SET command is designed for this purpose.

Using SET

If you use the SET command by itself with no parameters, like this:

```
SET
```

you can see the equations you currently have in your environment. Try it on your machine and see what you have. You may discover that, unbeknownst to you, DOS has created a COMSPEC= equation like the one in my example. Whatever equations you have in your environment, or if you have none at all, you can use the SET command to see what they are.

To create an equation, or change an existing one, just issue a command like one of these:

```
SET  NAME=VALUE
SET  FF=\THIS\DIRECT
SET  PROMPT=
```

Whatever equation you give in the command, SET will place it in the environment. If the equation is new, it'll appear for the first time. If it already exists, it'll be given the new value you've typed in. And if you set the value to nothing, as in the last line of the preceding example, the equation will disappear from the environment (that's how you get rid of equations you no longer need).

Special Versions of SET

As it turns out, DOS also gives us two commands that are really just special-purpose versions of SET. You already know about them; they're the PROMPT and PATH commands you encountered in Chapter 11. Although I didn't mention it at the time, both of these commands simply place information into the environment, for later use. Thus, any commands like these:

```
PATH     xxx
PROMPT   yyy
```

turn out to be the exact equivalent (and really just a disguised form) of these:

```
SET  PATH=xxx
SET  PROMPT=yyy
```

With that done, we're now ready to take a look at the subject of memory-resident programs and how they work with DOS.

15

DOS'S RESIDENT PROGRAMS

Introduction

Programs, like people, can be grouped in many different ways: by size, the work they do, the language they "speak," and so on. They can also be categorized according to how long and where they stick around in your computer's memory. Most programs do their work and then are replaced in memory by other programs. But some, which are called **resident programs**, remain in memory until you either turn off or reset the computer. These resident programs are one of the most mysterious elements in the world of DOS, and they are what we'll explore in this chapter.

Resident Programs and What They Do

When DOS runs a program, it finds space in the computer's memory for the program, copies it from disk to memory, and then, temporarily, turns control of the computer over to the program. Normally, when a program is finished working, it turns control of the computer back over to DOS, and DOS uses the memory where the program was loaded for the next program that you use. With resident programs things work slightly differently.

When a resident program finishes its initial operation, it hands control of the computer back to DOS, but it also instructs DOS to not reuse the memory area where it is loaded. The program asks DOS to leave it resident. DOS, in effect, puts a barrier in place where the resident program ends, and loads the next program that we use *above* the resident program.

What do I mean by "above" the resident program? Well, whenever we talk about memory, we refer to parts of it by number. These numbers start off low and get increasingly higher, much as house addresses on a street start low and get higher. DOS and resident programs settle in at the lower-numbered addresses, so when I say a program is loaded above another program, I mean it is placed in a portion of memory with higher-numbered addresses.

In effect then, a resident program incorporates itself into the small part of DOS that stays in the lower end of the computer's memory. All subsequent programs that you use operate at higher memory locations, leaving your resident program and DOS undisturbed in lower memory locations. Thus, the resident program stays, semi-permanently in the computer's memory, until you turn the computer off.

What is the point of having a program stay resident? Unlike most other programs, a resident program stays active after it seems to have finished. The program stays in memory and, through some technical tricks, manages to continue getting work done, even though you are running other programs after it.

There are many uses for resident programs, and you will get an idea of some of the things that they can do when we look at a few of them. DOS itself includes four different resident programs, which we'll discuss. There are other important resident programs, too, that are *not* an integral part of DOS, such as SideKick, SuperKey, and Lotus Metro. We won't be covering these programs in this book, but you should be aware of them.

Background Printing

The first of the DOS resident programs we'll consider is a command called PRINT, which acts as a variety of **print spooler**—a manager, so to speak, that handles information you want to send to your printer. The job of a print spooler is to print information without tying up the computer while the printing is going on.

If you've used your computer's printer, you've probably noticed that it's relatively slow compared to the computer's ability to get work done. While your printer is laboriously working away, almost all of your computer's working power is going to waste because printing really doesn't require all that much attention from your computer.

The resident program PRINT solves this problem by taking over the job of feeding data to the printer, while leaving the majority of the computer's power available for other programs to use. It's a bit like reading a book while you're stirring soup that's cooking. You don't have to give all your attention to stirring soup. Nor does your computer have to give its full power to printing information. What the PRINT resident program does is put just enough of the computer's power to work keeping a printer busy, while turning the rest of the computer's thinking power over to any other programs you want to run.

Because of the unobtrusive way it works, PRINT is what is known as a **background program**. Once you start up the PRINT command, it sits in the computer, and uses just enough of the computer's power to print out what you've asked it to do (just as you give a fraction of your attention to stirring soup while reading a book). If PRINT finishes its work, it remains in memory, ready for more work, but not taking up any computing power. When you ask PRINT to print something else, it occupies a fraction of the computing power to keep the printer busy, and leaves the rest of the computing power for our other programs; that's how a background program works.

Despite the intricacies of its work habits, PRINT itself is easy to use. The only thing you need to keep in mind is that PRINT is an **external program**—it is not automatically loaded when you start DOS, nor is it copied to a diskette you've formatted with the FORMAT /S command. Before you can use PRINT, DOS has to be able to find it on disk. If you use a system with floppy drives, that probably means you'll have to make the DOS disk available in one of your drives.

Using PRINT

The first time that you invoke the PRINT command, it loads itself into memory, and stays there until the computer is turned off or reset. From then on, any time you invoke the PRINT command, you just tell it what you want it to do. To get PRINT started, you type the command and tell it what printer to use, like this:

```
PRINT /D:PRINTER
```

For example, suppose you have parallel printers attached to the ports named LPT1 and LPT2, and you want PRINT to use LPT2. The command would be:

```
PRINT /D:LPT2
```

If you forget to tell PRINT about your printer, it will ask for the information like this:

```
Name of list device [PRN]:
```

and wait. Here, if you want, you can just press Enter and PRINT will use its default, LPT1.

Once you've got PRINT settled in, tell it to print information by giving it the name of a file that you want printed. PRINT only works with disk files, so if you want to use PRINT to print the output of one of your programs, you first have to get that program to store its print-style information into the disk file. Many programs, particularly word-processing programs, are prepared to do exactly that, for your convenience.

Assuming that your file is on disk, however, you tell PRINT to print a file like this:

```
PRINT MYFILE.DOC
```

If you've got your files organized by subdirectory, you can include a path name, like this:

```
PRINT \PATH\MYFILE.DOC
```

Print Queues

PRINT also has the ability to hold a list of work to be done in what is called a **print queue**. You can put up to 10 files in a print queue, and as long as there is work to be done in the print queue, PRINT will work away, passing information to your printer. When all work is done, PRINT goes to sleep, until you wake it up with a request to print some more information. If you've got some heavy-duty printing to do, you can increase the holding capacity of the print queue with PRINT's /Q switch:

```
PRINT /Q:SIZE
```

where SIZE can be any number up to 32 (that's probably many more files than you need).

To start a print queue, you use the PRINT \PATH\FILE.EXT form of the command. Once the queue exists, you can use:

```
PRINT \PATH\NEXTFILE.EXT
```

to add a file to the queue. (To add more than one at a time, you can also use the wildcards, * and ?).

If you change your mind about printing a file in the queue, you can type:

```
PRINT \PATH\THATFILE.EXT /C
```

to eliminate it from the queue.

If you change your mind about printing all the files in the queue, you can type:

```
PRINT /T
```

to cancel the job (and the queue).

Finally, if you only want to see what's in the queue, type:

```
PRINT
```

and PRINT will tell you.

Help with Screen Printing

The next memory-resident command we'll look at is GRAPHICS. When you learned about the things your computer will do, you no doubt learned about its built-in print-screen function, which lets you use the PrtSc (Print Screen) key to copy the contents of the display screen to your printer. The standard print screen operation, though, is only intended to print out normal character data, not any graphics pictures that might be on the screen. While most of us don't use graphics much, graphics screen displays can be quite important, and it's useful to be able to print out a full picture of a graphics display on the screen. If you have the right kind of printer, like the IBM Graphics Printer or a compatible model, then this GRAPHICS program can copy the screen image to the printer.

GRAPHICS

GRAPHICS is a slightly different kind of resident program from PRINT. While PRINT will work away simultaneously with your other programs (operating in the background), GRAPHICS is a program that replaces, and improves on, a standard operation you already have in the computer. IBM personal computers already have the ability to do the print-screen operation with text characters. The GRAPHICS program just augments that function by adding the ability to copy not just character text, but any graphics image as well.

When you invoke the GRAPHICS program by typing its name:

```
GRAPHICS
```

it loads itself into memory (and tells DOS to leave it resident), and then it does nothing. Nothing, that is, until you press the "print-screen" key, then the resident GRAPHICS program goes to work, working just like the regular print-screen program, but doing it for graphics images as well.

Using Special Characters with GRAPHTABL

The GRAPHTABL program is yet another variation on the idea of resident programs. GRAPHTABL leaves itself resident in memory, but what it leaves there isn't a working program, but some data. As it turns out, the IBM personal computers have a rich character set known as the **extended ASCII characters**. We can use all these characters when a program is working in text mode, but ordinarily we can't when we have the computer in graphics mode.

There's only one way to use this command:

```
GRAPHTABL
```

That's it.

Once it's resident, the GRAPHTABL program leaves in the computer's memory a definition of what the extended ASCII character set looks like. Without the GRAPHTABL program, you can't use the extended ASCII characters in graphics mode. With GRAPHTABL, you have those characters available, all through the magic of resident programs.

Controlling the Sharing of Data

The next of the resident programs that DOS provides for is the SHARE program. SHARE is used to control the use and sharing of data and disk files between programs. SHARE takes care of problems that arise when more than one program, or more than one computer, is making use of your disks. This is a special problem that can arise if you use a network to allow several computers to share a disk and pass data around. If one program, or one computer, is reading a data file, and another is changing it, things can get into quite a muddle. SHARE's job is to coordinate the sharing of data, so that nothing goes wrong.

SHARE is only used by advanced network applications of the PC, and there's really very little you need to know about it starting out. Mostly you need to be aware that it's there and that it concerns the use of networks. If the time comes for your PC to be connected to a network, then that's the time for you to learn the intricacies of network operations, including the SHARE program.

16

DOS AROUND THE WORLD

Introduction

Most of us write in one language on the familiar QWERTY keyboard, and generally don't need any currency symbol other than the dollar sign. If we need to use a word derived from another language, resume, for example, that really should have accent marks over each e—well, we do the best we can. It's the same for currency symbols: the pound symbol might end up as a capital L with a hand-drawn line through it.

But if we are usually not international, DOS is, or at least it can be. DOS has three commands, KEYBxx, COUNTRY, and SELECT, that can let us cross over the boundaries of language and custom. You may use these commands seldom or not at all, but they're interesting and best of all, they can be fun.

Keyboard Customization

There are two components to making DOS multinational: adjusting it to different keyboard layouts (which vary from one country to another), and adjusting it to different standards of displaying the date and time.

Adapting DOS to Different Keyboards

To adapt DOS to different national keyboards, use the KEYBxx command, replacing the xx with two letters that tell DOS which of five or more alternative keyboard layouts you want. The standard five are UK for the United Kingdom (Britain), FR for France, IT for Italy, SP for Spain, and GR for Germany. You may encounter another four for the Scandinavian countries of Denmark (DA), Norway (NO), Sweden (SV), and Finland (SU). It's a minor curiosity that the names used for the Scandinavian keyboards are taken from the names of the countries in their own languages, while the Spanish keyboard program uses the English abbreviation (SP) rather than the Spanish (ES); such is life. As the PC grows to widespread use in more and more of the world, we're likely to see more of these "native language" keyboard drivers.

Thus, for example, you tell DOS to switch to the British keyboard with the command:

```
KEYBUK
```

When you do this, DOS loads a resident program and "switches" its thinking from United States to United Kingdom. From then on, until you shut down your computer or press Control-Alt-F1 (which is the signal to deactivate any of these keyboard drivers), DOS reads and interprets your keystrokes as if they were typed on a British keyboard. That means, for example, that pressing Shift-3 produces the £ for British currency instead of the # symbol as it does on a United States keyboard.

Likewise, if you switch to the German keyboard layout with the command:

```
KEYBGR
```

DOS loads the resident program for the German keyboard. Now, if you try to type what would be a semicolon (;) on a United States keyboard, you see a lowercase o with an umlaut ö appear on screen.

It's important to remember here that what you're doing with the KEYBxx command is telling DOS to read your keyboard differently; as if it were a French, English, or Italian keyboard, which would have different characters printed on the keys. The command adjusts your PC's internals to match the layout. Unless you actually switch to an appropriate keyboard, the result could be a confusing muddle. If you want to see what I mean, type this:

```
KEYBFR
```

and then try to type the DOS command DATE. To get it right, you'll have to press the Q key to type A.

Adopting Other Conventions

Where the KEYBxx command lets you change the national layout of your keyboard, another command, called **COUNTRY**, lets you tell DOS to adopt other national standards for displaying date and time, numbers, and currency figures. This command, which we'll cover in more detail in Chapter 19, is used in a special file named

CONFIG.SYS that tells DOS about your computer system. Unlike
PRINT and KEYBxx, it is not a resident program you can load and
call into play during a session with DOS.

You've got more options with the COUNTRY command than you
do with KEYBxx, since it accepts the long-distance dialing code for
any of 15 or more countries, including Israel, Norway, and Australia.
The command itself is simple:

```
COUNTRY = code
```

where code is the three-digit international telephone dialing code for
the country. For example, the code for the United States is 001; for
France, it's 033.

What happens if you change the country code? Here's a directory
listing when country is set to the US:

```
KEYBFR      COM      8157      12-17-85      12:00p
KEYBGR      COM      8085      12-17-85      12:00p
KEYBIT      COM      7770      12-17-85      12:00p
KEYBSP      COM      8149      12-17-85      12:00p
KEYBUK      COM      7551      12-17-85      12:00p
```

Here's the same listing when you've set the country code to France:

```
KEYBFR      COM      8157      17-12-85      12:00
KEYBGR      COM      8085      17-12-85      12:00
KEYBIT      COM      7770      17-12-85      12:00
KEYBSP      COM      8149      17-12-85      12:00
KEYBUK      COM      7551      17-12-85      12:00
```

The only really obvious change is in the way DOS shows the date and
time, but other things change, too. For example, some countries use
commas in large number (like 1,000,000), others use periods. Some
countries place the currency symbol in front of a figure, others place
the symbol at the end. DOS and the COUNTRY command take care
of these details.

Automating the Country Set Up

Setting up DOS and your computer for a different country can, at times, be something of a chore. If you do this fairly frequently there's a way to automate the process: the SELECT command. Using this command, you can create a foreign-language start-up diskette for any country and keyboard DOS recognizes.

SELECT is basically FORMAT /S with a twist: At the same time it formats a system diskette it also does some special set up work to take care of turning DOS's attention to a particular keyboard and country. The command has two parameters—the keyboard code and the country code. This is how you use it:

```
SELECT COUNTRY KEYBxx
```

SELECT is designed to make the international customization of a boot system disk easier and more automated. That's simply all that it's about.

This command is only needed by people who are setting up DOS and PC computers for international use. For most folks, fortunately these complications don't apply.

With that look at DOS's internationalization commands, we're ready to move on to the special and useful subject of the DOS editing keys.

PART V

DOS EDITING

17

THE DOS EDITING KEYS

Introduction

In this chapter we're going to take a little side trip. Instead of concentrating on DOS commands, we're going to take a look at an interesting feature of DOS that can, maybe, make your use of the computer quicker and easier: the DOS editing keys.

I can't promise you anything in this chapter. Some people find this part of DOS exasperating, annoying, and useless; others find it very handy. (I find myself vacillating between the two.) You'll have to judge for yourself if this is something worth learning.

Setting the Stage for the Editing Keys

When you use your computer you're usually giving it instructions by typing at the keyboard. Sometimes, you're entering single keystrokes; for example, when you respond to a program's menu by typing the key that indicates your choice of commands. At other times, you're pounding away on the keyboard at length; for example, typing in a document to a word processor or an editor program.

But surprisingly often, what you key into the computer is something between those two extremes. Much of the time, what you do is key in a short line of information and press the enter key. A remarkably large proportion of your interaction with the computer involves typing single lines and then pressing enter. For example, whenever you give DOS a command, like COPY or FORMAT, you enter a single line of information—a line made up of the command name and whatever parameters it needs. Since you do this so often, there ought to be ways to make it easier, and that is what the DOS editing keys are about.

The DOS editing keys represent a set of operations and functions, all based on some special keys that help you enter or change a line of instructions. For example, one editing key lets you copy the last line you typed in, so that you can repeat an instruction without having to retype it, other keys help you change what you have already typed.

All this sounds rather handy—a fast and convenient way to speed your work and reduce the amount of key-pounding you have to do. But it isn't that simple, and before you decide they're your heart's desire, you ought to know about their drawbacks, so let's start with the down side.

Editing Key Problems

The first problem with the editing keys is that they don't always work, or at least, that's the way it sometimes seems. Of course, they do always work when they are available, but the problem is they aren't always available. Here's what I mean: DOS provides a line-editing service that any program, including all parts of DOS, can use to control what you key in. This line-editing service is where the DOS editing keys take effect. As you key in a line to DOS, you can use the editing keys to help enter and change the line. Only some programs take their input from this DOS service; many programs do not. Thus, you have to know which programs can, and which cannot, make use of the editing keys.

All the commands built into DOS naturally make use of the DOS editing keys, but you use plenty of other programs as well. And, as I mentioned, sometimes these other programs recognize the DOS editing keys, and sometimes they do not. Even worse, it isn't well advertised when you can and when you can't use them. The result is you have to set your working style to accommodate whether or not these DOS editing keys are available. If you can't count on being able to use them all the time, then they become tools you can't trust, friends you can't rely on.

The second problem with the editing keys is simply that you have to learn them. That's the biggest hurdle to overcome in working with a personal computer: There is much too much to learn. To master your computer, you have to learn how the machine works, how diskettes work, how DOS works, how each of your main programs—a word processor, a Lotus spreadsheet, or perhaps an accounting program—works. It's a lot to learn, and any added burden, especially one that applies to one situation but not to another, probably isn't something you need or want to tackle. Let's face it: No one can learn everything there is to know about a computer. So one of the major tasks that faces all of us in dealing with our computers is reducing the number of things that must be learned, and deciding what parts, out of all the thousands of things to learn, are the most important.

This brings us back to the DOS editing keys. They are something handy and productive, but mastering them is hardly essential to using your computer effectively. If you want to find out about them, fine. If you don't, that's fine, too. The DOS editing keys can be useful, particularly the simplest ones (only an enthusiast could benefit from some of the fancier ones). But if you decide that the DOS editing keys aren't important enough to be worth spending your time on, don't lose any sleep over it.

If you are going to learn about the DOS editing keys, you might as well learn the most basic ones right at the very beginning of your use of the computer, then they will become part of your general computer skills, and you'll use them all the time. Learning the editing keys later just means that you probably won't be able to integrate them into your comfortable style of computer use.

Now, make a quick decision: Press on in this chapter and read about the DOS editing keys, or skip over it. Either way, don't skip the entire chapter—the last section explains some special keys that you need to know about, even if you are not going to use the DOS editing keys.

How the Editing Keys Work

The DOS editing keys work on two simple concepts. The first is that you ought to be able to make simple revisions to what you have just typed before you press the Enter key to tell DOS to act on what you have keyed in. The second is that DOS should (and does) keep track of the last line you entered, so you can use all or part of that previous line to make it easier to enter a new line.

In this section I'll explain how each of the different editing key functions works, but remember that the DOS editing keys apply only in some circumstances. They work whenever you are entering DOS commands, when you are entering information into DOS command programs, and they work with some, but by no means all, other programs. In fact, they usually will not work with many of the major programs you use, such as a word processing program; where they do work, they can be quite handy.

Correcting Typing Errors

Let's start by assuming you've typed a line, but haven't yet pressed the Enter key. Let's say your left hand unwittingly moved one key to the right on the keyboard, and instead of typing FORMAT A:, you typed this at the C: prompt:

```
GOTMSY S:
```

It's obvious you made a mistake. How can you correct it? There are two ways.

The first way to make a correction is to cancel, or throw away, the entire line you typed. There is a DOS editing key specially devoted to this: The **Escape key** (marked **Esc** on your keyboard) is used for the cancel operation. When you press Esc, DOS displays a backslash at the end of the line you typed and moves the blinking cursor to a new line, like this:

```
C:>GOTMSY S:\
```

and waits for you to retype the line.

There is also another, completely separate key combination that sometimes has the same effect as the cancel editing key—the **break operation** (which is also sometimes called **Control-C**). You type this by holding down the key marked Ctrl and pressing the key marked Break. If you were to do this in our example, this is what you'd see:

```
C:>GOTMSY S:^C
C:>
```

Here, as you can see from the return of the C:> prompt, DOS just scraps whatever you typed and starts all over again.

The point to remember here is that sometimes break works just like the Esc key. The net effect in both of our examples is to start over. But there's a difference: Break can also terminate, or cancel, any program that you are running. Don't make a habit of using the break key to simply cancel or discard a line that you have typed in. If you make a habit of this, at some time you will make one of your programs come to an abrupt end when you didn't mean to. We'll take a closer look at Break at the end of this chapter.

Basically, then, to cancel, or throw away, a line of information that you have typed, use Esc, the escape key—the DOS editing key that's used for a cancel operation.

If you've typed in something really garbled, like our example, you probably want to use cancel to get rid of it all. More often though, all we want to do is correct some simple typing mistake. Suppose you had typed one letter wrong—say your finger slipped and you typed "FORMA5" instead of "FORMAT"—or you left a letter out—"FO-MAT" instead of "FORMAT"—and you want to correct that without retyping the entire line. The way you do this is using the DOS editing keys to back up to where you need to make the correction.

Backspacing

When you back up, you move one space at a time, back in the line you've typed in. As you back up, the character back over is erased, just as if you had never typed it. By backing up, you can erase what you have typed in, character by character, until you've erased the character you need to correct.

You have a choice of two keys to perform this back-up-one-space operation. You can use either the standard **Backspace key**, or you can use the **Cursor-left key**. Both of these keys will perform the same operation. The Backspace key is at the top right corner of the main part of your keyboard. On some keyboards it's marked with the letters BS (for backspace); on the IBM PC keyboards, it's marked with a bold, left-pointing arrow. The cursor-left key, on the other hand, is with the other cursor-control keys, on the right-hand side of the keyboard: It's the number four key on the numeric keypad, or the left-hand key on the special cursor section of some keyboards.

Recycling Your Keystrokes

Backspace or cursor-left key, after you have gotten rid of what you typed wrong, you can type in the right information, press enter, and your computer will act on your corrected command. In essence, both the cancel and backup keys let you correct something you typed. The rest of the DOS editing keys help you reduce the amount of actual typing you have to do, by letting you reuse what you've already entered.

This reuse only does you any good when you are doing some repetitive typing—when you are entering the same information again and again, with minor changes. Unless you are doing that, these other DOS editing key operations don't do a thing for you. So that you have an idea of when these keys might be useful, let's consider an everyday example.

Suppose you need to copy a number of files from one diskette to another. this is a common operation. You might have a working disk that has two kinds of files on it: ones that you're changing, and ones that stay the same. For the files that change, you ought to make backup copies onto another diskette, so you don't lose your latest data.

Here, you have a situation where you want to copy some of the files from a disk, but not all of them. It would be nice to be able to type the COPY command once, and thereafter just change the file name to copy the other files without having to retype COPY. This is the sort of thing the other DOS editing keys let you do.

As I mentioned, DOS keeps track of the last line you entered, so you can use it as a template to copy from. The reason you can do this is DOS not only keeps track of the last command you keyed in, it also lets you make all kinds of changes to this last command. This is the **template** idea.

The first editing key that works with this template is the **Copy-all** or **F3 key**, on the PC keyboard. This Copy-all key takes the last command you typed and copies it onto the screen, just as if you had retyped the entire line. If you want to duplicate exactly what you typed before, copy-all does the job. If you need to make minor changes, particularly at the end of the line, use the backup key to erase the part you want to change. For instance, in our copy example, you could type:

```
COPY THISFILE
```

and carry out the operation, then press the copy-all F3 key to duplicate the command and use one of the backup keys to change the file name like this:

```
COPY THISFILE
COPY TH
COPY THATFILE
```

What if it isn't convenient to copy all of the template? There are several ways you can copy only part of it. One is the copy-one-character operation. Every time you press a copy-one-character key, one character is copied from the template onto the display screen. In our example, pressing copy-one-character five times would duplicate "COPY " (including the space), and you could then type in the name of the file to be copied.

There are two keys you can use for the copy-one-character operation. One is the key marked F1; the other is the cursor-right key which, on most PC keyboards is marked with both a right-pointing arrow pointing and the number 6.

Another way—a quicker one—to do the same thing is to use the copy-up-to editing key. For this, you press the copy-up-to key, which is F2 , and follow it with one of the characters in your template. The copy-up-to, or F2, operation duplicates the template up to, but not including, the key you pressed. For the preceding example, you could get "COPY TH" all in two keystrokes by pressing F2 and A, which is the first character that you don't want to copy. Here's the sequence:

```
(F2)A
```

and here's what you get:

```
COPY TH
```

So far the DOS editing keys may seem somewhat handy, but perhaps trickier and more elaborate than they are worth. From here, though, it gets even more elaborate—which reinforces my argument that learning the DOS editing keys may be more trouble than you want to bother with.

If you want to skip over part of the template, and then pick up copying it from some point, you can use the skip-one-character and skip-up-to keys. They work just like the copy-one-character and copy-up-to keys, but they skip over the template rather than duplicating it. The skip-one-character operation is performed by the Del (delete) key, and the skip-up-to operation is performed by the F4 key. From the above example, if you wanted to drop "COPY" but use "THISFILE", you would press F4 (skip-up-to), then press "T", then press copy-all to duplicate the remainder of the template. If you are good at this, it's a quick, efficient operation; otherwise it's confusing.

Imagine you want to add something to the middle of a template. The Ins (insert) key lets you type in new information without typing over and replacing existing characters. Using insert thus holds your place in the template, while you type in new information. The way it works is very simple: Suppose you have copied part of a command from the template, and then you stop and press insert. At this point, the template is put on hold, and anything that you type is added to your new command line, without passing over any of the template. After you have finished inserting new material, you can then copy from the remainder of the old template. If all this sounds confusing, here's an example that may help.

Suppose you typed the COPY THISFILE command we've been using. You have a subdirectory named OLD_DOCS that contains an earlier version of the file, also called THISFILE. You decide to copy the earlier version for safekeeping. With the editing keys, you could use the DOS template and type:

    (F2)T

to produce this:

    COPY

press the Insert key and type the subdirectory name:

    COPY (INS)OLD_DOCS

and then press F3:

    COPY (INS)OLD_DOCS(F4)

to get this:

    COPY OLD_DOCS THISFILE

Naturally, there is an insert-exit editing key to reverse the insert operation. If your computer has an **Insert key**, as most do, this key will be used as a toggle, so you press it both to insert and to stop inserting characters.

The final DOS editing key lets you set up a new template to work with without actually entering a line for DOS to act on. If you are using the copy-from-a-template idea, you ought to be able to set up a template from scratch and not just use the last line that you entered into DOS. This is what the new-template command is for. F5 is the key used for this new-template operation. When you press F5, whatever shows on the screen as the line you've typed in so far becomes the new template that you can work with.

As you can see, these DOS editing keys are rather elaborate, so they are only good when two circumstances are combined:

- The DOS editing keys are active.
- You want to repeat the same or similar lines, several times.

If you don't have both these conditions, then the DOS editing keys do nothing for you.

The reason I suggest that you don't bother learning these editing keys is simple: Why learn the tricky rules for an operation you can only use sometimes? And when you can use the editing keys, they only save you a little work. But if they appeal to you, use them for all they are worth.

Here is a quick summary of the editing keys:

Table 17.1 DOS Editing Keys

Name	Operation	Keys Used
cancel	throw the line away	Escape
backup	erase the last character	Back space, left arrow
copy-all	copy the template, in full	F3
copy-one	copy the next template character	F1, right arrow
copy-up-to	copy up to the typed character	F2
skip-one	skip over one template character	Del
skip-up-to	skip up to the typed character	F4
insert	enter new stuff, keep place	Insert key
new-template	replace template with this line	F5

Other Special Keys

There are some other special keys DOS uses that can be very handy for you, and we'll go over them in this section. They are only loosely related to the DOS editing keys, and you can get good use from them even if you never try the editing keys. There's even one here that some computer makers don't tell their customers they can use.

There are five of these special codes, each of them entered as a combination of the control key and one of the letters of the alphabet. Like all of the control key combinations, they work by holding down the Control shift key and pressing the other key. When you're doing a control-letter combination, you don't have to worry about whether you type an upper- or lowercase letter; either works just as well.

Control-C

The most important of these five special control keys is break, which is also called Control-C. Break is a special instruction that tells DOS to stop, or break out of what it is doing. This break operation is very important, because it is your best way of stopping the computer, short of turning the power off. If your computer is going wild, or if you just want to interrupt what it's doing (a long directory listing you've seen enough of, for example), break is the best way to do it.

The break operation is so important that your IBM PC has a special key just for this operation. You can use this break key, but the Control-C combination will work just the same. In fact, Control-C is a universal code that means stop to all small computers. To make it easier to remember this code, you can think of the "C" as standing for Cancel.

When you're working on your computer, the record of what you're doing—what you type in and what the computer replies—rolls by on the display screen, and soon disappears. Sometimes, though, you might like a permanent written record of what's happening—a directory listing, for example, or a list of the mismatches DOS finds in a file-compare operation. DOS provides a way of doing this, with the echo feature. When echo is turned on, everything that is written on the display screen is also sent, or echoed, to the computer's printer. This works in a very straightforward way, so you can automatically get a printed copy of what has been appearing on the display screen.

Usually you don't want a printed copy of everything that's happening, so echo is normally off. To turn it on, press Control and the PrtSc keys. To turn it back off, press the same keys again. Each time you press this key combination, you turn the echo function on or off by "toggling"—using the same keystrokes to switch a function back and forth between on and off.

Like the break operation, there are also key codes that are used by all personal computers for this echo operation. If you want, you can also use Control-P to turn echo on, and Control-N to turn it off.

You should know, however, that echoing doesn't work with every program. Programs can produce display output many different ways. Only if the output goes through official DOS channels can it be echoed. Usually it is easy to tell if the output of a program can be echoed, even without experimenting to try it. If a program writes its information to the display screen just as if the screen were a typewriter, which means writing everything in consecutive lines that appear at the bottom of the screen, rather than jumping around to display some information here, and some there, then you should be able to echo the information. But if a program works in full-screen mode, displaying information in controlled locations rather than using the screen like a printer, then the output probably can't be echoed.

You probably won't be able to use echo with your word-processing programs, or with most accounting programs, or spreadsheet programs. On the other hand, it will work, and can be useful, with the commands that are a part of DOS. For example, if you are copying many programs, echoing your commands to the printer provides a quick and painless record of what you copied. Then too, unless you are really good at creating batch files, you might find it handy to echo everything you type, including mistakes, to the printer for later reference.

The next interesting and useful special key is the **suspend key combination**. It's not marked on most PC keyboards, but it's performed by holding down the Ctrl shift key, and pressing the NumLock key. When you suspend the computer, it just sits idling, not doing any useful work. This gives you an opportunity to read what's on the screen, or do anything else, without the computer running away. Pressing any ordinary key will end the suspension, and your computer will continue with its work.

Related to the suspend, or pause, function is another universal key code known as Control-S. While the suspend operation stops everything in the computer, Control-S just holds up the display. If the computer is computing or doing anything else, that work will continue. But once the computer tries to write to the display screen (through a regular screen-write operation), then it is suspended. The Control-S operation isn't advertised by IBM, but it's there, as a feature of DOS.

Remember the distinction: suspend/pause (done with Control-NumLock) stops the whole computer; Control-S stops only the display screen.

The last of the special control codes is Control-Z. Disk files with written text material include special codes to indicate such things as where one line of text ends and another begins, among these special formatting codes is a code that marks the end of the file. This end-file marker is quite important, and all programs that work with files of written text pay close attention to it. Normally, you never have to deliberately enter this Control-Z code at the end of a file—your text-processing program takes care of that for you. There are some special circumstances where it must be keyed in, and the Control-Z key combination is used to enter it from the keyboard.

I doubt that you will ever need to use the Control-Z code. It is more likely, though, that you will see it mentioned in a book or article on personal computers, and so you should know what Control-Z is used for. Table 17.2 is a summary of the control-key conbinations

Table 17.2 DOS Control Keys

Control Key	Function
Control-C	Cancel operation, or end program
Control-S	Suspend screen output
Control-P	Start echoing screen output to the printer
Control-N	Stop echoing
Control-Z	Enter an "end file" marker

This ends our discussion of the special key codes used with DOS. Next we'll move on to some DOS topics that are more advanced, complicated, and fascinating.

18

THE EDLIN EDITOR

Introduction

In this chapter you'll find out about a text-editing program that comes with DOS: the **EDLIN program**. To begin, let's see what an editor is for and how EDLIN fits into the world of editing.

Ordinary written material, such as a letter or report, is dealt with in a special way by computers: It's stored in the format known as an ASCII text file, which you encountered briefly in Chapter 9. Here, in more detail, are a few key things you need to know about ASCII text files.

ASCII Text Files

The data that is stored in an ASCII text file is the ordinary stuff of written material—alphabet letters, numbers, and punctuation symbols like the comma and the period. The words you are reading here are ASCII text, stored in my computer in as an ASCII text file.

One very important thing to remember about ASCII text files is that they are organized as distinct lines of text. The punctuation you put into a text file—the commas or the periods—don't mean much to the computer, but there are two kinds of punctuation added by the computer to an ASCII file that are quite important. These special "punctuation marks" indicate the end of each line and the end of the entire ASCII text in a file. Both the end-of-line and end-of-file punctuation is invisible to you. The computer will show you your commas and periods and other punctuation, but it keeps its own special punctuation hidden. The result is that, within any ASCII file, you don't see any end-of-line markers themselves, but you do see the results of this punctuation: the separation of your text into distinct lines.

ASCII text files are widely used in computers, and three of those uses are particularly interesting: word-processing data, source code of programs (**source code** is what computer programs look like when you write them), and batch-processing files. Since most computer users do word processing, many write programs, and all should know how to create and change DOS batch-processing files, everyone who uses a personal computer needs to know how to work with ASCII text files.

Editor Programs

Whenever you want to enter and change ASCII text, there is a special kind of program, known as an **editor**, to help you. A word-processing program is basically an editor, but one with many fancy frills, such as the ability to justify text, produce boldfacing or italics or even check spelling. The frills are important in a word processor, but the heart of word processing is still just the entering and revising of written text: editing.

It is hard to use a computer well without an editor program on tap. Not only will much of your computer work call for an editor, you'll need one to create batch-processing files. The key to effective use of a computer lies in using good batch commands, and you need an editor to create the files that define what a batch command is to do.

Editor programs are so important that most computer users buy them specially, often getting a complete word-processing program that includes an editor. But having an editor is so important that DOS doesn't rely on you to buy one, it includes a simple editing program called **EDLIN**. If you don't have another editor, you will need to use EDLIN. Even if you do have a word-processing program, you may find that you still need to use EDLIN, simply because your word processor may be too powerful to be handy for simple editing tasks. You don't hunt mice with an elephant gun, and you may find that you don't want to use your word processor to create simple batch files.

There is another very practical reason why you should learn how to use EDLIN. For quick work with batch files, you ought to have a copy of an editor program on each of your program disks, but your main editor, or word processor, may be too large to fit on each disk. It is good to have a small, compact editing program available, and EDLIN fills that bill.

EDLIN and How It Works

To use EDLIN effectively, you have to understand how it works, and that calls for a little discussion of different ways of doing editing. EDLIN is a type of editor known as a **command editor**, or **line editor** (the latter is where the name EDLIN comes from). Most good editors, including word processors, are **full-screen editors**, which means they show as much as possible of the material being edited on the display screen, and new material is entered right in its proper place on the screen.

While a full-screen editor shows as much of the file as possible, a line editor like EDLIN works in smaller units. It thinks of a file as a collection of lines. This makes working with it more cumbersome, because you must enter commands in order to display any part of a file, or to do anything else for that matter. If you want to see or change something in the fifth line of your file, you must first tell EDLIN to show you the line, then you must tell it what change to make. Whatever you do, when you're working with a line editor like EDLIN, you do it all in terms of commands that operate on the lines of a file.

EDLIN always refers to a file in terms of the numeric order of the lines in the file. If you had a file with three lines in it like this:

```
This is the first line
This is the second line
This is the third line
```

EDLIN would refer to these as line numbers 1, 2, and 3. To help you keep track of the line numbers, EDLIN always gives the line number when it displays lines from the file. If EDLIN were to display the above lines, they would appear like this:

```
1: This is the first line
2: This is the second line
3: This is the third line
```

The line numbers EDLIN shows are not part of the data in your ASCII text file—they are only shown for reference.

Another thing that you need to know about EDLIN and line numbers is that the lines are renumbered after any change. In our three-line example, let's say you delete line 2. The old line 3 immediately becomes the new line 2, so the file now would look like this:

```
1: This is the first line
2: This is the third line
```

Likewise, if you insert a new line below line 1, line 2 becomes line 3 again:

```
1: This is the first line
2. This is the new second line
3: This is the third line
```

To make work easier, EDLIN keeps track of its current place in a file and indicates the current line by marking it with an asterisk (*). For example, if the current location in our original three-line file were the second line, then it would be displayed like this:

```
1: This is the first line
2:*This is the second line
3: This is the third line
```

When you tell EDLIN to do something, you can either tell it to work with a particular line number or to work relative to the current line. For anything you are typing into EDLIN, whether it is a command to EDLIN or data you are entering, you can use the DOS editing keys you learned about in Chapter 17, to help you.

File Protection

Before we move on in the actual use of EDLIN, you ought to know that, for your protection, a safety feature is built into EDLIN (and many other editors). When you use EDLIN to change a file, it does not destroy the old file. Instead, it saves the old file data under a slightly different name—the file keeps the original filename, but EDLIN adds a filename extension of BAK, short for backup copy.

If you happen to make some disastrous error in editing a file, the BAK copy will help you recover from the mistake. Because of this backup convention, you can't edit a file while it has an extension of BAK, but you can rename the file to something else with the DOS RENAME command. Now let's move on to see EDLIN in action.

Starting EDLIN

EDLIN is an external DOS command, whenever you want to use it DOS must be able to find the EDLIN program file on disk. Other than making the program file available, you begin using EDLIN by typing the EDLIN command name, followed by the name of the file you want to edit. For example:

```
EDLIN B:FILENAME.EXT
```

Although many editors don't have to be given the name of a file when they're started up, EDLIN does. The file name can either belong to an existing file that you want to look at or change, or it can be the name of a new file you want to create.

When it starts up EDLIN looks for the file you've named. If the file already exists, EDLIN reads it into memory. After EDLIN begins, it will give you one of three messages. If EDLIN hasn't found the file you named, it reports:

```
New File
```

If you're creating a new file, this message is fine. But if you want to work with an existing file, this message means EDLIN wasn't able to find the file you named. Perhaps you misspelled the filename, or maybe the file does exist, but it's not in the current directory. If that's the case, you need to quit EDLIN by typing:

```
Q
```

and (as you'll soon find out in more detail) press:

```
Y
```

to confirm your intentions. You can then either change directories to the one that contains your file (with the CD, or CHDIR, command) or restart EDLIN, giving it the full pathname that will lead it to the file.

That's the first message you might see. Now, what if you requested an existing file, and EDLIN finds it?

If EDLIN finds the file, and there is room enough, it reads the complete file into memory. It's unlikely you'll use EDLIN with a file too large to fit into memory, but it could happen. However, if EDLIN has enough memory space for the file, it reports:

```
End of input file
```

This message tells you that EDLIN did find the file, and had enough room for all of it.

If there isn't room for the entire file, then EDLIN gives a "message" of a different kind: no message at all. This is a little cryptic (and the sort of thing that makes EDLIN a weak editor), but if you know how to read EDLIN's signs, no message means "the file was found, and it's too big to fit into memory." When a file is too big to fit into memory, EDLIN reads part of it into memory, leaving a cushion of about 25% of available memory to give you some working room.

Once EDLIN is up and running and has given one of its three messages, it tells you it is ready for a command by giving its command prompt. EDLIN's prompt is a simple, but distinctive asterisk (*) that helps distinguish it from DOS or any other program.

Ending an EDLIN Session

At this point, since you've learned how to start using EDLIN, your next order of business might as well be knowing how to end it. There are two different commands used to end EDLIN's operation. One, E (for end), writes the file you're working on from memory to disk, replacing the old file with a new version, and saving the old version as a BAK file. E both writes the file and ends operation. To have EDLIN carry out the E command, you type in the single letter at EDLIN's asterisk prompt:

```
*E
```

and press the enter key.

The other way to end EDLIN's operation is Q (for quit), which you saw briefly already. The **Q command** is used when you want to stop using EDLIN, but don't want to write a file back to disk: perhaps because you haven't made any changes and don't need to save anything new, or because you've made some mistakes and want to discard them. Whatever the reason, if you want to throw away whatever record of the file that EDLIN has in memory, you use the Q command. As a protection against accidentally losing some work you have done, EDLIN will ask:

```
Abort edit (Y/N)?
```

and unless you answer "Y" for yes, EDLIN will continue operation.

Be careful to keep these two commands straight, otherwise you may write a bad file to disk when you don't want to, or throw away changes you wanted to keep. E is end, including writing the changes; Q is quit, without writing any changes to the disk copy of the file. If you've been tinkering with a file and have made a mess of it (deleting lines you need to keep, or whatever), then be sure to use Q, not E, so that you discard the changes you don't want to make a permanent part of the file.

Both of the commands you have seen so far are given as single letters—E and Q. In fact, all of the EDLIN commands are single letters. This makes them very quick and easy to type, as long as you can remember the right letter to use. You always press the enter key to tell EDLIN to carry out our commands, just as you do in entering DOS commands.

Using EDLIN Commands

While the two commands you've seen so far are used by themselves, the other EDLIN commands take some parameters that tell them where to act and what to act upon. For example, the **D** (Delete-lines) **command** needs to know which lines to delete. Before you get into the details of each command, let's see how you specify which lines you want the command to act on.

When an EDLIN command needs us to tell it what line to act on, you have five different ways to indicate the line you're interested in:

1) Type the specific line number, such as 27 or 32500. If you type in a line number that is too big (a higher number than the last line in memory), EDLIN acts just as if you had put in the number immediately after the last line number.

2) You can explicitly refer to the line after the last line in memory by typing in a pound sign (#). This has the same effect as entering a line number that is too big.

3) Indicate you want to work on whichever line is the current line by putting in a period (.). A period means, "use the current line number." You'll recall that EDLIN indicates the current line by marking it with an asterisk. Although keeping mental track of the current line may be a little confusing at first, it will become easy after some experience with EDLIN.

4) Leave the line number blank, and EDLIN will use some default line number. This number will vary with what makes most sense for each command.

5) With all but the earliest versions of DOS, you can indicate a line above or below the current line by entering a plus or minus sign and a number, such as +25 or −200. This will refer to the line which is that number of lines before (−), or after (+) the current line.

With that background, let's look at some more commands.

Adding Lines

To add some lines to a file, you use the **I** (Insert) **command**. The command is given like this:

line-number I

This command sets you up to begin inserting lines into the file. The insertion begins before the specified line number. If you leave the line number off, the insertion goes before the current line. Here, for example, is how a new line is inserted above line 3 in an existing file:

```
 *3i
 3:*this is going above old line 3
```

and here's what the result looks like:

```
 1: this is the first line
 2: this is the second line
 3: this is going above old line 3
 4:*this is the third line
```

If you are creating a new file, there is nothing in the file, and you would expect you could just start typing lines into it. EDLIN doesn't work that way. Even with a brand-new file, you have to use the I command to start entering lines. With a new file, the first command you give EDLIN is the I command. Here, however, you don't have to specify a line number, just type I all by itself:

```
 *I
```

When you give EDLIN the Insert command, it lets you enter not only one line, but line after line—very convenient. Along the way, press the Enter key to signal the end of one line, and EDLIN lets you begin the next and the next and the next. How do you stop entering new lines? You give EDLIN the Break or Control-C command to tell it that's all. One special warning about breaking out of insert mode, though: Press Break only after you have pressed Enter for the last line you inserted. If you press Break with a line partly entered, the line will be thrown away. Keep that in mind—losing the last line you've entered is very easy to do until you're familiar with EDLIN's rules.

Once you press Break, EDLIN switches back into command mode, where it waits for your next command. To signal this, EDLIN shows its command prompt, the asterisk.

Removing Lines

The opposite of the I command is the **D** (Delete) **command**. D removes one or more lines from the file you are editing.

To delete one line, you enter the command like this, with one line number:

line-number D

For example, you would delete line 3 of our earlier example like this:

```
*3D
```

When you press Enter, that one line will be deleted; naturally, all the following lines will be renumbered.

```
1: this is the first line
2: this is the second line
3: this is going above old line 3
4:*this is the third line
```

with this result:

```
1: this is the first line
2: this is the second line
3:*this is the third line
4:
```

If you want to delete a group of lines, you give two line numbers, separated by a comma, like this:

starting-line-number, ending-line-number D

Both of the lines specified, and any lines in between, will be deleted.

You'll recall that we can always leave a line-number specification blank, and a default will be used. If you enter just a D, without a line-number, like this: D then the current line is deleted. With the range form, if you leave out the first number, like this:

,ending-line-number D

then lines are deleted from the current line through the line specified. The reverse doesn't work. If you specify

starting-line-number, D

it will only delete one line, and not (as you might think) a range of lines from the starting point to the current line.

Listing a File

Naturally you can't edit a file blind, you need to be able to see what you are doing. The **L** (List) **command** lets you list (display on the screen) lines from the file. Remember that EDLIN doesn't voluntarily reveal anything about the file you're editing. It will only show you exactly what you ask to see, and nothing more. (Full-screen editors show much more information.)

The L command has a format similar to the D command. You can enter it with no line number, or one line number, or a range of lines:

L
line-number L
starting-line-number, ending-line-number L

As I mentioned, each command has its own defaults, which are tailored to what makes the most sense for it. The defaults are quite different for L than they are for D. If you give no numbers, then EDLIN lists 23 lines, centered around the current line—it will show 11 lines before and 11 lines after the current line. This is an easy and convenient way to get a quick snapshot of the lines you're currently working on in the file.

If you enter only the first line number, with or without a comma, EDLIN also shows 23 lines, but starting with the specified line, no matter where the current line is. If you put in just the second line number (with a comma before it, to indicate that it is the second number), then lines are displayed from 11 lines before the current line, up to the specified line.

Do you find this a little confusing? One of the problems with EDLIN is that its rules are too complicated (even a little more so than what you've seen). This is unfortunate, but with a little practice you'll find that the commands like L are reasonably easy to use.

Changing Lines

The next thing you need to learn about EDLIN is how to make changes to a line that is already in the file. Say you've used the L command to find the part of the file you're interested in, and now you are ready to make changes. You've seen how to delete and insert whole lines, but how do you change part of an existing line?

You make such changes with the **Edit-line command**. For this command, you don't use a letter of the alphabet; instead, you just enter the number of the line you want to edit. In response, EDLIN displays a copy of the line, as it exists, and then gives you a (seemingly) blank line with the same line number. You can then use the DOS editing keys to make changes to the line, including copying any part of it that you don't need to change. When you have the line the way you want it, press Enter and the line is changed. If we decide we don't want to make any changes to the line, we can just press Enter, without typing in any changes and the line will be left as it is.

So you can see what this process looks like, let's assume you want to change the word "second" in line 2 of our earlier example from lowercase to capital letters. First, let's list the file:

```
*L
    1:*this is the first line
    2: this is the second line
    3: this is the third line
    4:
```

Now, tell EDLIN you want to change line 2:

```
*2
```

This is what you see:

```
2:*this is the second line
2:*
```

To make the change, let's just copy the whole line (with the F3, Copy-all key), then backspace to erase characters and retype the end of the line. First, press F3 to copy all:

```
2:*this is the second line
2:*this is the second line
```

Then, backspace to get this:

```
2:*this is the second line
2:*this is the
```

Finally, correct the line:

```
2:*this is the second line
2:*this is the SECOND line
```

and list the result:

```
1: this is the first line
2:*this is the SECOND line
3: this is the third line
4:
```

The edit-line command has a default line number, just like any other command. So, when the asterisk prompt is displayed, if you just press Enter without typing a line number, EDLIN will assume that you want to edit the current line. It will display the current line and you can then change it, as we just did, using the DOS editing keys if you want.

Also, if you repeatedly press Enter, EDLIN will switch back and forth between command mode (with the asterisk prompt) and editing the current line. Each time it switches, the current line location is moved down one. This makes it possible to move through the file, line by line, by repeatedly pressing Enter. As each line is set up to be edited, you can either change it or move on to the next line. This is a convenient and quick way to go through a small file, making changes as you need to.

Finding Text

One of the things an editor needs to be able to do is search through a file to find the location of some text you are interested in. EDLIN has two commands to do this: the **S** (Search) **command** and the **R** (Replace) **command** (which is really a search-and-replace command). We'll start with the S command. There are several variations on the S command. The simplest one is like this:

starting-line-number, ending-line-number S *what-to-search-for*

The search command searches through the range of lines, looking for the "what to search for." If it is found, then the line with the infor- mation is displayed (and made the current line). For instance, you could search for the word "third" in our example like this:

```
*1,4Sthird
```

and EDLIN would display this:

```
3: this is the third line
```

If EDLIN doesn't find what it is searching for, then it will report the a message: "Not found." Each of the three parameters is optional. If the starting line is left off, the search begins with the line following the current line; if the ending line is left off, the search goes on to the end of the file in memory. If the "what to search for" is left off, then EDLIN uses whatever you last told it to search for.

These three default values make it very easy to continue a search after one instance has been found. After you have had the Search command search once, just entering the command S with no more parameters, will continue the search from where EDLIN left off.

EDLIN will only report exact matches of the information that you ask it to search for. If you had typed the Search command like this:

```
*1,4STHIRD
```

EDLIN wouldn't have found it. It can find a word in the middle of a sentence, but it can't make the connection between "THIRD" and "third". Thus, for example, EDLIN can find a match if the word you're looking for is capitalized at the beginning of a sentence. Some editors can make matches in either upper- or lowercase, but EDLIN does not—it requires exact matches.

There is another variation on the S command, when we put a question mark just before the S; for example

```
1,35?Swhere
```

S is prepared to repeat the search over and over when the question mark is used, until it finds the instance that you are looking for. Each time EDLIN finds an occurrence of the search text, it displays what it found, and asks:

```
O.K.?
```

If you answer N for no, then EDLIN will go on looking. If you answer Y for yes, then EDLIN will stop looking, so you can work with the line it found. Here's another opportunity for confusion. To me anyway, this yes/no convention seems backward. Whether you find it logical or not, remember the rule: Y-yes means stop and work here; N-no means no go searching.

Related to the S command is the R (Search-and-Replace) command. This command is entered like the S command, including the optional question mark. But Replace is designed to replace what it finds with something else, thus you have to enter two sets of characters after the R command. The two items are separated by a special character, Control-Z. This separator is the same Control-Z character you encountered as the end-of-file marker in Chapter 17. You can enter it either by holding down the Ctrl key and pressing Z, or by pressing the F6 DOS editing key. In either case, Control-Z will appear in your command like this: ^Z. (Even though it's represented as two characters, ^ and Z, DOS considers the two together as one Control-Z character.)

To see what the R command looks like, let's go back to our example and tell EDLIN to replace third with THIRD. Here's the command:

```
*1,4Rthird^ZTHIRD
```

and here is the result:

```
Ⅎ:*this is the THIRD line
```

Now, here's something to remember. The S command stops at the first instance that it finds, so that you can do whatever you want with what it found. But the R command has something active to do, so it will automatically repeat its search-and-replace operation all through the range of lines that you give it. For example, if you had a 300-line file, and you used the command:

```
*1,ЗООRjellybeans^Zlicorice
```

Every time EDLIN finds "jellybeans" anywhere in lines 1 through 300, it will replace it with "licorice". Each replacement will also be displayed, so you can see what is going on.

While the ordinary form of the R command will replace each instance that it finds, the question mark version will stop each time and ask you, okay? If you answer Y, the replacement is made; if you answer N, the line is left as it was, unchanged. But the search-and-replace continues, even if you answer N to any particular query.

You will notice that this is an important difference between the S and R commands. With S, answering yes stops the search, while no continues it. With R, answering yes lets the replacement take place, while no prevents that one replacement, but the search still continues, whether the answer is yes or no. So while these two commands are very similar, they respond very differently to the yes-or-no answer.

As you might imagine, it is very easy to make an accidental mess out of using the S and R commands. Proceed cautiously until you are comfortable with them.

Working with Large Files

There are two commands that are used in that special case I mentioned at the beginning of this chapter: When a file is too large to fit into memory. One command is used to write some of the file back to disk, to make more room in memory, and the other is used to read in more of the file.

The **W** (Write) **command** is used to write some lines out of memory. The command is given like this:

number-of-lines W

As many lines as were specified are written from the beginning of the lines in memory. If you don't specify a number of lines, then EDLIN will write just enough lines to get the 25% working cushion that it likes to have. After the lines are written, the part of the file that remains in memory is still numbered from line one, so your line numbers don't tell you where the lines are relative to the beginning of the entire file—only relative to the beginning of the part that is in memory.

When some space has been made free by writing out part of a file (or by deleting some lines), you can then read in more of the file into memory. This is done with the **A** (Append) **command**. The A command is given just like the W command:

number-of-lines A

If there is enough room, EDLIN reads in as many lines as you asked it to. If you don't specify the number of lines, then EDLIN will automatically read until memory is 75% full, leaving its 25% cushion of working space.

If EDLIN finds the end of a file while reading it with the A command, it will report it with the message End of input file, just as it does when it first begins editing a file.

When to Use EDLIN

As you can probably tell from the discussion of the ordinary EDLIN commands, EDLIN is not really a convenient and easy editor to use. In practice EDLIN is very clumsy and inconvenient to use, except when you are using it with very tiny files. That, though, is the one thing I recommend using it for: creating and changing batch files. Little work, like a batch file, is just EDLIN's speed. For anything larger, you should use a more capable editor.

Advanced EDLIN Commands

From the commands that you've seen so far, it would appear that EDLIN doesn't give you any way to move data around or to duplicate it. If you need to rearrange your file data, it looks like you would be stuck. Not so, unless you are using the earliest versions of DOS. Beginning with DOS 2.00, you have three special commands, **C** (Copy),

M (Move), and **T** (Transfer), that let you move lines of a file from one place to another.

The C command lets you duplicate lines, copying them to another part of the file. There are four parameters in this command:

starting-line, ending-line, where-to, how-many-times C

Each of the four parameters is optional, expect for the "where to" specification, which must be given. If either the starting or ending lines are left off, then the current line is assumed. If the number of times is left off, then only one copy is made. The copied material is placed before the specified "where to" line, just as it is with the I command.

You would usually use the copy command only to duplicate material once, but there are times when you might want to use the "how many times" parameter to make several copies. As an example, if you were creating a table or list in a file, you might create a skeleton line (with all the repeated information), copy it as many times as needed, and then fill in the details in each line. Every table and list that you see in this book was created using this technique.

To show how you would use this command, here's a rather silly example using the lines you've been seeing throughout this chapter. Let's say you wanted to make three copies of lines 2 and 3 at the end of your short file. Here's the command:

```
*2,3,4,3C
```

which, translated, means "take lines 2 and 3 (2,3,), go to line 4 (4,), and make three copies (3C)." This is what you'd get:

```
 1: this is the first line
 2: this is the SECOND line
 3: this is the THIRD line
 4: this is the SECOND line
 5: this is the THIRD line
 6: this is the SECOND line
 7: this is the THIRD line
 8: this is the SECOND line
 9: this is the THIRD line
10:
```

Obviously, you'll have better uses for the command.

The **M** (Move) **command** performs a similar function to the C command, but takes lines out of their current place, and puts them somewhere else. With a C, the original copy stays in place; with M, it is gone. Duplication makes sense for a C command, but not for M, so M doesn't make multiple copies. There are three parameters for the M command:

starting-line, ending-line, where-to M

As with C, the third parameter, "where to," is required and not optional. The starting and ending line numbers will default to the current line if they are not specified.

Here's our three-line example once again, this time with lines 2 and 3 moved above line 1. First, the Move command:

```
*2,3,1M
```

meaning, "take lines 2 and 3 (2,3) and move them before line 1 (1M)." This is the result:

```
1:*this is the SECOND line
2: this is the THIRD line
3: this is the first line
```

The third special command that can be used to rearrange data is the **T** (Transfer) **command**. T is used to read the contents of another file, and to place it into the file being edited. The command is given like this:

line-number T *file-name*

The contents of the file are placed in memory, ahead of the specified line number, just as it is with I, C, and M. The file must be specified, naturally enough, but the line-number is optional. If it is not specified, then the current line indicates where the new data is to go. For example, if you had a two-line file named NEWDATA that looked like this:

```
1:*this is the name line
2: this is the address line
```

and you wanted to place it at the top of our much-edited three-line sample file, the command would be:

```
*1TNEWDATA
```

and the result would be:

```
1:*this is the name line
2: this is the address line
3: this is the SECOND line
4: this is the THIRD line
5: this is the first line
6:
```

There is one further advanced command which EDLIN provides, the **P** (Page) **command**. The P command is intended for browsing (paging) through a file, and it works just like the L command, with one handy exception. The L command leaves the current line unchanged, which might be far from what is being displayed on the screen. The P command makes the last line displayed the current line, so that the working location in the file follows what is displayed.

PART VI

Customizing DOS

19

THE CONFIGURATION FILE

Introduction

In this chapter you're going to be digging into one of the most complex and intriguing aspects of DOS. What you'll be seeing here are some ideas and some software parts that are not completely related to each other. They *do* have one thing in common: In one way or another, they modify, revise, or customize the way DOS operates.

The Configuration File

When DOS first begins operation, when it **boots up**, it does some start up work, or **initialization**, that sets the stage for how it will work and what things it can work with. You can participate in this initialization, through something called the **configuration file**.

In the last stages of its initialization, DOS looks on the disk it is booting up from for a special text file named CONFIG.SYS. This file tells DOS about your computer system, and you can use this file to specify some of the ways that the system will be configured.

The CONFIG.SYS file itself is a plain ASCII text file containing a series of commands to DOS that tell it how we want it to be customized. These commands fall into two groups, those that perform particular functions, and one, named **DEVICE**, that allows you to load external software (device drivers) into DOS. In the next section we'll look at the various distinct commands, and then we'll finish up this chapter with a discussion of the device drivers.

Configuration Commands

There are eight separate, special-purpose commands you can put into your CONFIG.SYS file. Let's begin with the BREAK command.

BREAK

The **BREAK command**, which you can set as either BREAK = ON or BREAK = OFF, controls the default setting of the Control-Break switch, which you learned to use in Chapter 14. As you know, BREAK regulates, to some degree, whether or not you can interrupt a program by using the Control-Break key combination.

During normal DOS operations, you use the BREAK command to change the setting of the break switch. When you include a BREAK command in CONFIG.SYS, you are using the command to control the default setting that's in effect whenever you start DOS. If the state of the break switch matters to you, this CONFIG.SYS command will help you have control over it.

BUFFERS

To improve the performance of your programs—especially its own performance—DOS sets aside some memory space for disk buffers, which can, under the right circumstances, reduce the amount of reading and writing of disk information that has to be done. To conserve memory, DOS by default doesn't set aside many disk buffers, usually just two or three. But for many PC users, particularly those with hard disks, DOS's default buffers are far from enough for efficient operation. Fortunately, you can control the number of disk buffers that DOS uses, by including the **BUFFERS command** in CONFIG.SYS.

This command lets you set the number of buffers you want, from a minimum of 1 to a maximum of 99. In my experience, a PC with a hard disk needs at least 16, maybe even 20, 30, 40, or more. (I happen to use 64 in my computer and don't regret having that many at all.) There is a price to be paid in setting aside buffers, though: Each buffer takes about one-half K of memory away from your main programs. Still, if you have enough memory and the right number of buffers, they can greatly speed up much of your computer's disk work.

You can easily test to see if you need more or fewer buffers in your machine. Set up a CONFIG.SYS file with this BUFFERS command in it like this:

```
BUFFERS=8
```

Then, reboot your machine and try some of the program you use the most. If you don't know what program to try, use the DOS program CHKDSK as a test. Observe how much time DOS takes to start up, how long it takes to load programs, and how long it takes the programs to do their disk-intensive work. Next, try using the values:

```
BUFFERS=16
BUFFERS=32
BUFFERS=64
```

and see what happens with each. Don't worry about minute differences, but if you see a dramatic change, you know you've hit paydirt.

COUNTRY

The next CONFIG.SYS command to consider is the **COUNTRY command**, which we looked at in Chapter 16. As the use of personal computers and DOS has spread from America to the rest of the world, there's been a growing need to have DOS (and the programs that run under it) adapt to different customs and conventions used in each country. Originally DOS did everything in the way that was most congenial for Americans, but now DOS can adapt to the country it is working in. This is done with the COUNTRY command, like this:

```
COUNTRY=061
```

which happens to set up DOS for Australia. The default code for the United States is 001 and there are numerous codes for all the countries that DOS has been developed for.

Setting the country code allows DOS to adjust its own operations. For example, the way it shows the date and time on the screen when you use a command, such as DIR, that displays date and time information. In America, dates are shown in the form month, day of the month, and the year, as in 8-14-87. But some other countries use the convention of the year first; others put the day of the month first.

The COUNTRY command not only adjusts some of the way DOS works, it allows other programs to adjust the way they work, too. To do this, a program (behind the scenes and invisible to us) asks DOS for a table of country-specific information, which DOS passes along to the program. This table of information includes not only things like the preferred format for date and time, but also the currency symbol that's used (such as the dollar sign, $, or the pound sign, £) and many other things as well. Few programs make use of this feature of DOS, but it's there, available to any program that wishes to adjust to local national conventions.

The Other CONFIG.SYS Commands

There are also CONFIG.SYS commands that allow you to expand or contract some of DOS's internal limits. The **FILES command** lets you control how many disk files DOS will allow a program to use at one time. DOS's default is eight files; a higher number (it can go as high as 255) lets a program use more files, while a smaller number saves a little bit on memory use.

Another similar command, **FCBS**, controls a more old-fashioned limit on how many files a program can be using at once. Unless you get error messages indicating trouble in this area (which is possible, but unlikely), you can ignore this facility.

A similar command, called **LASTDRIVE**, lets you tell DOS how many logical disk drives to allow for. DOS will always accommodate as many disk drives as your machine has, and will also always accommodate as many apparent drives as the device drivers need. (We'll get to them in the next section.)

Beyond that fixed requirement, you can make disk drives seemingly come and go by using the **SUBST** command. DOS, though, can't accommodate new drives indefinitely. It needs to know in advance how many drives will be called for, and that's what the LASTDRIVE command is for. It's used like this:

```
LASTDRIVE=LETTER
```

where you make LASTDRIVE equal to a letter between A and K, which would allow for a total of eleven drives. You'll only need this command if you're making use of the SUBST command or any other software tools that makes disk drives (seemingly) come and go.

SHELL

The last of the CONFIG.SYS commands is an interesting one. It allows you to control some of the workings of DOS's **command interpreter**, COMMAND.COM which, if anything is, can be called the heart of DOS. The **SHELL command** is used like this:

```
SHELL=COMMAND.COM  /P  /E:256
```

There is actually a variety of things that the SHELL command allows you to do. First, if you want to activate a command interpreter other than DOS's standard COMMAND.COM, you can use the SHELL command to give the name and disk location of that program. Even if you are using COMMAND.COM, in the SHELL program you can specify a special disk path or drive where you want DOS to find the command interpreter.

The two parameters in the example, /P and /E:256, allow you to control two features of COMMAND.COM. The first one, /P, tells the program to do what it normally would if you didn't include a SHELL command—to perform the start up commands that are located in the AUTOEXEC batch-processing file (more about this in the next chapter). The other parameter, /E:256, allows you to tell DOS how much memory to set aside for the environment space. DOS's **environment** is the location where it stores the information from the PATH, SET, and PROMPT commands. If, as may happen, the standard amount of space allowed for this information isn't enough for the use your programs make of it, you can make the environment larger with this option of the SHELL command.

Device Drivers

DOS automatically knows certain things about your computer and the devices (such as printers, and disk drives) that are attached to it. These are the default devices, and DOS knows about them because IBM designed them into DOS. But, of course, you can attach all sorts of other devices to your computer. How does DOS learn about them and any special commands that they might require? The answer is the **DEVICE command**, which you can put in the CONFIG.SYS file.

Unusual devices call for special support programs that are called **device drivers**. DOS is able to incorporate device drivers into itself, through the use of this DEVICE command. For any device driver that you might want to incorporate into DOS, you have to have the program code of the driver stored in a file on your DOS disk. Thus, for example, if the file that holds a device driver is named X, then your CONFIG.SYS file would contain a command like this:

```
DEVICE=X
```

Then, when DOS encounters that command in the CONFIG.SYS file, it will read the device driver, X, into memory, and attach drive to the rest of itself—in effect, absorbing the device driver as a native part of DOS.

As you might imagine, writing a device driver is a highly technical subject, for expert programmers only. Any device driver has to follow strict DOS rules, so that it cooperates with the rest of DOS. Normally, people like you and me don't write device drivers; instead, we get them as part and parcel of any exotic equipment we want to attach to our computers that happens to require a special device driver.

This equipment might be an unusual type of disk drive, a mouse, or whatever. For example, if you equip your PC with a Microsoft Mouse, you'll find that the mouse hardware comes with a software disk that includes the device driver support the mouse needs. Similarly, some other exotic hardware add-ons for your PC may come with their own custom device drivers.

Device Drivers as Software

The concept and use of device drivers is even more broad than what I've suggested. Device drivers can be used strictly for hardware, such as the mouse driver mentioned, but they can also be used to perform services that are more closely related to software. I'll describe several of them, including three that come with the latest versions of DOS and one that comes with some Compaq PCs.

VDISK.SYS

The first that comes with the latest versions of DOS is named **VDISK.SYS**. (SYS is the common filename extension for device drivers, so you'll find that many, if not most device drivers have that extension.)

You use VDISK to create a **memory disk**. A memory disk uses part of your computer's memory to simulate an ultra-high-speed disk drive, and VDISK allows you to set aside part of your computer's memory to act as such a simulated, or **virtual disk** (which is what the name VDISK stands for). Memory disks allow you the fastest possible access to your data—roughly ten times faster than a real disk could, but at a price. Memory disks get their storage space by dedicating part of your computer's memory to the task, thus removing that part of memory from any other use.

Unlike regular disks, memory disks are ephemeral. They exist only as long as your computer is turned on and working. You must copy the files to which you want high-speed access to the memory disk before they can be used, and any new information created on the memory disk needs to be copied to a regular disk before your computer is turned off. So, there can be a real nuisance factor in setting up and using a memory disk, but the pay-off is extra-fast access to frequently used data.

VDISK is not the only program that can create a virtual disk, but it is the standard one that comes with DOS. The VDISK program allows you to control how much memory will be set aside for the virtual disk, and whether the memory will be taken from the PC's regular main memory or from the extended memory that the AT-class of PCs can have installed. VDISK also allows you to control some of the internal characteristics of the virtual disk, such as the number of directory entries that it will accommodate. Here's the form in which you use this command, including the parameters you can set:

```
VDISK DISK-SIZE SECTOR-SIZE DIRECTORY-SIZE /E
```

and here's what those parameters mean.

Disk size is how many kilobytes you want to dedicate to your virtual disk. This value can be anywhere from 1K (small) on up to all the memory in your computer (large and not very useful). Sector size tells DOS how large each sector on your virtual disk should be. Here, you're limited to one of three choices: 128, 256, or 512 bytes (512 is typical on a PC diskette or hard disk). Directory size is how many file entries you want your virtual disk's root directory to be able to hold; for this, pick a number from 2 to 512. (Normally, a disk directory holds something in the range of 64 to 512, depending on the disk you use, but for your virtual disk you're likely to want a low number, assuming you won't load a lot of files in at once.) Finally, the /E switch is what you use to take advantage of AT-type extended memory for your virtual disk.

ANSI.SYS

Our next device driver is called **ANSI.SYS**. It's a very special kind of device driver, and can do wonders for you. What ANSI does is provide two special facilities to modify the routine keyboard input and screen output that goes on in your computer. The full details are complicated and surprisingly hard to explain, but the essence of it is this: If you have ANSI.SYS installed as a device inside your DOS, you can give it commands that make it perform two special kinds of magic.

One kind of magic is **keyboard translation**, which can turn one keystroke into something quite different, including a long series of keystrokes generated by ANSI.SYS. For example, you could tell ANSI.SYS that every time you press the ! key, that single keystroke should be changed into this entire phrase: "Now isn't that magic!"

The other magic ANSI.SYS can do is accept **special commands** that fully control the information that appears on the display screen—including such things as where the cursor is located, or what color is being written on the screen. Some programming languages, such as BASIC, include features like this, but ANSI.SYS can give this kind of screen-control to any program that wishes to use it.

The ability of ANSI.SYS to perform screen-control magic was created to provide a standard way for programs to gain full control over the capabilities of the computer's display screen, without having to know just how the screen works. This could assist people in writing programs to be used on a wider variety of computers. In fact, though, very few programs make active use of the facilities of ANSI.SYS, and it's unlikely that you'll have any use for it. But since it's a facility in your DOS, you ought to know about it. Besides, ANSI.SYS can be a lot of fun to play with.

DRIVER.SYS

Another device driver that comes with DOS is called **DRIVER.SYS**. DRIVER.SYS allows you to create another disk drive letter (for example, drive F) and make it refer to one of the disk drives you already have. This may sound silly, but it has its uses.

You already know that for PCs with only a single diskette drive, DOS makes the one diskette drive act as both drive A and drive B. This makes it easier for you use the same diskette drive to copy files from one diskette to another. Now suppose—as more and more people are doing—that you add one of the new 3½-inch diskette drives to your computer. The DRIVER.SYS device driver would allow you to tell DOS to treat that drive as two drive letters (say, drives E and F), so you can use it to copy files on its particular kind of diskette. That's a handy facility!

ENHDISK.SYS

Finally, to give you another example of what a device driver can do, consider this one, which comes with many Compaq models of PC. This device driver is called **ENHDISK.SYS**. It allows you to take a hard disk that is larger than DOS's ordinary working limit of 32 million bytes and access additional partitions on the same disk. That means you can use all of the space in a disk that is larger than 32 megabytes, although you do have to use the space in separate partition-chunks no larger than DOS's 32-megabyte limit. The concept behind this program is not unique to Compaq; any hard disk that's larger than 32 megabytes should come with a similar program to perform the same function.

20

STARTING UP WITH AUTOEXEC

Introduction

As you saw in Chapters 7 and 8, batch files are one of the most useful and powerful tools DOS puts into your hands. In this chapter you're going to see how batch files can be put to further use through DOS's own automatic start-up batch file, AUTOEXEC.BAT.

The Where and How of AUTOEXEC.BAT

Whenever DOS starts up its operation, the command interpreter, COMMAND.COM, checks to see if you have any initial instructions for it. It does this checking by looking for a special batch file with the name of AUTOEXEC.BAT. If DOS doesn't find a file with this name, it performs its two automatic start-up commands, DATE and TIME. If DOS *does* find an AUTOEXEC.BAT file, it carries out the commands in that batch file as part of its start-up routine. (In this case, DOS doesn't automatically perform the DATE and TIME part of its start-up, so if you want to set the date and time, you have to make sure these commands are part of your AUTOEXEC.BAT file.)

To make AUTOEXEC.BAT work, follow two simple rules. First, like any other batch file, AUTOEXEC.BAT must be a plain ASCII text file, which you can create with any editor program, including DOS's own EDLIN or with the non-document mode of your word processor. In the file, put the commands you want carried out during start-up, each command on a separate line. Second, the AUTOEXEC.BAT file must be located where DOS will go looking for it, and that's in the root directory of the DOS system disk you use to start your computer. That's basically all you need to know about what it takes to make an AUTOEXEC.BAT file work for you.

Otherwise, there's no particular magic to an AUTOEXEC.BAT file. It works just like any other batch file, and can be as simple or as elaborate as you want it to be. The only thing special about an AUTOEXEC.BAT is that DOS automatically carries out its commands, which can be a big help in getting your computer going just the way you want it. How you can take advantage of that help is what we'll cover next.

Using AUTOEXEC.BAT

Now we're going to look at suggestions for things you might want to put into your own AUTOEXEC.BAT file. Before we do that though, consider a possibility you might never think of: an AUTOEXEC.BAT with nothing in it at all.

As I mentioned, if there's no AUTOEXEC.BAT DOS automatically performs the DATE and TIME commands before letting you go on with other operations. That habit comes from the days when PCs didn't have permanent clocks built into them. But now many—not all—PCs have permanent clocks. The AT-class of PCs come with them, and many other PCs are equipped with multifunction boards that include a clock feature.

It's very worthwhile to have DOS know the proper date and correct time (among other reasons, so it can put an accurate time-stamp on your files). But having one of these permanent clocks means you don't have to bother setting the date and time anymore; the clock takes care of that for you. Yet, without an AUTOEXEC.BAT file, DOS will still ask you for the date and time.

To avoid this slight, but otherwise unavoidable nuisance, you can create an empty AUTOEXEC.BAT file with no commands in it at all. Just having an empty AUTOEXEC.BAT file is enough to tell DOS to not bother performing its standard DATE and TIME start-up commands. How would you create an empty AUTOEXEC.BAT FILE? Try this sequence of commands from the root directory of your start-up or DOS disk:

```
EDLIN AUTOEXEC.BAT
E
```

That's it, and that's how you can benefit from an empty, command-less, AUTOEXEC.BAT file.

Start-Up Commands in AUTOEXEC

Handy though an empty AUTOEXEC file might be, chances are you have plenty of useful start-up commands you'd like DOS to perform, so let's look at some you might want to consider putting in your AUTOEXEC.BAT file. We'll cover them in what's probably the most sensible logical order to place them into your AUTOEXEC file.

The first set of commands ought to be the ones that help DOS (and other programs) carry out their work. First and foremost of those is the PATH command introduced in Chapter 11. You'll recall that PATH tells DOS where to go looking for the programs that will be performed in response to your commands. Since you're going to be giving DOS a series of commands (both in the rest of the AUTOEXEC.BAT file, and later with the commands you type in), you really should start by telling DOS where your various command files are located. I always begin my AUTOEXEC.BAT files with the PATH command.

```
PATH C:PROGS\DOS;C:PROGS\123;C:PROGS\MISC
```

Related to the PATH command are two others that you might as well put at the beginning of your AUTOEXEC.BAT. One is the PROMPT command which, as I mentioned in Chapter 11, I consider invaluable. You'll recall that PROMPT lets you set the command prompt that DOS shows when it's ready for you to give it a command. The standard DOS command prompt is like this:

```
A>
```

But, especially if you're working with subdirectories on a hard disk, I think it's much more sensible and helpful to have DOS report not only the drive, but also the directory path that it is currently set to. Seeing a prompt like this:

```
C:\DATA\123>
```

lets you know immediately where you are. This can be such an enormous benefit, particularly when you're working with many subdirectories, and you can soon feel lost without your helpful prompt.

I recommend that you include the command

```
PROMPT $P$G
```

in your AUTOEXEC.BAT file to tell DOS to generate a more informative command prompt. (Incidentally, the "$P" part of the command tells DOS to show the path along with the drive; the "$G" part tells DOS to show the greater-than symbol, >, that's so familiar.)

If you're going to include a PROMPT command in your AUTOEXEC.BAT, there's no real need to have it at the beginning of the file, but putting it next to the PATH command seems to me both sensible and well-organized.

The PATH and PROMPT commands are actually just special versions of the general purpose SET command, which was discussed in Chapter 14. Just as DOS uses the PATH and PROMPT commands to direct how it carries out some of its operations, other programs can use information created by the SET command to help them in their work. What sort of information is completely up to the needs of the program that uses it. Typically the information is needed for one of two purposes: to tell the program where to find the disk files it will be working with and to give the program some details about the computer it's working on, such as the kind of display monitor you're using.

If any of the programs you use call for SET commands to help them do their work for you, you might as well get the SETs done automatically in your AUTOEXEC.BAT file. My recommendation is to place the SET commands next in the file, right next to the PATH and PROMPT commands.

```
SET FF=C:\DATA\COMMON
```

Other candidates for inclusion in your AUTOEXEC.BAT file are any commands that help set up the operation of your machine. Examples of these are the MODE command, which is used to set up the operation of your printer or to set your display screen for color or monochrome. I'd recommend that any commands of this sort that you have be placed next in the batch file.

```
MODE CO80
```

If you use a memory disk, you may need to load it with files each time you start up your computer. If the files are ones you routinely put onto your memory disk, this is another natural candidate for your AUTOEXEC.BAT file. This point in your file is a good place for it:

```
COPY PROGS\MISC\*.* E:
```

Next come the RAM-resident programs discussed in Chapter 15—both those that come with DOS, such as the PRINT command, and those that you buy separately. Your AUTOEXEC.BAT file is the natural and sensible place to activate all of the resident programs you want in your computer all the time . So, the next thing I'd recommend is putting in your AUTOEXEC.BAT whatever list of resident programs you use.

Another obvious advantage of using an AUTOEXEC.BAT file to activate them is that, sometimes, these programs have to be invoked in a certain order. Of course, once you've worked out the right order, the batch file will do it right for you every time. Incidentally, if any of your resident programs make heavy use of help files or data files, you may want to keep those files in a RAM disk—that's why I suggested that you load up your RAM disk before you activate your resident programs.

The next step I would suggest including in your AUTOEXEC.BAT file is final, or nearly final, preparation for DOS handing control back to you. That means setting your current working directory with the CD (or CHDIR) command. If you want to set up your computer to work in a particular directory, say a document directory for your word processor, rather than the disk's root directory, here is the place to do it, just as your AUTOEXEC.BAT file is coming to an end.

The final step in an AUTOEXEC.BAT file is not for everyone, but you may want your AUTOEXEC file to activate a particular program before it ends. This program might be a standard **application program**, such as 1-2-3, that you use all the time. If you normally go right into using a particular program whenever you turn your machine on, you might as well have your AUTOEXEC.BAT file activate that program as its last step.

123

Alternatively, if you use a DOS-helper program of the type that's known as a **shell**, then activating that shell should be the last step in your AUTOEXEC.BAT. Examples of such shells include Microsoft Windows, IBM's TopView, X-Tree, and my own Norton Commander program. In either case, whether you want your computer to start up with an application or a shell (such as Windows), the very end of your AUTOEXEC.BAT is the place to put the command. The reason for putting such commands last is, of course, that whatever program you activate is the one you want to use when the AUTOEXEC.BAT is done.

That's a short outline of the kind of commands you may want to build your own AUTOEXEC.BAT file out of. The exact mix of commands and the order you put them in will be up to your own needs, your preferences, and also your skill. I hope that my suggestions will be useful in guiding you on your way.

PART VII

Notes and Comments

21

AVOIDING PITFALLS

Introduction

Everything you do on your computer involves information of some sort. Programs, facts, and figures—they're all types of information. But there are danger areas in using a computer, areas where just the wrong moves could wipe out a lot of valuable information. We'll use this chapter to do something a lot of computer books don't do. Let's look at some of the ways you could make a dangerous mess of things and lose much of your data. We'll see the sources of these pitfalls and dangers and as we go, you'll see what you can do to avoid them.

Mixing Your DOS Versions

Mixing up different versions of DOS presents one subtle and insidious danger to your data, and there are more versions of DOS than you might imagine. For example, I've used nine different, official versions of DOS over the years. Also, many of the various PCs I have around the office can use any recent version of DOS, whereas others require a particular version of DOS that's matched to their special mix of hardware features.

Because the parts of DOS work very intimately together, it is important for me—and for you—not to get them mixed up. If you do get them confused, the results are very unpredictable, but one potential, and unhappy result, is the loss of an entire disk's worth of data. I've helped rescue two Hollywood screenwriters who lost their data this way.

To avoid this danger, you need to know how a mix-up can happen, and what you need to do to prevent any damage. To begin with, let's see how you might end up having different versions of DOS in the first place.

Periodically, changes are made to DOS—to revise it, extend it, or improve it. Even if your computer currently has only one version of DOS, it is almost certain that there will be new ones in the future, and you may want or even be forced to switch to them.

You might end up with a different version of DOS in three ways. One is simply that you receive a new improved version; this is the safest situation, since you are aware that you have two versions. Another is by exchanging disks with colleagues who might be using a different version of DOS; in exchanging disks, you might unintentionally be mixing your DOS program files together. The third way can happen when you buy a **copy-protected program**.

Customarily, a copy-protected program must be used from the disk it is distributed on, and that disk is supposed to be formatted with a blank space reserved for the DOS system. When you buy the program, you're supposed to transfer DOS onto that reserved space on the disk. Sometimes, however, things aren't done this way, and the disk already contains a copy of DOS—a copy that might not match your version of DOS.

You're most likely to encounter a different version of DOS, and one you are unaware of, either by exchanging disks with friends or by receiving copy-protected disks. And, not knowing, you can accidentally start mixing it up with your own version. The problem is insidious, since you don't really know that it is happening. Things might work just fine for you for awhile, until you get just the wrong combination of programs and operations and—bang—you've lost a disk's worth of data.

How can you prevent this from happening? First, be aware that there are three different parts to DOS—the two hidden system files, the command processor (COMMAND.COM), and the various DOS command programs, such as FORMAT. For DOS to work properly, all three parts must match, all must be from exactly the same version of DOS.

Verifying the DOS Version

For COMMAND.COM and the various DOS command programs, it is relatively easy to check to see if you have a matched set, thanks to the date and time stamp that is placed in each disk's directory. To find out the date-and-time marking of your DOS, take your original master disk of DOS (or an unaltered copy of that disk), and do this DIR command:

```
DIR *.COM
```

You should see listed COMMAND.COM, FORMAT.COM, and numerous other program files. The dates and times on all of them should match, and this gives you the official reference point for checking any other disk.

With that in hand, you can check any other disk, to see if the visible DOS program files match that version. Using DIR commands to list all of the COM and EXE files, you can see all the DOS files on your disks and check their dates. When you do this, you need only check the DOS COMMAND.COM, COM, and EXE files. Any other program files aren't an integral part of DOS and can safely have any date and time on them.

If you find that there is any mismatch of dates and times, you should copy a coordinated set of program files onto the disk, so that there is no question of a mix-up.

Checking Hidden Files

That's the procedure for checking and fixing a mismatch in the visible DOS files. But there are also two hidden system files that are used when DOS starts up. There isn't any ordinary way to check to see if they match the rest of your DOS, but you can force them to match your master DOS version. Here is how it is done.

First, you have to see if a disk even has the two hidden files. Do this, as explained in Chapter 6, with the CHKDSK command. If CHKDSK reports two (or three) hidden files, and you know you have more than one version of DOS, these hidden files may need to be matched with your master version of DOS.

To do this, use the SYS command, which was discussed in Chapter 6. The SYS command is designed to transfer these two hidden files from one disk to another. The COPY command can't be used, because hidden files are invisible to the copy operation, but SYS has a special x-ray vision that gives it the ability to copy these two files. To make sure that a disk with the two files has the version you want it to have, use SYS to transfer the files from a disk you are sure of (such as a copy of your master DOS disk) to the questionable disk.

With this as background, you can see what you need to do when you change to a new version of DOS, or when you receive a new disk that you want to match your current version of DOS. For each disk that you need to update or confirm:

1. Check for the presence of COMMAND.COM and other DOS files with DIR.
2. If any DOS programs have the wrong dates, COPY the right version to the disk.
3. Check for the hidden files with CHKDSK.
4. Transfer the hidden files, as needed, with SYS.

This operation involves enough looking and deciding that you must do it more or less by hand, but it is possible to reduce the work involved by setting up batch files for the repetitive work.

Using More Than One DOS

What if you want to have two different versions of DOS? This is all right, as long as you take care to not mix them up. If you do set up two versions of DOS, for any reason, you should carefully mark your disks with the version they contain. (If they don't contain any part of DOS, note that, too.) Keep the use of those disks distinct. Remember DOS will sometimes reload COMMAND.COM from a disk. If you have started DOS from one disk version, and then insert a disk that has another version of DOS, it is possible that the wrong COMMAND.COM will be loaded. Fortunately, this is one error that all versions of DOS are good at checking for, so the worst that will happen is that DOS will complain that you have the wrong COMMAND.COM on the disk.

Also, if you use recent versions of DOS you will find that most parts of DOS contain internal checks to avoid a mismatch in any of the programs. This provides you with some partial protection against a mix-up, but it is far from completely solving the problem. You cannot, and should not, rely on DOS to protect you from the dangers of mixed versions.

Disastrous Interruptions

Another thing that can destroy your data is interrupting the writing of disk information before it is complete. There are several ways this can happen. One way is if the power goes off on your computer while something is being written. In this case, anything that hasn't been saved on disk is gone, irretrievably. Other than buying a backup power supply, there's little you can do about this except save your work frequently on windy or stormy days.

It's also possible to lose data if you remove a disk while it is being written to, or if you use the break command, Control-C, to tell DOS to interrupt the write operation. Here, however, even though your disks are spinning, the computer may not necessarily be writing to them at the time of the interruption—it might have been reading from the disk, and that can't do you any harm. If it was writing, damage might be done, but even then you might get off scot-free.

In general terms, any of the interruptions I have mentioned run the risk of damaging a file, but there is less risk that any of these interruptions will ruin everything on the disk. Sometimes no harm is done at all, and you are lucky. Occasionally one file, the file that was being written, will be messed up. Very rarely will there be more harm, but in either case you can check both the disk and the file you were writing.

Checking a Disk

The first and best way to check a disk is with the CHKDSK command. CHKDSK will tell you if there is any logical scrambling of the disk for one file or any others. If CHKDSK gives no error messages, then you know that the disk as a whole is okay, and that the one file that was being written might be all right. But you don't know for sure yet, so the next check to do is to use the DIR command to look at the file's directory entry. If you know which file was being written, ask for it; if you don't, then ask for the full directory listing (DIR *.*).

When you see the directory listing, the main thing to check for is a reasonable size for the file (or for all files). If a file size is given as zero, then the creation of the file was cut off in midstream, and the data that was being written (or any old data that the file had before) has been lost.

Suppose you *do* find that your file has a size of zero bytes. Does that mean you have to start all over from scratch? Not necessarily, most application programs create automatic backup copies of files you are using, and you may find a backup version of your lost file. If so, all you've really lost are the changes you made to update the file. Then, too, files are sometimes created under a temporary working name and only given their official name when the creation process is finished. If you suspect that a file was cut off as it was being created, you should check for unusual file names; common possibilities are names with extensions of $$$ or TMP. If you do find such a file, at least some of your work may be salvageable. (Backup BAK, $$$, or TMP files may have to be given a different extension with the DOS RENAME command before you can load them into your usual application program.)

Switching Disks

There is one kind of interruption of the computer's writing to disk that can do much more harm: If you switch disks in the middle of an operation. The problem relates to the disk's record of its used and unused space, which we covered in Chapter 9. After a file is written, a record of the space the file occupies is written to the disk—this record applies to every file, and not just one. If this space table, called the **File Allocation Table** or **FAT**, is lost or damaged, then every file will be damaged or permanently lost.

This problem can occur in quite an innocent way, and I know of many people who have had it happen to them. You think that you are just beginning to write out a file, and DOS reports that something is wrong with the disk, so you substitute another disk. DOS finishes writing out the file and the File Allocation Table. However, DOS doesn't know you switched disks, and so it writes the FAT that was read from the first disk onto the second disk. Every file that was stored on the second disk is now lost.

DOS versions 2.00 and later have more protection against this problem built into it, but the danger still exists. The way to protect against this danger is simple: Whenever DOS tells you that there is trouble with a disk, never switch to a disk with good data on it. Either fix the one disk, switch to a blank disk, or abort the operation. Don't put in a good disk with existing files, because they may all be lost.

This potential problem with disks is a good reason for always keeping a supply of formatted blank diskettes handy. Unless you are using a program that gives you access to DOS, encountering disk troubles while trying to save hours of work may put you in a no-win situation: In order to format a good disk on which to save your work, you have to quit the program. But if you quit the program, you lose your work anyway, so you don't need the disk.

Ordinary Ways to Lose Your Data

So far I've mentioned the more interesting and exotic ways that you can lose your data. Now we'll get down to the dull, prosaic, and common dangers. There are exactly three ordinary ways to lose your disk data: by copying over it, by erasing it, and reformatting a disk.

Of these three dangers, the least frequent is to copy old, or bad data onto new, good data. Although there are a million ways you could do this without meaning to, the most common is when you intend to make a backup copy of your data, but copy in the wrong direction: Instead of copying from your newly updated original to the backup disk, you copy from an old backup, overwriting your latest data.

There are several ways that you can protect against this problem. One is to follow a strict physical pattern in the way you copy data. For example, with the original always in drive B, the backup disk always in drive A. Another is to keep using the same disk as your original, instead of rotating between the original and the backup. Another is to keep more than one backup and rotate them (perhaps one backup disk for odd-numbered days, another for even). Another is never to make the copies manually, but instead use a batch file to make sure that the copy is made correctly. Among the advantages of a batch file is that you can have it display the file dates before any copying is done, as a precaution—if the dates don't look right, you can stop before any damage is done.

The next problem, and probably the most common destroyer of data, is the DEL/ERASE command. It is incredibly easy to accidentally erase files you didn't mean to erase. This happens most often through the unintended, or misguided, use of the asterisk wildcard, which will match any filename or any extension. DOS does contain one small precaution against this: If you use the DEL/ERASE command and enter the complete wildcard name *.*, then DOS will pause to ask for confirmation. That's not a lot of safety. It's pretty easy to think to yourself, "Of course that's what I want to do," press Y for Yes, and a second later—a second too late—wish with all your heart you hadn't done that.

There are two things that you can do to protect against losing files through erasure. One, as I mentioned in Chapter 12, is to get an "un-erase" program, if one is available for your computer. The other is to avoid using the DEL or ERASE command manually. If you have any routine need to erase files, don't do it by entering the command by hand; instead, build a batch execution file that will then have the names of the files being erased specified correctly. If you use a batch file, instead of manually entering the erasure command directly, you guard against an accidental mistyping of the names to be erased (provided you get it right in the batch file).

The last of the dangers I'm going to cover is the danger of reformatting a disk that has valuable data on it. This is the worst of all the dangers to your data, because it is completely unrecoverable. If you erase your data, you may be able to un-erase it. If you copy over your data, some of it may still be left on the disk. But when you format a disk, everything that was on that disk is gone. Every part of every file is gone, beyond any hope of recovery. You can't ordinarily un-format a disk the way you might be able to un-erase a file (although there are some programs that can help make it possible, under the right circumstances).

The best way to protect against formatting over your data is to only use the FORMAT command through a batch file, and have that batch file first check the disk for any files that are there. Here is an example of what such a batch file might be like:

```
REM             About to format a disk--check for files
CHKDSK  B:
DIR     B:
PAUSE Any valuable files?  If so, BREAK, don't continue
FORMAT  B:
```

By doing all of your formatting with something like this batch file, you add a measure of protection to your data.

Beyond all these things, the best protection for your data is simply meticulous care. Be careful to always label your disks, indicating what is on them. Be careful not to do physical damage to your disks. Be particularly careful about the particularly dangerous operations of copying, erasing, and formatting.

22

AVOIDING OTHER MISTAKES

Introduction

If you are new to personal computing or even if you aren't, you may be worried about making expensive mistakes with your computer. First, expect to make plenty of mistakes, and don't worry too much about it. Personal computing is still a young field, and many people don't have a lot of experience with it. Making mistakes comes with the territory; expect it, and be prepared for it. What I'll try to do in this chapter is to help you avoid some mistakes that are especially shortsighted or especially costly.

Hardware Mistakes

Since computer equipment is so modular and computers are so expandable, it is hard to make a mistake by getting too little equipment. If you end up needing an expansion feature that you didn't need at first, you can always add it. This seems to argue in favor of under-buying at first and adding on to your computer later. The simple fact is, it usually works the other way: You are generally better off buying more equipment than you think you might need. Why is this so? Here is the simple reason. Only rarely do people buy a piece of computer equipment and then later realize they never needed it at all. Conversely, it is a common experience for computer users to waste time because they don't have a piece of equipment that they need but are reluctant to add to their system, or to waste money by replacing some part of their system with a bigger, better, or faster component. The market for used parts of personal computers is weak, so if you need to replace your printer or disk drive with a better one, you may not be able to recover much, if any, of the cost of your first one.

Unless your budget is severely constrained, it is wiser to over-buy in computing than to under-buy. The history of computing shows that people almost always need more, more, more as time goes by. If you get plenty to start with, you are usually better off. Obviously you shouldn't buy everything in sight and spend your money wildly. Yet it is a simple fact of computer life that you are better off, when equipping your computer, to get more rather than less—more speed or more capacity than you might think you will need.

What mistakes are you most likely to make in under-buying? Too little memory, for one, although these PCs tend to come fully loaded with their maximum complement of standard memory, 640K. If the PC model you choose doesn't necessarily come with that much memory, I'd recommend you make sure the system you buy has it added. Memory is relatively cheap, so you can get plenty. Of course, memory is something you can add on but rarely have to replace, so there's no great problem in adding it later. Usually, though, there is a large savings in buying memory in big chunks. For example, if you add 128K of memory to your system, and then later add another 128K, it will probably cost much, much more than if you had bought 256K to begin with.

Another common under-buy is too little disk capacity. Your data storage needs are likely to grow beyond anything you imagined possible. Adding disk storage is likely to mean discarding your old disk devices, and this can be a real money-waster. If you can add capacity by adding equipment, don't worry about under-buying. But if adding capacity will mean replacing equipment, you would be better off over-buying than under-buying.

The third most likely under-buy is printer quality. Printers that produce a high-quality appearance, especially what's called **letter-quality printing**, are usually expensive. This is a natural area for computer buyers to economize, but is also one of the most common areas in which people become dissatisfied with their equipment. Since printers can be so expensive, it is harder to recommend that you buy a better printer than you may need. I do recommend that you think carefully. Upgrading to a better printer can be a real waste of money. In my own experience, this is where I have wasted the most money—buying printers that were in the price range I might have preferred, but were less useful than what I needed.

The biggest thing to consider, of course, is the computer itself. Personal computers today don't come with many limitations on them, particularly the PC family. It is only in buying game-oriented computers that you are likely to get a computer with too many limitations. If you are choosing between one model of computer and another, consider deeply the expansion options and the raw computing horsepower. The last thing you want to have to replace, and the most expensive thing to replace, is the computer itself. So if you are choosing between one computer and another, err on the side of more power and more expandability, rather than less.

To recap, the most common and expensive mistakes that are made in buying personal computer hardware are buying too little disk storage capacity and too low a quality of printer. An even more common mistake, though a less costly one, is to buy too little memory; this won't waste much money, but it can waste your time. Finally, the most expensive mistake of all is to buy too little computer—too little expansion capability or too little computing speed.

Software Mistakes

Making mistakes in buying software can be very expensive, and even more wasteful of your time and effort than of your money. It's easy to waste your money in basket loads, if you make the wrong moves in buying software for your computer. You are more likely to make mistakes in buying software than in buying hardware.

Probably the most important mistake is in underestimating how much you will want to tie your software uses together. By that, I mean how much you'll be using one piece of software in conjunction with another. Integration is the key here; the more integrated the software, the better.

This is a strong argument in favor of multifunction packages. You may, quite wisely, want to buy the best available word processor and the best spreadsheet program. But you may be even wiser to get an integrated package that does both, even if neither the word processor nor the spreadsheet is first-class. The same rule obviously applies to accounting packages. If you are going to need payroll processing in the future, it would be very shortsighted to buy a general ledger that doesn't have an accompanying payroll module, no matter how superior the general ledger might be.

Another common software mistake is to underestimate how important speed and ease of use will become to you. When you start out in computing, speed may not seem extremely important. You may think that it is no big deal if it takes a few keystrokes to tell one program to do some operation, while another program can do the same thing automatically through a batch processing command. As time goes by, it is likely that your use of the computer, and your dependence on it, will grow. Then, the speed and ease of use of your computer programs will become major factors in how efficiently you can get your work done.

Still another shortsighted mistake in buying programs is to underestimate how important it is to be able to transfer programs to fast-access storage, such as hard disks and electronic disks. As the number of programs you use grows and the amount of time you spend working with your computer grows, the worth of hard and electronic disks grows. When that happens, copy-protected programs that cannot be transferred to other disk systems, become real enemies of your system.

Operational Mistakes

There are three main mistakes that you can make in organizing the operation of your computer. The first one I don't really have to hammer into you, since you will hear it from so many sources: Make backup copies of your data. You'll hear it again and again and again.

Computers are so thoroughly reliable it is easy to feel that your data is quite secure, but that isn't the case. Your data is in danger, two ways. The lesser danger is from failure of the computer—or its programs—resulting in destruction of your data. The greater danger is from inadvertent erasure of your data. As I mentioned in Chapter 21, it is extremely easy to lose your data by a mistaken DEL/ERASE for FORMAT command.

The all-around solution to this operational danger is to frequently make backup copies of your data. Because this can be a time-consuming process, it is tempting to skip or put off doing it—don't. As you saw in Chapters 7 and 8, the best and safest way to safeguard your data is to incorporate backup procedures into your working methods, through batch files.

The second shortsighted mistake in the operation of your computer is not taking the time to get organized. It is easy to think that you don't need to devote much effort into organizing your use of the system. But the simple fact is that one of the best investments you can make of your time is to carefully organize how you use your computer, including placing the right programs together on your disks and, especially, working out the most effective batch-processing files.

Once you've done that, do it again when your work patterns change, or when you develop a better way to get organized. The payoff in smooth, easy work is tremendous. I find that it pays off for me to take the time to refine my working procedures roughly once a month. Even after a full year of heavily using the same computer, I still reorganize every month or so. It takes me about a half-hour's effort, and then what I'm working on goes more smoothly.

The third operational mistake is about neglecting to use batch files altogether. There is nothing else in the DOS operating system that can more enhance the smooth and effective operation of your computer system than automating working procedures with batch processing files. Turn to Chapters 7 and 8, and to the previous chapter, 21, for more information about batch files. When you think you've got the hang of putting them together, try some out. Start with the easy, but useful commands like DIR, PROMPT, PATH, and COPY. Leave the tougher ones—the IFs, SHIFTs, and GOTOs—for a more experienced you.

PART VIII

Technical Parts of DOS

23

SPECIAL PROGRAMMER'S COMMANDS

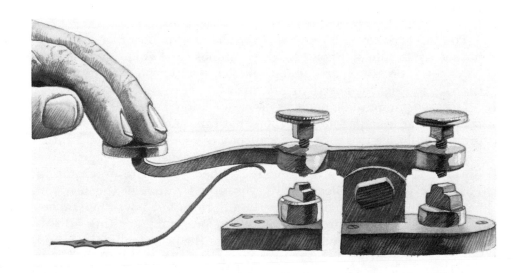

Introduction

In this chapter we're going to move on to a quick survey of two commands that are included in every copy of DOS, but are only used by programmers. These two commands, called **LINK** and **EXE2BIN**, are used to put together a program from its pieces (LINK) and to convert a finished program from one format to another (EXE2BIN). Since they're in your DOS, I'll explain what they are for.

I've written this and the next chapter primarily as introductions to the programmer's parts of DOS, thus they're mainly for people who are interested in programming. Even if all you know is that BASIC comes before C in the alphabet, you should find these chapters helpful for the insights they give into the way programs are put together.

Building Programs with LINK

The LINK program is designed to do the programming task of combining parts into a whole. LINK combines, or "links together" or "link edits" program parts, and it takes care of the job of making sure that all the right connections are made.

Most programming languages use a collection, **a program library**, of useful and standard subprograms that take care of routine work. A program library is kept in a form that is ready to be used by the LINK program. Most programming languages come with subroutine libraries, and their use is automatic. When you write programs in Pascal or C or Compiled BASIC, you aren't aware of the use you make of the accompanying subroutine library, but nevertheless, behind the scenes you are using it. When programs are link edited, LINK finds the parts that are needed from the program libraries and automatically incorporates them into the programs.

When you buy a program compiler, for example, the Microsoft C compiler, version 4, which I use for most of my program development, you may find that it comes with another copy of the LINK program. There's a simple reason for this: The programming language may require more advanced linking features than those that come with some older versions of DOS. To make sure that you have the right linker, a new one comes with the compiler. Check the version numbers on your linkers (which they'll report to you when invoke them) and use the latest. If you're in doubt, use the one that came with the language.

Programming languages, such as BASIC, C, or Pascal, come with ready-made libraries of subprograms that are an important part of the programming language itself. You may wish to build your own libraries of subprograms, or even make changes to the standard libraries. There's a command that's designed to do that, called **LIB.** It comes with some versions of DOS and it's often included with any compiler you buy.

With LIB we can build libraries from scratch or make changes to existing libraries—adding, replacing, or removing subroutines from the library. If you have the LIB program, you can use it for program library work. You should understand, though, that library maintenance is a sophisticated chore, and few programmers have much of a need for it. It is unlikely that you, or anyone working with you, will have much need for LIB. But again, it is interesting to know about.

Converting Programs

When computer programs are stored in disk, in a ready-to-use form, they can be—and must be—in one of two formats that have been specially defined for storing programs. These two formats are known as **COM** and **EXE**, after the filename extensions used for them.

There are two formats for the simple reason that some programs require more help from DOS, and others require less. The EXE format is used for those programs that need the full range of DOS services in loading them for execution. For programs that do not need as much help, the COM format provides a more compact and efficient form of disk storage.

Incidentally, since all programs must be stored in files with filename extensions of either COM or EXE, you can see a complete list of all the programs on a disk by using the DIR command to list the two types of files. For example, these two DIR commands will list the programs on drive C:

```
DIR  C:*.COM
DIR  C:*.EXE
```

EXE2BIN

Any program can be kept in the richer but less efficient EXE format, but only a program that meets the necessary technical rules can be kept in COM format. There is a program provided with DOS to convert programs from the EXE format to the COM format; this DOS command program is called **EXE2BIN**. Incidentally, this rather cryptic-seeming name describes the conversion process itself: The COM format is also known as **binary,** so EXE2BIN converts programs from EXE to (or 2, if you don't mind some bad English) BI-Nary.

The LINK program always produces programs in the EXE format. Eligible programs can then be converted to COM using EXE2BIN. As I mentioned, the COM format is not for every program. The EXE format provides special kinds of technical aid to programs. If a program doesn't make use of the particular features of the EXE format, then it can be converted to COM format; otherwise, it can't.

For your interest, here are all of the stages that a program might have to go through to be prepared for use:

- First the program is written, using an editor.
- Next it is compiled or assembled, using a language translator.
- At this point it might be placed in a library, using LIB.
- Then it is link-edited, using LINK and, possibly, incorporating parts of a library.
- Finally, it may be converted to COM format, using EXE2BIN.

That's a summary of the mechanical stages of preparing a program. Of course, lots of thinking, toil, and testing goes into the creation of a program for our PC family of computers. When it comes to producing a PC program though, those are the steps used to build one.

24

Using DEBUG

Introduction

In this chapter we delve into the technical part of DOS. Our topic is the DOS programmer's tool command, **DEBUG**. DEBUG is really a quite advanced tool, and is not intended for the ordinary DOS user. But DEBUG may provide capabilities you need, or you may just want to know what can be done by DEBUG. This chapter will give you a low-level introduction to DEBUG.

If you don't need to know about technical matters like this, or you're not interested in them, don't feel you have to read through what's in this chapter. If you don't need it, you won't be cheating yourself—this is technical material for those who want to know everything about DOS.

DEBUG works very much like the DOS text editor EDLIN, thus some of the methods we'll be going over here, and particularly the very linear style of using the commands, should already be familiar.

Some DEBUG Background

Almost everything in DOS is designed for civilian use by the likes of you and me. But there are some special things that need to be done by qualified, technically expert people, and DOS's DEBUG is designed to provide the means to accomplish many important tasks that can't be done without such a sophisticated and complicated tool.

In order for a truck to do its job, it can't be made as pretty, or as easy to drive, as an ordinary car, and so it is with DEBUG. Much of what DEBUG works with is technical by nature, thus the use of DEBUG is equally technical. This isn't to say that DEBUG is necessarily over your head; you can judge that for yourself. I can assure you that it is substantially more complicated and technical than any other element in DOS.

The details of using DEBUG are closely tied to the details of the particular microprocessor that is in your computer. Our discussion here will be based on the Intel 86 series of microprocessors, which are used in the IBM PC. Most of the features of DEBUG require a rough understanding of the microprocessor; some of them call for a very thorough understanding.

Hexadecimal Arithmetic and DEBUG

The first thing you need to know about DEBUG is that it does all of its work in hexadecimal arithmetic. Unfortunately, DEBUG doesn't even give you the option of using decimal numbers; everything in DEBUG is done in **hexadecimal**, or **hex**, as it is called.

Hexadecimal arithmetic uses 16 as its base, or radix, instead of 10, which we use. All computers work with binary numbers, and so they need to be given, in one way or another, **binary numbers**. Hexadecimal is simply a shorthand for binary, with each hexadecimal digit standing for four separate binary digits (**bits**). While our decimal arithmetic uses the ten digits 0 through 9, hexadecimal arithmetic uses sixteen digits, which are represented by 0 through 9, followed by A (with a value of 10) through F (with a value of 16).

Here is a table giving a quick outline of the hexadecimal digits:

Table 24.1 Hexadecimal Digits and Equivalents

Hex Digit	Decimal Equivalent	Binary Equivalent
0	0	0000
1	1	0001
2	2	0010
3	3	0011
4	4	0100
5	5	0101
6	6	0110
7	7	0111
8	8	1000
9	9	1001
A	10	1010
B	11	1011
C	12	1100
D	13	1101
E	14	1110
F	15	1111

Hex numbers are interpreted like decimal numbers, but with a base of 16, rather than 10. Thus, whereas you could interpret decimal 12 as a number meaning "one times ten plus two equals twelve," the hexadecimal 12 would be interpreted as "one times sixteen plus two equals eighteen."

Numbers can be up to four hexadecimal digits long, so they can range from 0 to FFFF, which is equivalent to the decimal number 65,535.

DEBUG and Memory

The use of DEBUG involves referring to locations in memory called **addresses.** For computers like the IBM PC family that are based on the Intel 8086 family of microprocessors, complete memory addresses are five digits long, but they have to be represented by numbers no longer than four digits. This is accomplished by using two numbers to represent an address. The first number, called the **segment part**, is treated as if it were shifted one place over, the equivalent of multiplying it by 10. The second number, called the **relative part**, is added to the segment part (shifted over), to get a complete address. It is done like this:

```
1234
 5678
179B8
```

When addresses are written out, they are shown with the two parts separated by a colon, like this:

```
1234:5678
```

When DEBUG shows you addresses, it always shows them in that form. When you give DEBUG addresses, you can type them in that way, or you can leave off the segment part and the colon and give only the relative part. In that case, DEBUG will use a default segment value, which will be the first free segment.

There is one other way you can specify the segment part of addresses. The microprocessor has **registers**, which are used to hold numbers for addressing memory. Each of the registers has a symbolic name; for example, **CS** is the name of the **code-segment register**, which customarily provides the segment portion of addresses within a program itself (as opposed to the program's data). Any of the standard symbolic register names can be used, if you know and understand them.

There is much more of a technical summary we could go into, but rather than lay it all out here, we'll let it emerge as we cover the commands that DEBUG can perform.

The DEBUG Commands

You begin operating DEBUG in one of two ways. You can give the command name, DEBUG, and DEBUG will begin operation by showing you its command prompt, which is a hyphen (-). DEBUG, like EDLIN, has its own command prompt, different from the main DOS command prompt. When you see a hyphen prompt, you know that DEBUG is asking for a command.

The other way to start DEBUG is similar to the way you start EDLIN. You give the name of a file after the command, like this:

```
DEBUG    A:FILENAME.EXT
```

When you start DEBUG this way, it begins by reading the file into memory, so you can work with the data in the file.

After you've started DEBUG, you need to know how to stop it. The **Q** (Quit) **command** tells DEBUG to end its operation. In response to DEBUG's hyphen command prompt, you type Q, press the enter key, and DEBUG ends. As with the EDLIN editor, all of DEBUG's commands are single-letter abbreviations.

Now, the first thing you might want to do with DEBUG is display the information stored in some of your computer's memory. Displaying is done with the **D** (Display) **command**. You have to tell DEBUG what you want displayed. It's always part of your computer's memory, but DEBUG needs to know two things about what to display: where in memory to start, and how much of it to show.

You must specify where to start as an address (as you saw in the last section), but there are three ways to tell DEBUG how much to display. You can leave this part of the command blank and DEBUG will show a standard amount, 128 bytes. You can give the relative part of a second address, and DEBUG will display through that address. You can indicate the number of characters you want displayed by keying in L (meaning you're specifying the length you want displayed) followed by the number of bytes, which must be given in hexadecimal.

Here are examples of all three ways of invoking the D (Display) command:

```
D  F000:6000                 display from an address, default length
D  F000:6000  6800           display from one address, through another
D  F000:6000  L 100          explicit length, for 100 (hex) bytes
```

These three ways of specifying a section of memory are collectively called a **range**, and several more of the DEBUG commands use ranges; whenever we indicate that DEBUG needs a range, you can give it to DEBUG in any of these three formats.

As a convenience, D keeps track of where it has displayed last, so that just entering the D command, with no parameters, will display successive parts of memory—convenient for browsing. (The U command, which we are coming to, gives us another way of seeing memory, but let's concentrate on D here.)

The information shown by D shows the contents of memory in both hexadecimal and character formats, so you can read what is there either way. Here is what a typical D command shows:

```
-D 0:0
0000:0000  43 31 E3 00 3F 01 70 00-C3 E2 00 F0 3F 01 70 00   C1c.?.p.Cb.p?.p.
0000:0010  3F 01 70 00 54 FF 00 F0-47 FF 00 F0 47 FF 00 F0   ?.p.T..pG..pG..p
0000:0020  A5 FE 00 F0 87 E9 00 F0-DD E6 00 F0 DD E6 00 F0   %~.p.i.pf.pf.p
0000:0030  DD E6 00 F0 60 07 00 C8-57 EF 00 F0 3F 01 70 00   f.p'..HWo.p?.p.
0000:0040  65 F0 00 F0 4D F8 00 F0-41 F8 00 F0 56 02 00 C8   ep.pMx.pAx.pV..H
0000:0050  39 E7 00 F0 59 F8 00 F0-2E E8 00 F0 D2 EF 00 F0   9g.pYx.p.h.pRo.p
0000:0060  00 00 00 F6 86 01 00 C8-6E FE 00 F0 F2 00 71 05   ...v...H~~.pr.q.
0000:0070  53 FF 00 F0 A4 F0 00 F0-22 05 00 00 00 00 00 F0   S..p$p.p"......p
```

Here's a D command that will show the date of your computer's built-in BIOS programs, if you have one of the models with a standard date-stamp:

```
D  FFFF:6 L 8
```

The information from D, and all other DEBUG commands, appears only on your computer's display screen, but you can save a record of it in several ways. One is to turn on your computer's echo-to-printer switch, which we covered in Chapter 7. Another is to redirect the output of DEBUG, say to a file. The display shown here is actual DEBUG output, which was captured in a file using redirected output and then incorporated into the text of this chapter.

Besides displaying memory, DEBUG also lets you compare two parts of memory with the **C** (Compare) **command**. To work, C needs a range to indicate the location and length of one part of memory, and a second address to indicate the location of the other part of memory. DEBUG will then compare them, byte for byte, and report any differences. Here what the C command looks like:

```
C F000:1000 L 200 F000:2000
```

Similar to the C command, is the **M** (Move) **command**, which will copy the data in one part of memory to another. Like C, the M command needs a range to indicate the move-from locations, and an address to indicate the move-to locations. For example, this would move 1K of read-only BIOS data into the regular memory:

```
M F000:0 L 1000 100
```

Since you have to use hexadecimal numbers with DEBUG, it would be nice to have some aids. Unfortunately DEBUG offers no help in converting between decimal and hexadecimal, so you are on your own in this department and must turn to a programmer's pocket calculator, or to BASIC (which has easy ways to convert decimal and hex).

Even if it doesn't convert back and forth between decimal and hexadecimal, DEBUG does give you a tool to do addition and subtraction in hexadecimal—the **H** (Hexarithmetic) **command**. To use the H command, you key in H followed by two hex numbers. H will then display their sum and their difference, which gives you easy access to hex addition and subtraction—something very useful in working with addresses. For example, the command,

```
H 1234 ABCD
```

will get you the result

```
BE01 6667
```

One of the things you might want to do with DEBUG is make changes to the information that is stored in memory. DEBUG gives you two ways to do this, the Enter and Fill commands, E and F. Let's start with E.

The **E** (Enter) **command** lets you make direct changes to memory. There are two ways to use this command, one that lets you just enter data, and one that lets you first see what you are changing.

The first way of using the E command is done like this:

E *address* *list-of-data*

With this command, the list of data is entered in memory, starting at the address, and continuing until everything in the list has been placed in memory. For your convenience, the list-of-data can be any mixture of character and hexadecimal data. If you use characters, just enclose them in quotation marks to make them distinct from hex numbers. Here is an example:

```
E OF32:0100 25 "If you figure this out, you're" 63 6C 65 76 65 72
```

The other way to use E is interactive, with DEBUG showing you the old contents of each byte of memory before you change it. This is very important and useful, because it provides a safeguard against changes to the wrong part of memory. One way in which you might use this form of the command is if you receive a **program patch**—changes that need to be made to a program. Patches are often given in the form of DEBUG's interactive E commands, so that you can confirm that you are changing what you are supposed to, and not something else.

The interactive form of the E command is invoked by giving E an address, but no list of data to store. E will then display, in hex only, the data at that address and wait for you to key in a new value, also in hex. You either key in a new value, or press the spacebar to leave the value unchanged. DEBUG will continue, presenting you with byte after byte, until you call the process to a halt by pressing Enter.

You can confirm the changes you make in two ways. You can do it later by using D to show where you made the changes, or you can confirm the changes on the spot by using another feature of E, the hyphen. While you are using the interactive form of the E command, keying in a hyphen will move you back one byte (just as pressing the spacebar will move you forward one). This makes it easy to back up and confirm what you have done.

The **F** (Fill) **command** can also be used to change the contents of memory. F is used like the automatic form of E, except that you specify a range of memory and not just a single starting memory address:

F *range* *list-of-data*

The reason for the range is that F will duplicate the list-of-data as many times as necessary to fill up the range of memory. The list of data can be as long and complicated as you wish, but the most common use for the F command is to set a block of memory to one byte value, such as zero.

If, instead of putting something into memory, you want to search through memory for some particular data, you can do so with the **S** (Search) **command**. S needs the same kind of parameters as F: a range (indicating what part of memory to search) and a list of data, in hex or character formats. S will report the address location of each set of data in the range that matches the data list. If you are using DEBUG for snooping and patching—two of the most popular uses of DEBUG—then the Search command is definitely for you.

DEBUG and Registers

Besides the main memory, your computer also has **registers**, which it uses to hold working addresses and temporary results of arithmetic operations. DEBUG provides the **R** (Register) **command** to let you display and change the register values. If you enter the R command by itself, DEBUG will display the contents of all the computer's registers, along with some related information. If you enter R followed by the name of one particular register, then DEBUG will display its contents, and give you an opportunity to enter a new value similar to the way you do with the interactive E command. To use this command successfully, you must understand quite well how registers are used by your computer, and you must understand how DEBUG uses the registers when it is working.

Here's an example of how DEBUG shows the register values to you:

```
AX=0000  BX=0000  CX=0000  DX=0000  SP=FFEE  BP=0000  SI=0000  DI=0000
DS=4531  ES=4531  SS=4531  CS=4531  IP=0100  NV UP EI PL NZ NA PO  NC
4531:0100 0A496E        OR CL,[BX+DI+6E]                      DS:006E=20
```

DEBUG and Ports

One of the ways your computer talks to its various parts and also to the world around it is through an element known as a **port**. Ports are data paths into and out of your computer's microprocessor, so each port can pass data in or out. Each port has an address that identifies it, an address that is similar to, but completely distinct from, memory addresses. There are very many possible ports, and your particular computer will use some of them for special purposes. Generally, you must have a detailed knowledge of your particular computer's inner workings to be able to understand and use ports.

If you know enough about the ports in your computer, DEBUG gives you two commands to move data through them: **I** (In) reads data from the port, and displays it; **O** (Out) sends data out the port. The commands are used like this:

```
I    port-address
O    port-address   data
```

DEBUG and Disks

While DEBUG gives you the means to display and change data in memory, often your real goal is to display or change data that is on disk. DEBUG provides you with a way to read and write disk data to and from memory. The **L** (Load) and **W** (Write) **commands** are used for this. L and W work in two distinct ways. They can read and write either entire files or specific parts of the disk storage. Let's cover the file part first.

Reading or Writing to Files

As you'll recall from the beginning of this chapter, when you start DEBUG, you can either start it by itself, or with the name of a file you want DEBUG to read into memory automatically. If you make changes to the file's data in memory, how do you write it back to the disk? The **W** (Write) **command**, without any parameters, writes the memory copy back to the disk, replacing the original disk copy of the file.

Suppose you want to read another file into memory? How can you do this? Oddly enough, it takes a combination of two commands. The first command, **N** (Name), tells DEBUG the name of the file to be read; the second command is **L**, without any parameters (just like writing a file is done with W, with no parameters). To read a file, you do something like this:

```
N  A:FILENAME.EXT
L
```

and then the file is read into memory, just as it would be if you had used that file name when you started DEBUG.

Reading Disk Data

The "naked" form of L and W is used to read and write complete files, but another form of these commands is used to read specific parts of the disk data. In this case, you specify the memory address you want the data read into, and what part of the disk you want to read from. The command is like this:

L *address* *drive-number* *sector-number* *sector-count*

The address is the location in memory the data is to go to. The drive-number is the equivalent of the letter that DOS uses to identify disk drives, with 0 representing the A-drive, 1 the B-drive, and so forth. This indicates which disk drive the data is to be read from. The sector-number indicates what part of the disk is to be read; the exact number used depends upon your particular computer, the particular disk format, and the version of DOS. The sector-count indicates how many disk storage units, or sectors, are to be read into memory.

Writing to specific locations is done with the W command, using the same kind of specifications used for a L command.

DEBUG and Programs

Everything discussed so far has been about and has been working with abstract data. DEBUG also has the ability to work with programs in several interesting ways.

With the D command, you saw how to display data in a combined hex and character format. That is just fine if what you are displaying is data, but it doesn't tell you much if the information is part of a program. To translate raw programs into a more intelligible format, DEBUG gives you the U (Unassemble) **command**.

The U command translates the hexadecimal of machine language programs into the form of assembly language. Ordinary users still won't be able to comprehend the result, but anyone who can at least stumble through assembly language programs will be able to decipher some or all of what is being done. Here is an actual example of an unassemble done on my computer:

```
F600:0000  E98F7E    JMP    7E92
F600:0003  E8A76B    CALL   6BAD
F600:0006  CB        RETF
```

The display, as you can see, includes the address locations, the data in hex format, and the equivalent assembly language instructions, such as "JMP" and "CALL". The assembly language format does not strictly follow what is needed to create an assembly program, but it is a close equivalent.

DEBUG also provides the flip side of U, the **A** (Assemble) **command**. The A command allows you to key in assembly-like instructions, like the "JMP 7E92" that appears in our example, and have them translated into machine language and stored in memory. While anyone can use the U command, and some will also be able to understand it as well, only those who are fluent in assembly language can use the A command successfully. It is more difficult to use DEBUG's A command than it is to write ordinary assembly programs, since an assembler provides more aid and assistance than DEBUG can. The assemble command is only for proficient experts.

There are two more program-oriented commands that DEBUG offers. Both of them are quite advanced, and are really only for use by very proficient assembly-language programmers. Even then, these two commands are used only in fairly extreme circumstances, when programming problems can't be solved by more routine methods. These two commands are **T** (Trace) and **G** (Go).

The **T command** is used to execute a program step by step. With a program ready in memory, T will execute the program's instructions, one at a time, and display the status of the computer, as reflected in its registers. T can be told to stop after each instruction or to continue for a number of instructions, displaying the results of each one. The T command is mostly used when a programmer is uncertain about the exact results of some instructions or a very small part of a program. T is too laborious to be effective for extensive program testing.

The **G command** also executes a program, but without tracing its results. G will execute, or carry out, a program as quickly as DEBUG is able to. With the G command, you can specify locations in the program, called **breakpoints**, where DEBUG will stop executing it.

This is the difference between executing a program by itself, and executing it under the control of DEBUG's G command. With breakpoints set, you can run a program and then stop to check the results when it reaches an interesting or important part.

This has been a quick, and only slightly technical overview of what the facilities of DEBUG are. In the next section we'll look at how to use DEBUG to **patch**, or change programs.

Using DEBUG to Patch

Whatever else you might do with DEBUG, there is one common use that anyone might need it for: modifying or patching programs.

There are two different kinds of patching that you might be doing with DEBUG. One is making actual detailed changes in hexadecimal to correct a program, or to alter its operating characteristics. For example, some editing and word processing programs are patched with DEBUG in order to customize the way they operate. When you do this kind of patching, you should be following very careful and detailed instructions that tell you exactly how to make the patches.

The other kind of patching you might do on your own. In this type of patching, you don't have to know the exact details of the program that you are changing. Instead, you want to change something more obvious and more easy than the program code. One example of this kind of patching is changing a message that a program displays.

A Patch Example

In order to illustrate how this is done, let's imagine a typical example of how such patching might be done. Suppose you have a program, called SUPER, and you find that this program really is super in every respect but one: SUPER insists on reading its data from your disk drive B, when you would like it to use whatever default disk drive DOS is currently using. If you can change SUPER so that it doesn't specify a disk drive, then you can move SUPER's data to a hard disk or an electronic disk or, in fact, any disk other than the B-drive that SUPER insists on.

Here is what you would do to try to change SUPER. You don't know in advance if this is going to work—the method is experimental, but there is a very good chance that you will succeed and do no harm in the process.

First find the SUPER program, it ought to be in a file named SUPER.COM or SUPER.EXE. If SUPER happens to be a BASIC program, it might be stored in a file named SUPER.BAS. Whatever the name, find it and copy it to a separate disk (so that you can safely change it without endangering your main copy). In the process, you should note the size of the program file.

Next, you have to consider one detail. If the program file has an extension of EXE, then DEBUG will treat it in a special way that makes it possible for DEBUG to use the T and G commands. You don't want this, for reasons that are rather technical. The main thing is, if you have an EXE file, you don't want DEBUG to know about it. If the file has an extension of EXE, you get around it by using the DOS RENAME command, to change its extension to anything other than EXE. Let's assume that SUPER is an EXE file, so you rename it like this:

```
REN  SUPER.EXE  SUPER.XXX
```

Next, start DEBUG and tell it to load the program file. The command is like this:

```
DEBUG  SUPER.XXX
```

At this point, DEBUG has a copy of the SUPER program file in memory. You suspect that inside this program file are specific references to the B-drive, in this form: "B:". Now you are going to ask DEBUG to search for them. To use the search command, you have to tell DEBUG how much to search, and that is the length of the SUPER.XXX file. If you can translate decimal into hexadecimal, figure it out. If you can't, tell DEBUG just to search as much as possible. Here is the S command that you use:

```
S  0  L  FFFF  "B:"
```

Step-by-step, this is what you are asking DEBUG to do: The "S" tells DEBUG you want to search for something. The "0" tells it to look from the beginning of its working memory. The "L" tells it to search for some length. The "FFFF" tells it to search for as many bytes as possible. (If you knew the exact length of the file, in hexa-decimal, you would substitute the length here.) The last part, in quotes, tells DEBUG to look for the drive specification "B:".

In response to this command, DEBUG will report where it found "B:". If it doesn't report it anywhere, you are out of luck, and you have to give up. But instead, DEBUG is likely to report one or even several addresses. Now, if you want to, you can display the data fol-lowing each address. If DEBUG reported an address like this: 04EF:0220, then you would use the D command to show information from there:

```
D 04EF:0220
```

using exactly the same address that S gave you.

When you do this display, you may see only the "B:", but more likely you will see a complete filename, with the "B:" at the front. You're likely to see something like this:

```
04EF:0220 42 3B 46 49 4C 45 4E 41-4D 45 32 32 32 32 32 32  B:FILENAME
```

The combination of the "B:" and the filename is a tip-off that you have found what you want. Your goal now is to remove the "B:" part. You can use the E command to replace it with blank spaces, which you do like this:

```
E 04EF:0220" "
```

Repeat this process for each memory location at which the search command reported that it found "B:". When you are done, you write the file back to disk with the W command.

Now you have your modified program file, ready to test. If you renamed it from an EXE file, you need to change its name back—with the RENAME command:

```
RENAME SUPER.XXX SUPER.EXE
```

Finally, you are ready to test your version to see if it works. To play it safe, make copies of any current data that SUPER uses, just in case the new, modified version gets up to any mischief. You'll test the new SUPER with one copy of your data, knowing that if anything goes wrong, you have another, undisturbed copy. Then you try running the SUPER program, and see if it now looks for its files not on the B-drive, but wherever you have pointed the DOS default drive. If the test works, you can start using the modified program with your ordinary data.

The same methods I've described here can be used to locate and change messages that are built into programs. I can think of two plausible reasons why you might want to do this sort of thing. One would be to replace DOS's **starting message** with your company's own logo; if you want to do that, you'll find the DOS starting message located in the COMMAND.COM file. Another reason would be to translate program messages from English into another language. Whatever your reason, you can use the techniques here to make any kind of reasonable changes that you want. Even if you have no real reason to do this sort of patching work, you might want to give it a try, simply to learn the skill of how to do it. It's a skill that might come in handy some day.

Making patches or changes to programs, however, is a potentially dangerous process, for you take the risk of ending up making a program unusable—either due to some error on your part or some trick in the program. You need to proceed with caution when you do this kind of work. Under normal circumstances though, what I have described works fine and is surprisingly easy to do.

PART IX

References

Appendix A

NARRATIVE GLOSSARY

Introduction

This narrative glossary is intended to provide a very brief rundown of the most common and fundamental terminology used in discussing computers. You can use this narrative glossary in two ways—either by reading it all, or by scanning the boldface words for the terms you are interested in and then reading the surrounding discussion.

Numbers and Notation

Computers work only with **binary numbers**—numbers made up of zeros and ones (0's and 1's). These binary digits are called **bits**, for short. No matter what a computer is doing, it is working with bits. Even if the subject matter is alphabet characters, or decimal arithmetic, the method is still binary numbers.

Writing many bits, for example 0101010011101010101, is inconvenient, so several shorthand notations have been developed. The most common is **hexadecimal**, or base-16, notation. Hexadecimal digits have sixteen possible values, from 0 through 15; they are written as 0 through 9, followed by A (representing the value ten), B (meaning eleven), and C through F (with a value of fifteen). Hexadecimal digits, also called **hex**, represent four binary digits, or bits, at a time. (Another notation, called **octal**, uses the digits 0 through 7 and represents 3 bits at a time.)

The bits that a computer uses are grouped into larger units. A group of eight bits is called a **byte**. Since hex notation represents four bits at a time, it takes two hex digits to represent the value stored in a byte (hex digits are sometimes whimsically called **nibbles**, or **nybbles**). A byte can be used to store two to the eighth power of values— 256 different values. The values can be interpreted as numbers or as characters (such as letters of the alphabet). One byte can hold one **character**, and therefore the terms bytes and characters are sometimes used interchangeably. The letters of the alphabet and the ten digits, together, are called the **alphanumerics**, although the term is sometimes used loosely to mean any text data.

When bytes are used to hold characters, some code must be used to determine which numeric value will represent which character. The most common code is the American Standard Code for Information Interchange (**ASCII**). In ASCII, the capital letter A has the value 65 (in hex notation, 41), B is 66, and so forth. ASCII includes codes for letters, numbers, punctuation, and special control codes.

ASCII proper has only 128 different codes, and needs only 7 bits to represent it, but since ASCII characters are almost always stored inside 8-bit bytes, there is actually room for the 128 ASCII codes, plus another 128 codes. The other codes are sometimes called **extended ASCII**. ASCII codes are standardized, but extended ASCII varies from computer to computer.

Traditionally, IBM computers have not used ASCII coding to represent characters. Instead, they use **EBCDIC** (the Extended Binary Coded Decimal Information Code). Although EBCDIC has been very little used in personal computers, it may become more important to us, as data is transferred more and more between the two types of machines.

ASCII data, or an **ASCII file**, is data that consists of text—letters of the alphabet, punctuation, and so forth—rather than numbers or other data. Sometimes the term ASCII is used loosely to mean text data. Properly speaking, an ASCII file not only contains the ASCII codes for letters, spaces, punctuation, and so on, but also contains the standard ASCII codes for formatting, such as carriage return and end-of-file.

When a byte is used to represent a number, the 256 different byte values can be interpreted as either all positive numbers ranging from 0 through 255, or as positive and negative numbers, ranging from -128 through 127. These are referred to as **unsigned** (0 to 255) or **signed** (-128 to 127) numbers.

To handle larger numbers, several bytes are used together as a unit, often called a **word**. For different computers different meanings are given to the term word, but most often it means either two bytes (16 bits) or four bytes (32 bits). For the IBM PC family of computers a word usually means a two-byte, 16-bit, number.

A two-byte word has two to the sixteenth power different possible values. These can be used as unsigned numbers, with a range of 0 through 65,535, or signed numbers, with a range of $-32,768$ through 32,767.

Integers, or whole numbers, are not satisfactory for some tasks. When fractional numbers are needed, or a very wide range of numbers is needed, a different form of computer arithmetic is used. This is called **floating-point.** Floating-point numbers involve a fractional portion, and an exponent portion, similar to the **scientific notation** used in engineering. To work with floating-point numbers, computers interpret the bits of a word in a special way. Floating-point numbers generally represent approximate, inexact values. Often more than one format of floating-point numbers is available, offering different degrees of accuracy. Common terms for these formats are **single-precision** and **double-precision**. Floating-point numbers are also sometimes called **real numbers**.

Due to the nature of computer arithmetic and notation, items are often numbered starting from 0 for the first element; this is called **zero-origin**. Counting from zero is done especially when figuring a memory location relative to some starting point. The starting point can be called many things, including **base** and **origin**. The relative location is most often called an **offset**. Starting from any base location in memory, the first byte is at offset 0, and the next byte is at offset 1.

Computer Fundamentals

All of the mechanical and electronic parts of a computer system are called **hardware**. The programs which a computer uses are called **software**.

The idea of a computer starts with the concept of **memory**, or **storage**. A computer's memory consists of many locations, each of which has an address and can store a value. For most computers, including the PC family, each location is a byte; for others, each location is a word.

The addresses of the locations are numbers. The values stored in each location can either be discovered (**read**) or changed (**written**). When a value is read or written, the address of the location must be given.

Some computers organize their memory storage into large modular units, often called **pages**. IBM PC computers do not use pages, but for addressing purposes they divide their memory into units of 16 bytes, called **paragraphs** (a term that was chosen to suggest a smaller division than a page). The memory-addressing mechanism for these computers uses two parts: a **segment value**, which points to a paragraph boundary, and a **relative value**, which points to a byte located at some displacement, or offset, from the segment paragraph. The two values, segment and displacement, are needed to specify any complete address; together, they are sometimes called an **address vector**, or just **vector**.

Amounts of computer memory are frequently referred to in units of 1,024, because 1,024 is a round number in binary notation, and almost a round number in decimal notation. The value 1,024 is known as **K**, from the metric kilo—64K is 64 units of 1,024, or exactly 65,536.

When referring to general capacity, K almost always means 1,024 bytes. However when referring to semiconductor chips, K means 1,024 bits. When magazine articles refer to 16K and 64K chips, they mean 16K bits (equivalent to 2K bytes) or 64K bits (equivalent to 8K bytes).

A computer has the ability to perform operations on the values stored in its memory. Examples of these operations are arithmetic (addition, subtraction) and movement from location to location. A request for the computer to perform an operation is called an **instruction**, or **command**.

A series of computer instructions that together perform some work, is called a **program**. Programs are also called **code**.

The part of the computer that interprets programs and performs the instructions is called the **processor**. A very small processor, particularly one that fits onto a single computer chip, is called a **microprocessor**. The development of microprocessors made personal computers possible. Properly speaking, a computer is a complete working machine that includes a processor and other parts; but the processor part of a computer is sometimes also called a computer.

The **memory** of a computer is used to store both programs and data. To the memory, there is no difference between programs and data. However to the processor, only those stored values that represent valid instructions can be a program. The processor reads and writes from its memory both to carry out a program and to access the data that the program uses.

To help it carry out its work, a computer may have a small amount of very specialized memory that does not have addresses. This specialized memory is referred to as **registers**. Registers are used to make arithmetic more efficient, or to assist in handling addresses.

Many modern computers, including the PC family, use a push-down **stack** to hold status information. Data is pushed onto and popped off of the top of a stack, on a last-in-first-out (or LIFO) basis.

When a computer uses a common data path to pass data from one part to another, this path is called a **bus**. Standard PC models have an 8-bit bus; the AT-class of PCs (which use the 286 microprocessor) use a 16-bit bus, while the 386-class of PCs use a 32-bit bus. This **bus width** is a partial reflection of the speed and power of a PC.

The memory and processor are the internal part of a computer. There are many external parts, generally called **peripheral equipment**, or **peripherals**. Most peripherals must be connected to a computer through some supporting electronic circuitry, called an **adapter**. For a complex peripheral, such as a diskette drive, the adapter will include some special logical circuitry called a **controller**. A controller is often a specialized computer in its own right.

Peripherals may be of many kinds, but they fall into a few simple categories. **Storage peripherals** are used to hold programs and data that can be moved into the computer's internal memory. Examples of peripheral storage devices are floppy diskettes, cassette tape recorders, and high-capacity hard disks. (For more on this, see the section, Disk Vocabulary.)

Other peripheral equipment is used to communicate with people. The pieces of equipment used to communicate between people and computers are usually called **terminals**. A terminal most often consists of a typewriter-style keyboard, and a television-like display screen, called a **CRT** (for cathode ray tube). A printer of some kind may be used instead of a CRT. A **display screen** is called a **monitor**, or simply a **display**. A color display may accept its color signal information in a combined form, called **composite**, or separated into its red, green, and blue components, called **RGB.**

Large computers may have many terminals, but small personal computers usually work with only one terminal, which may be built right into the computer system. Having only one terminal is a large part of what makes a personal computer personal.

Other kinds of peripherals, besides storage and terminals, are printers and telephone connections. Connections between computers and telephones are referred to by the names of some of their parts, such as **modems** and **asynchronous adapters**; all of these terms, in general use, refer to the entire computer-telephone connection, which is generally called **communications**. The most common format for communications connections follows a design standard known as **RS-232**. The speed, or data rate, of a communications line is measured in **baud**, which is bits-per-second. Twelve hundred baud is a common speed for personal computer communications; 1200 baud is about 120 characters per second. On personal computers, an RS-232 connection is also called **serial**, since it transmits data one bit at a time. A **parallel** connection can transmit more than one bit at a time.

Computer **printers** come in many varieties. Many personal computers use an inexpensive **dot-matrix printer**, which creates its printed results by writing a series of dots. **Letter-quality printers** produce results comparable to good typewriters. Most letter-quality printers use a print element that is either a flat disk, called a **daisy-wheel**, or one that is shaped like a large thimble.

There are two exciting new kinds of printers that more and more are being used in place of traditional dot-matrix and daisy-wheel printers. One type is the **ink-jet printer**, which squirts very tiny drops of ink, and paints its information with these small dots. Some ink-jets print as crudely as dot-matrix printers, while others print as finely as a typewriter that uses a fabric ribbon. The other new printer technology is called **laser printing**. A laser printer is essentially a computer-driven photocopier, but where a photocopier gets its image from taking a camera-like picture of something you're copying, a laser printer creates an original image of what you want to print. A computer-controlled laser beam paints the image inside the photocopier, which then prints the image onto paper.

An **interface** is a connection between any two elements in a computer system. The term interface is used both for connections between hardware parts, and software parts, as well as the human interface.

Much of the equipment that can be connected to a computer is generally referred to as **input/output equipment**, or **I/O**.

The smallest physical parts that make up a computer may be called **chips**. Chips and other parts are wired together electrically and held mechanically on **boards**. If there is one principal board, it is called the **system board**, or **motherboard**. Openings for the addition of more boards are called **expansion slots**, into which are placed **memory boards, disk boards, asynchronous communi-**

cations boards (telephone connections), and other expansion or peripheral boards.

A microprocessor interacts with its world through three means, **memory accesses**, **interrupts**, and **ports**. Ports have a port number or **port address**, and are used for passing data to or from peripheral devices. **Interrupts** are used to get the computer's attention. There are three kinds of interrupts (although all three are handled in the same way). An **external interrupt** is from the outside world (for example, from a diskette drive). An **internal interrupt** reports some exceptional logical situation (for example, division by 0). A **software interrupt** is a request from a program for some service to be performed. A software interrupt is an alternative to using a program call to activate a subroutine. Memory accesses are used to read or write from the computer's memory.

The computer's memory can be of several types. Ordinary memory, which can be read or written to, is called **RAM** (random access memory). Memory that contains permanent data is **ROM** (read only memory). Memory can be dedicated to some particular use, for example, to hold the data that appears on the computer's display screen. If a display screen uses the computer's memory to hold its information, then it is a **memory-mapped** display.

Programs and Programming Languages

Series of computer instructions are called **programs**. Parts of programs that are partially self-contained are called **subroutines**. Subroutines are **procedures** if they do only some work. They are **functions** if they also result in a value ("open the door" is analogous to a procedure; "tell me your name" is analogous to a function). Subroutines are also called **subprograms**, and **routines**.

Many subroutines use **parameters** to specify exactly what work is to be done; for example, a subroutine that computes a square root needs a parameter to specify what number to use. Many subroutines will indicate how successful their operation was through a **return code**.

Computers can only execute programs that appear in the detailed form known as **machine language**. However, for convenience, programs can be represented in other forms. If the details of a machine-language program are replaced with meaningful symbols (such as the terms ADD or MOVE), then the programming language is known as **assembly language** (also called **assembler**, **symbolic assembler**, or **macro-assembler**).

Assembler is called a **low-level language**, because assembly programs are written in a form close to machine language. Other forms of programming languages are more abstract and produce many machine instructions for each command written by the programmer. These are called **high-level languages**; examples are BASIC, Pascal, FORTRAN, COBOL, PL/I, C, and Forth.

Programs that translate high-level language programs into a form usable by the computer are called **compilers**; for low-level languages, the translators are called **assemblers**. There is no real difference between a compiler and an assembler—they both translate from a human programming language to a form of machine language.

When a person writes a computer program, the form it takes is called **source code**, or **source**. When the source code is translated (by an assembler or compiler), the result is often called **object code**. Object code is nearly ready to be used, but it has to undergo a minor transformation, performed by a **link editor**, or **linker**, to produce a **load module**, which is a finished, ready-to-use program.

An error in a program is called a **bug**, and the process of trying to find errors, or trying to fix them, is called **debugging**.

There are usually many ways to accomplish an objective with a computer program. The scheme, formula, or method that a program uses is its **algorithm**. For many tasks—even as simple a one as sorting data into alphabetical order—there are dramatic differences in the efficiency of different algorithms. The search continues for better and better methods.

A program works with symbolic entities called **variables**. In effect, a variable is the name of a place that can hold data of some type. Specific data can be moved into and out of a variable, and the purpose of the variable is to provide a mechanism for manipulating data. Variables usually have a fixed type, which indicates what sort of data it can accommodate: for example, **integer** type, **single-** and **double-precision floating-point**, and **string** (a collection of text characters). In a program, a **file** is just a special kind of variable, one that can be connected to a diskette file or some device, such as the display screen.

Human Roles

On a personal computer, one person can do everything that is to be done. However, in traditional large computer systems there is a division of labor, separating human involvement with a computer into various roles. Users of personal computers may wonder about the meaning of various job titles used.

The **user**, or **end-user**, is the person for whom computer work is done.

The **systems analyst**, or **analyst**, determines the details of the work that the end-user needs done, and decides on the general strategy of how a computer will perform the work.

The **programmer** converts the analyst's general strategy into the detailed tactics and methods to be used. This usually includes writing (and testing) the actual program. However, actually writing and testing the program is sometimes left to a **coder**.

The coder turns the programmer's detailed methods into the program instructions.

The **operator** runs the program on the computer to produce the results needed by the user.

Data Organization

Data is organized and viewed differently, depending upon who or what is looking at it. To the computer itself, data consists of just bits and bytes. To programmers who manipulate data, there are some traditional logical boundaries for data. A complete collection of related data is a **file** (as an example, a mailing-list file). One complete unit of the information in a file is called a **record**; in a mailing list file, all of the information connected with one address would be a record. Finally, within a record are **fields**, the information of one type. For example, the ZIP code would be one field in an address record in a mailing list file.

The records that a program reads or writes are **logical records**. Logical records are placed in the storage medium's **physical records**—the pieces actually read or written to a diskette. A program sees logical records, while the operating system performs any necessary translating between logical and physical records. On a disk, a physical record is called a **sector**.

The terms **data base** and **data base manager** are used, and abused, so widely, that they have no precise meaning. When data is large, complex, and spread across several files, it might be called a data base. A data base manager is a program—usually large and complex in itself—that can control and organize a data base. Full-scale data base management is far beyond the capabilities of a personal computer.

Disk Vocabulary

Data on a **disk** is stored on **sectors**, which can be individually read from or written to. Typically, for DOS, a sector is 512 bytes. Sectors are the disk's physical records—the units that are actually read or written. A **track** is the collection of sectors that will fit into one circle on a disk; a typical disk format has nine sectors in a track. If there is more than one surface on a disk drive, then a **cylinder** is all of the tracks that are the same distance from the center. Sectors that are in the same cylinder can be read without moving the disk drive's read/write mechanism. Moving the read/write heads from one track/cylinder to another is called **seeking**, and it is relatively slow. Typically there are forty or eighty tracks on each surface of a diskette and several hundred on a hard disk.

A disk needs a table of contents for its files. This is called a **directory** in DOS. Some means must be used to keep track of used and unused space on a disk and with DOS it is done with the **FAT** (**File Allocation Table**). The first sector of each disk is dedicated to holding the first part of the operating system's startup program, called the **bootstrap loader**, or **boot record**. On each disk there are four kinds of sectors—boot record, FAT, directory, and data space (where files are stored).

A diskette is flexible, thus it is called a **floppy**. A **hard disk** has a rigid platter in place of the flexible plastic of a floppy; the rigid shape allows more precise data recording, and thus higher density and more capacity. IBM calls the hard disks in their personal computers **fixed disks**; everyone else calls them hard disks or hard files. The sort of hard disks installed on personal computers today use a collection of methods called Winchester technology, so hard disks are also called **Winchester disks**.

There are other sorts of diskettes as well. While standard-sized diskettes for personal computers are $5\frac{1}{4}$ inches across, a new type of diskette, called a **mini-diskette**, is only around $3\frac{1}{2}$ inches across. It is small enough to fit into a pocket and enclosed in a hard shell, so that it's not floppy (even though the magnetic disk inside is just as flexible as the one inside a floppy diskette). Also, advanced technology has made it possible to pack much more information onto standard-sized diskettes. These are called **high-capacity diskettes**. On the AT-type PCs, high-capacity diskettes hold 1.2 megabytes of information.

Operating Systems

An **operating system** is a program that supervises and controls the operation of a computer. Operating systems are complex and consist of many parts.

One element of an operating system is its **BIOS**, or **Basic Input-Output System**. The BIOS is responsible for handling the details of input-output operations, including the task of relating a program's logical records to a peripheral device's physical records. At the most detailed level, the BIOS contains routines tailored to the specific requirements of each peripheral device; these routines are called **drivers**, or **device handlers**.

Usually an operating system is organized into a hierarchy of levels of services. At the lowest level, the **device handlers** insulate the rest of the operating system from the details of each device. At the next level, relating logical data to physical data is performed. At a higher level, basic services are provided, such as accepting output data from a program to be placed into a file.

Besides device and data handling, an operating system must supervise programs, including loading them, relocating them (adjusting their internal addresses to correspond to their exact location in a memory), and recovering from any program errors, through an **error handler**.

Another element of an operating system is the **command processor**, which accepts and acts on commands given by the computer's user. Commands usually amount to a request for the execution of some service program. The command processor is the part of an operation most people think of as the operating system. In DOS, the command processor is a file named COMMAND.COM.

Appendix B

COMMAND SUMMARY

Introduction

Here is a reference summary of the DOS commands and CON-FIG.SYS commands. To avoid getting bogged down in the elaborate and almost unreadable syntax notation that you'll find in DOS's own manual, I've simplified the notation here. The required parts of each command are <u>underlined</u> ; the other parts are optional. The use of **files** stands for a full, elaborate file-specification; it must include a filename (with or without any of the wildcard characters * and ?). It may also include the optional parts of a path specification and a file-name extension. The word **paths** stands for a path specification that may optionally include a drive letter. The abbreviations **d:** and **e:** stand for disk drive specifications. You'll find similar abbreviations defined along the way.

DOS COMMANDS

ASSIGN   Reroutes activity from one disk to another. For example, if a program insists on working with diskettes A: and B:, AS-SIGN allows us to redirect both to our hard disk, C:.

<u>ASSIGN</u> d=e

d and **e** are drive letters; you can give more than one assignment "equation" in a command; specifying no equations resets any previous ASSIGN.

When a program asks to use drive d DOS reroutes the activity to drive e. We can give a series of assignments in the same command. ASSIGN without any parameters resets any previous assignments.

ATTRIB   Controls the file attribute settings for read-only and archive.

<u>ATTRIB</u> *settings* <u>*files*</u>

The *settings* are either +R or −R or +A or −A to set on or off the attributes of read-only or archive. Without any **settings** specified, this command will list the **files** and show how the attributes are currently set.

BACKUP   Makes a backup copy of files from one disk to another (usually to a series of diskettes).

<u>BACKUP</u>   *files* <u>*d:*</u> *switches*

The operation copies from the **files** to the **d:** drive. The **switches** are /S for subdirectories; /M for modified (archive) files; /A to add to the target disk (otherwise, over-write the target); /D:mm-dd-yy select on or after the given date.

This command makes its copies in a special way which, among other things, allows backup copies of files that are bigger than the diskettes they are being copied onto. Copies made with BACKUP can't be used until they are copied back with the RESTORE command.

BREAK   Sets a switch that controls when DOS checks for the Control-Break key.

<u>BREAK</u>   ON   or   OFF

Setting BREAK ON allows DOS to respond to the Break key under a wider set of circumstances.

CHDIR   Changes the working directory for a disk.

<u>CHDIR</u>   *paths*

CHDIR may be abbreviated CD. Changes the current working directory to the specified path or if no path is given, displays the current path.

CHKDSK   Analyzes a disk to test for logical errors in the directories and space allocation for files. Reports on the results and can fix some errors.

<u>CHKDSK</u>   *files switches*

If *files* are specified, CHKDSK will report on specific files. The *switches* are /F to fix any errors detected; /V to list all files.

CLS   Clears the display screen.

```
CLS
```

COMMAND   Activates a secondary command processor; mostly used to allow nested batch file processing.

```
COMMAND  paths  switches
```

If a **paths** is given, the command processor is found on that path. The **switches** are: \C-string, which causes the new command processor to carry out the command on that string (typically a batch file) and then finish operation, returning control to the original command processor; /P to stay working permanently; and /E:size to set the environment size.

COMP   Compares two groups of files.

```
COMP  files1  files2
```

The two groups of files are compared. If either of the **files** isn't specified, the command asks for a specification. The second **files** is usually either just a drive or path to search for names matching the first **files.**

COPY   Copies files from one disk location to another.

```
COPY  switches1  files1  switches2  files2
```

The **switches** may be /A to treat the files as ASCII text files or /B to treat the files as binary files; a /V verify switches may also be used. Several files may be copied together into one by having **files1** list more than one file combined with a + sign.

CTTY   Allows another device (typically COM1, a communications line) to act as the command console (keyboard and display screen).

```
CTTY  device
```

The **device** may be COM1 or COM2; or CON to reset to the normal console.

DATE   Sets and displays the current date.

DATE *dates*

If the **dates** isn't given, DOS asks for it. The format of the date will depend on the country-setup DOS is working with. For the USA it is like 12-31-87 or 12/31/87.

DEBUG   Starts up DOS's interactive debugger. See Chapter 24 for details.

DEBUG *files parameters*

DEL   Deletes files from a disk.

DEL *files*

The **files** are deleted. If all files are specified, DEL will pause for confirmation. ERASE is a synonym for DEL.

DIR   Lists the files in a directory.

DIR *files switches*

The **switches** are /P to pause when the screen is full; /W to show the files wide format with names only (without sizes and dates).

DISKCOMP   Compares entire diskettes for an *exact* match.

DISKCOMP d: e: *switches*

The **switches** are /1 and /8 to compare only 1 diskette side or only 8 sectors per diskette. Two diskettes may have exactly the same file data, but not match by DISKCOMP simply because the data is recorded in different locations.

DISKCOPY   Copies entire diskettes.

DISKCOPY d: e: *switch*

The **switch** is /1 to copy only one diskette side. DISKCOPY will make an exact duplicate of a diskette, copying both file data and the exact location where it is stored.

ECHO Controls the display of commands during batch file execution.

```
ECHO ON or OFF or message
```

OFF suppresses subsequent display of the commands in a batch file, until its end; ON turns it back on; **message** shows the message even when ECHO is OFF.

EDLIN Starts up DOS's interactive text editor. See Chapter 18 for details.

```
EDLIN files parameters
```

ERASE Deletes files from a disk.

```
ERASE files
```

The **files** are deleted. If all files are specified, ERASE will pause for confirmation. ERASE is a synonym for DEL.

EXE2BIN Converts program files from EXE format to COM format.

```
EXE2BIN file1 file2
```

EXIT Ends the execution of a secondary command processor and returns control to the previous one. Used in nested batch commands.

```
EXIT
```

FDISK Activates the interactive disk partition control program.

```
FDISK
```

FIND Filters out any input lines that do not contain the specified text.

```
FIND switches string files
```

The **switches** are /V (Vice-versa) to pass lines that do *not* contain the string; /C to count the number of matches; /N to give the line

number of each match. The **string** should be in double quotes. If
FIND is not used in a pipeline then **files** gives the files to be searched
(it may be a list of files rather than a single file-spec).

FOR   Specifies repetitive execution of a command for each file in a
specification.

FOR *variable* IN *(set)* DO *command*

The **command** is any DOS command that will be repeated individually for each file generated by the FOR operation; the command
may have parameters which include the **variable**. The **variable** is a
dummy name of the form "%%x" (with x being any characters) that is
used to substitute the file names generated from the **set** in the **command**; use one % when this is a direct command, two %%'s when this
is part of a batch file. **set** is a list of file specifications.

FORMAT   Prepares a disk for use by DOS.

FORMAT d: *switches*

The **switches** are /S to make the disk a system disk; /V to add a
volume label; /B to make a system disk without actually copying the
copyrighted system files; /1 for a single-sided diskette; /8 for an 8-
sector disk; /4 for a non-high capacity diskette in a high capacity
drive.

GOTO   Allows looping and branching logic in a batch file.

GOTO *label*

Batch file processing jumps to the line where the **label** is found.
The **label** line must begin with a colon followed by the **label** symbol.

GRAFTABL   Loads a set of character images for the high-order
characters. Only used for the Color Graphics Adapter.

GRAFTABL

This command permits the graphics modes of the Color Graphics
Adapter to use the special top-half of the PC's character set. It does
not have wide application.

GRAPHICS   Allows the print-screen operation to be used with the Color Graphics Adapter.

GRAPHICS *printer switches*

This command only applies to certain specific IBM-brand printers (or their exact equivalents) and only to the Color Graphics Adapter. The **printer** options are COLOR1, COLOR4, COLOR8, COMPACT, and GRAPHICS. The switches are /R to *not* reverse black and white when printing and /B to print the background color (with a color printer). This command does not have wide application.

IF   Controls conditional execution in a batch file.

IF NOT *condition command*

The **condition** may be any of three kinds of tests: ERRORLEVEL **number** (which is true if any previous program ended with an error condition equal or higher than the **number**); **string1** = = **string2** (is true if the strings, which usually include one of the batch files's parameters, match); or **EXITS files** (which is true if the named file exits). The optional NOT reverses the result of the **condition** test. The **command** may be any command; often it is a GOTO.

JOIN   Makes a disk appear to be a subdirectory on another disk. This is the opposite of the SUBST command.

JOIN d: *paths switch*

The disk **d:** may be accessed through the paths specification on another drive—making it appear to be a subdirectory. The **paths** directory specification must be empty of any files or subdirectories and attached to the disk's root. The switch /D deletes an existing join. With no parameters, JOIN displays all joins that have been set.

KEYBXX   Loads a keyboard translation routine to adapt DOS to keyboards other than the USA format.

KEYUK or KEYGR or KEYFR or KEYIT or KEYSP

LABEL   Controls adding, changing, or deleting disk volume labels.

```
LABEL d: label
```

The label is applied to the disk; if none is specified, the command interactive prompts for one.

LINK   Combines compiled program modules into an executable program.

```
LINK various-link-parameters
```

See programming manuals for the details of how to use this specialized command.

MKDIR   Creates a new subdirectory.

```
MKDIR paths
```

MKDIR may be abbreviated MD.

MODE   Controls various hardware features.

```
MODE LPTn:width,height,P
MODE screenmode,L or R,T
MODE COMn:baud,parity,databits,stopbits
MODE LPTn:=COMn
```

See Chapter 14 for the elaborate details of these commands. The *screenmode* is any of these: 40, 80, BW40, BW80, CO40, CO80, or MONO.

MORE   Displays input data and pauses when the screen is full.

```
MORE
```

MORE is designed to be used in a pipeline of commands, but it can be used as a pausing version of the TYPE command when it is combined with input redirection.

PATH   Specifies the list of directories where DOS will search for command files.

```
PATH paths
```

The **paths** is a series of path specifications, separated by semicolons.

PAUSE   Pauses during the execution of a batch file.

PAUSE *message*

Suspends batch file processing until a key is pressed; the Break key may be used to avoid continuing after the PAUSE command.

PRINT   Activates the background printing of files while the computer is free to continue other commands.

PRINT *files switches*

The **files** specifies the files to be printed. The **switches** are rather technical in nature and are: /D:device to specify the output printer device; /B:buffersize to specify the working buffer size; /U:count to control how long the program waits; /M:count to control how much working time the program takes; /S:count to control the time-slice sharing; /Q:count to control how many files may be queued up to print at a time; /T to cancel printing (terminate); /C to cancel specific files; and /P to print specific files (needed only in combination with /C).

PROMPT   Sets the form of DOS's command prompt.

PROMPT *prompt-command*

See Chapter 11 for the details of this command. PROMPT with no **prompt-command** returns to DOS's default prompt. PG is the **prompt-command** that I recommend.

RECOVER   *Either* removes an unreadable portion of a file *or* reconstructs a dummy directory for an entire disk.

RECOVER *files*
RECOVER d:

With a file specification this command removes any unreadable portion from the middle of a file. Without a file specification, this command discards a disk's entire directory structure and rebuilds a dummy directory based on the file storage map (FAT). Note that the first form of this command is relatively harmless while the second form can devastate a disk—**losing the names of every file.**

REM   Displays a comment in a batch file.

`REM comment`

RENAME   Changes the name of a file or group of files.

`RENAME files1 files2`

REN is another name for this command.

REPLACE   Copies files from one disk to another, either replacing all like-named copies on the target or added missing files to the target.

`REPLACE files paths switches`

The **files** are the files to be copied from; **paths** is the location to check for matching files. The **switches** are /A to only add missing files to the target path; /S to replace all matching files in any subdirectory; /R to allow replacing read-only files; /W to wait between reading and writing (to allow changing diskettes); and /P to prompt before copying each file.

RESTORE   Restores files backed-up with the BACKUP command.

`RESTORE d: files switches`

The operation copies from the d: drive to the **files** specification. The **switches** are: /S to restore subdirectories below the **files** specification and /P to pause before replacing newer or read-only files. Note that a copy made by BACKUP contains control information and cannot ordinarily be used until it is reconstructed by the RESTORE operation.

RMDIR   Removes a subdirectory.

`RMDIR path`

RD is another name for this command. A directory cannot be removed if it contains any files or subdirectories; also, the root directory of a disk cannot be removed.

SELECT   Installs DOS with a specified national keyboard driver and country code (for date and time format).

SELECT d: e:paths *country-number keyboard-code*

The optional first drive, **d:**, is a diskette to be copied from; the required second drive, **e:**, is the target disk (which may, optionally, include a target path). The **country number** is the numeric country code (see the COUNTRY command) and the **keyboard-code** is the code used in the KEYBxx command.

SET   Sets an equation in DOS's environment space as control information for various programs.

SET *name=value*

The equation is placed in the environment, where any program may inspect it. If no equation is given, all the equations in the environment are listed. If no value is given, the named equation is nullified (removed from the environment).

SHARE   Creates support for file sharing on a network.

SHARE *switches*

The **switches** are /F:size to set the space for recording shared files and /L:count to set the number of sharing locks allowed.

SHIFT   In a batch file, shifts the parameters to allow looping through them.

SHIFT

The batch file parameters are shifted over so that what was the second becomes the first, what was the third becomes the second.

SORT   Sorts the lines in the input stream.

SORT *switches*

The **switches** are /R to reverse the sort order (Z . . . A); / + n to specify that sorting begins with column n (ignores the first n − 1 columns in each line). SORT is designed to be used in a pipeline of commands, but it can be used as a conventional command to sort a text file, by redirecting its input and output.

SUBST   Makes a directory appear to be a separate disk drive. This is the opposite of the JOIN command.

```
SUBST d: paths switch
```

The paths directory may be accessed through the **d**: drive specification. The switch /D removes a specific substitution. The command with no parameters displays all active substitutions.

SYS   Copies the two key hidden files that form the core of DOS onto another disk.

```
SYS d:
```

The two hidden files are usually named IBMDOS.COM and IBMBIO.COM, but with other names on some computers. This command is usually used to update a disk to a new version of DOS or to transfer the operating system to a disk formatted with the /B option.

TIME   Sets and displays the current time.

```
TIME times
```

If the **times** isn't given, DOS asks for it.

TREE   Lists the directory tree for a disk.

```
TREE d: switch
```

The **switch** /F lists all the files in each directory.

TYPE   Copies a text file to the display screen.

```
TYPE files
```

VER   Displays the version ID of DOS.

```
VER
```

VERIFY   Turns disk-write verification on or off.

VERIFY ON or OFF

VOL   Reports the disk label (volume) information for a disk.

VOL d:

The LABEL command allows you to add, change, or delete these volume labels.

XCOPY   Copies groups of files, including subdirectories.

XCOPY *files1 files2 switches*

The first ***files1*** specification must contain at least a drive, path or filename part. The ***switches***, which are the key element of this command, are: /S to copy files in all subdirectories; /A to only copy archive files *without* resetting the bit; /M to only copy archive files *with* resetting the bit; /E to copy even empty directories; /D:dates to copy files dated on or after the specified date; /V to verify all copies; /P to pause for permission before copying each file; /W to wait to change diskettes between source and target.

CONFIG.SYS COMMANDS

ANSI.SYS   This device driver provides extended screen and keyboard control, using a series of command forms defined by the American National Standards Institute. It allows programs to control the screen output formatting in a machine-independent way and it allows keyboard input to be transformed or "macro-ized" to a degree.

DEVICE=ANSI.SYS

BREAK   Sets the default Break key checking (which may be overridden by the BREAK command of DOS).

BREAK=ON or OFF

BUFFERS   Sets the number of disk buffers that DOS uses.

BUFFERS=n

The default, without this command, is 2 or 3 buffers. I recommend many more, say 32 for a large hard disk.

COUNTRY   Sets the country code that determines the date and time formats, currency symbol, and other country-specific elements.

COUNTRY=*number*

DEVICE   Used to load device drivers into DOS; the device drivers available include ANSI.SYS, DRIVER.SYS, and VDISK.SYS.

DEVICE=*files*

DRIVER.SYS   Defines the characteristics of extra drive specifications.

DEVICE=DRIVER.SYS *switches*

The ***switches*** are /D:number the physical device number (1–128 for diskettes, 129–255 for hard disks); /S:number for the sectors per track; /H:number for the number of heads per cylinder; /T:number for the number of tracks; /C to indicate a "changeline" (the drive senses when a diskette is changed); /N for nonremovable drives; and /F:type for a formfactor type.

FCBS   Specifies the maximum number of file control blocks (FCBs) that can be used at the same time.

FCBS=*max,min*

The ***max*** parameter specifies the total number of open FCBs allowed; ***min*** specifies how many are protected from being forced closed when DOS needs to free some FCBs.

Note: FCBs refer to the old-fashioned file control used in the earliest versions of DOS. See the following FILES entry.

FILES   Specifies the maximum number of new-style files (file handles) which can be open at the same time.

```
FILES=number
```

The **number** can range from 8 to 255; default is 8. This file handle limit is independent of the old-style FCBs (see page 329).

LASTDRIVE   Specifies the maximum number of logical drives that may be used.

```
LASTDRIVE=d
```

This specifies—through a drive letter, rather than a count—the maximum number of drives that may be used. This command is used to make room for *additional* drives beyond those already in use for physical drives (and for other device drivers). These additional drives may be needed for commands such as SUBST.

SHELL   Specifies the name and the directory location of the default command processor.

```
SHELL=files switches
```

The normal DOS command processor is found in the boot disk's root directory and is named COMMAND.COM. This command allows the command processor to have another name or be located in another directory. It also provides a means to pass control parameters or switches to the command processor before it begins operation. For the standard COMMAND.COM two switches are defined: /E:size, which sets the size of the environment (measured in bytes for some versions of DOS and in 16-byte paragraphs for others), and /P, which instructs COMMAND.COM to execute the default batch file, AUTOEXEC.BAT.

VDISK.SYS   This device driver creates a virtual or RAM disk using the computers regular or extended memory.

```
DEVICE=VDISK.SYS parameters switch
```

The ***parameters*** are three numbers (which may be preceded by alphabetic comments) giving the size of the disk in K-bytes, the (simulated) sector size in bytes and the number of directory entries in the disk's root. The ***switch*** is /E:transfer which specifies that extended memory will be used and determines the number of sectors which will be transferred between regular and extended memory.

INDEX

About the Author

Peter Norton is well known in the personal computing arena for both his writing and programming. Starting in the earliest days of the IBM Personal Computer, he began writing about the IBM/PC, helping other people understand how these wonderful machines work. He has written a half a dozen books on the PC family, including the best-selling *Inside the IBM/PC*; his column appears in each issue of *PC Week* magazine. His set of programs called The Norton Utilities has helped many PC users rescue lost data and explore the inner workings of their computers. Peter grew up in Seattle, Washington, attended Reed College in Portland, Oregon; he now lives in Santa Monica, California with his wife.